A GARDEN OF ONE'S OWN

A GARDEN OF ONE'S OWN

A Garden of One's Own
A Collection of Modern Chinese Essays, 1919–1949

Edited and translated by
Tam King-fai

The Chinese University Press

A Garden of One's Own:
A Collection of Modern Chinese Essays, 1919–1949
Edited and translated by Tam King-fai

ISBN: 978-962-996-423-8

THE CHINESE UNIVERSITY PRESS
The Chinese University of Hong Kong
Sha Tin, N.T., Hong Kong
Fax: +852 2603 7355
E-mail: cup@cuhk.edu.hk
Website: www.chineseupress.com

Printed in Hong Kong

Table of Contents

❁❧❦❁

Introduction

Names

The time is around the New Year. The chilly wind outside is still blowing strong, discouraging people from venturing out. The paper windows of the study are tightly closed, and the doors are carefully locked up. Works of calligraphy and paintings by ancient artists hang on the wall of the study, and a pot of narcissus in full bloom sits on the table. Fragrant incense comes wafting from the golden burner shaped like the mythic animal ni *on the desk. The master takes a snuffbox from his pocket; after taking a few sniffs, he caresses the jade ring on his thumb. All of the sudden, he seems to think of something, gets up, and walks toward the pot of narcissus to see whether the few buds that have remained unopened have bloomed. He stands there and looks at the plant for a while. Then, holding his hands behind him, he begins to pace back and forth in the study.*

The day feels as long as a year. Not knowing how to pass the time, he walks up to the bookshelf and picks out a book at random. He lies down on a couch and begins to read. Thus does he come to enjoy a conversation with the ancients, as his spirit roams in a realm of timeless enjoyment, forgetting the frigid wind outside and the hustle and bustle of the city. By the time he puts down his book, he feels as if, in this world of turmoil, only he has remained unsullied.

And what is the book that he reads, one might ask? It is not Dream of the Red Chamber *or* The Western Chamber, *but a volume of Ming essays.*

Qian Gechuan (1935, 200)

Like the essays that the man of leisure in this passage picks up to while away a long wintry day, the works introduced in this anthology are known in Chinese by the name *xiaopin wen*.[1] Having a common name is but one of the resemblances between essays of the Ming and those of the modern period, which echo each other in many significant ways across a time span of three centuries. Modern scholars of *xiaopin wen* of either period have often felt obliged to include in their studies speculations on their similar aesthetic orientations and cultural underpinnings, as well as the social and intellectual climates that account for their emergence.[2] Indeed, our understanding of essays from both periods has benefited from many such instances of mutual illumination.

Unlike the majority of essays found in the West nowadays, *xiaopin* essays are almost always meditative, casual, and intimate in tone.[3]

---

[1] While the meaning of *xiaopin*, the first component of the term *xiaopin wen*, will be the subject of this introduction, it should be noted here that the other component, *wen*, in the present context simply means either writings or essays. The traditional philosophical connotations of the concept of *wen* or *wenxue*, so crucial in the investigation of prose writings up to the late Qing period (see Huters 1987 and 1988), have very little relevance here. For all intents and purposes, *xiaopin wen* simply means the kind of prose known as *xiaopin*; in other words, *xiaopin* essays. *Sanwen*, which means prose as opposed to verse, is also sometimes paired with *xiaopin* in the place of *wen*, in which case it has the same meaning as the latter.

[2] See Chen Shaotang (1981) and Gong Pengcheng (1994) for examples of scholarship on late Ming *xiaopin wen* that also touch on modern *xiaopin wen*. Even though Chen thinks that modern *xiaopin wen* should not be confused with the kind found in the late Ming, he deems it necessary to devote five pages to comparing the two. Gong's topic is a late Ming *xiaopin* collection, *Caigentan*. In accounting for its popularity in present-day Taiwan, he goes to considerable length in discussing the different ways in which Lu Xun and Zhou Zuoren interpreted late Ming *xiaopin*.

Early twentieth-century writers and critics of *xiaopin wen* were just as obsessed, if not more so, with late Ming *xiaopin wen*, betraying no doubt an anxiety of influence. See the section on "Disputes" below for a discussion of their interminable arguments over the relationship between the two periods.

[3] A word of qualification is called for here. Surely, as my account below will show, Chinese essayists have often regarded the tradition of the familiar essay in the West as addressing the same aesthetic concerns as their own works. Yet, the present-day Western understanding of the word "essay" is predominantly "expository essay," to which the Chinese essays included in this anthology bear little resemblance, if any at all. See, for example, William Zeiger, 1985. There are, however, indications that the tradition of the familiar essay

Argumentation is not their forte, but philosophizing is. They tend to shy away from topics charged with political and social significance, but are inclined instead to explore ethical and interpersonal situations. Their scope ranges widely, from ruminations on large existential issues to contemplation of mundane daily objects and activities. And though their medium is prose, they more often recall the characteristics of poetry.

This kind of essay is definitely not what the literary reformers of early twentieth-century China had been expecting. New poetry, yes, and new fiction and new drama, too, all of which they sought to promote in their ambitious cultural agenda; but modern *xiaopin wen*, so new in its sensibilities and yet so old in its associations, so unmindful of social issues and yet so in tune with the expression of individuality that the search for modernity seemed to call for, no. At first, critics were perplexed. Although they were quite ready to acknowledge the remarkable success of these essays, they could not help but register a note of surprise and, in some cases, dismay. In offering the first summation of the success of modern Chinese literature, Hu Shi (1922, 149–150) wrote:

> Vernacular prose has made remarkable improvement. There is no need for us to go into the progress made in the genre of long argumentative essays here; rather, in recent years, the most notable development in prose has been the "*xiaopin sanwen*" promoted by writers such as Zhou Zuoren. This kind of essay [is able to express] profound meanings in plain and casual language. At times these essays appear awkward, but in fact they are quite witty (*huaji*). The success of this type of writing has once and for all exploded the myth that "aesthetic writing cannot be done in the vernacular language."

Similarly, Zhong Jingwen (1927, 33) also had this to say:

> Since the beginning of the New Literature Movement, most of us have seemed to rush in droves to the major thoroughfares of fiction, poetry, and drama. Prose—the *xiaopin wen*—has seemed to remain a path in the wilderness covered with thorny bushes. Few have been willing to blaze that path.

---

is experiencing a revival in the West. For example, two publications in recent years are devoted to such essays. See Phillip Lopate, 1994, and Joseph Epstein, 1997.

I have used the English word "essay" for the convenience of English readers, in much the same way as Martin Woesler (2000a, 2000b) and David Pollard (2000). Unless specified by the context, the term "modern Chinese essays" in my discussion should be taken to refer to modern Chinese *xiaopin wen*.

Despite the general lack of interest in this form of writing, however, Zhong went on to point out that the very few who had ventured down this path had produced impressive results. Zhou Zuoren, Yu Pingbo, Zhu Ziqing, Ye Shengtao, and Xu Zhimo were the few that he held up as models of success.

Although Hu Shi and Zhong Jingwen used the names "*xiaopin sanwen*" and "*xiaopin wen,*" respectively, in their accounts, these were by no means commonly accepted terms. Instead, until at least the late 1920s, a plethora of names were used, a few of which will be discussed below. The proliferation of terms went even further due to the many sub-genres of this type of essay: *kexue xiaopin* (*xiaopin* about science), *lishi xiaopin* (*xiaopin* about history), *shuqing xiaopin* (lyrical *xiaopin*), and so on. Understandably, these terms have proved as confusing for general readers as for professional critics, indicating as they do the multifaceted nature of this genre of writing on the one hand, and the entrenched positions from which critics have chosen to articulate their understanding of its aesthetics and social significance on the other. Chinese literary critics have been well known for their contentiousness throughout the ages, but in the period covered in this anthology, encompassing what are generally called the May Fourth and post-May Fourth generations, literary disagreements were further fueled by political convictions. In this context, literature was but one of the many venues for people to air their thoughts about the future of China. Whether and how one wrote or read essays, and what brand one chose, very often became a litmus test of one's political stance, whereby more than one's literary reputation was at stake. An exercise in naming thus soon descended into a battle of name-calling. One recalls, for instance, the utter contempt with which Liang Shiqiu and Zhou Zuoren were viewed in some quarters.[4] In this regard, the polemics surrounding *xiaopin wen* were not too much different from other debates in the history of modern Chinese literature.

---

[4]   See Gaylord Kai Loh Leung (1990) for a discussion of the ostracism that Liang Shiqiu suffered at the hands of writers of the All-China Federation of Literary and Art Workers for the War of Resistance. Liang's essay collection, *Yashe xiaopin*, moreover, had often been singled out for criticism for its pointed silence on anti-Japanese themes that pervaded writing of the time. See also Chen Suyu (1989) for a description of Liang Shiqiu's antagonistic reception in the Yan'an area during the 1940s.

   The case of Zhou Zuoren will be discussed below.

Part of the confusion over nomenclature no doubt came as a result of foreign influences. According to the prevalent views of the time, there were many forms in foreign literature similar to that of the modern Chinese essay, and critics were fond of weighing the relative importance of foreign and indigenous elements in the works of contemporary essayists. From the West, they discerned a tradition of essay writing that started with Montaigne, was popularized by Francis Bacon, and came to develop and prosper in the hands of English and American essayists of subsequent generations. Charles Lamb, William Hazlitt, Washington Irving, G. K. Chesterton and Ralph Waldo Emerson are just a few of those mentioned in this connection. From Japan, the genealogy was not as clear-cut, although it was generally recognized that the works of Lafcadio Hearn (who went by the Japanese name Koizumi Yakumo in his most productive years), Matsuo Bashō, Kobayashi Issa, Abe Jiro, Saitō Mokichi, and a few others belonged to this literary family that had yet to come up with a name acceptable to all. If indeed all of these literary dignitaries had a shaping hand in the formation of modern Chinese essays, then perhaps one could borrow a foreign term to label them. But which term? Which of the foreign literary forms most approximated what modern Chinese essayists were producing? Was it the British familiar essay, the French *essais* and prose poem, the Japanese *zuihitsu*, "sketches" of the kind introduced by Lafcadio Hearn, or the Japanese *manga*, which, as a form of drawing, was somehow believed to share the spirit of the essay as well?[5]

While all of these foreign terms have been proposed as names for the modern Chinese essay, serious contenders for the title remain few in number, namely, *meiwen*, *chun sanwen*, *xuyu sanwen*, and, of course, *xiaopin wen*, all of which I will examine below.

---

[5]   The most systematic articulation of Western influences in Chinese *xiaopin wen* is to be found in Liang Yuchun (1930). Citing an unnamed English critic, Lin Yutang (1934a) further outlined two lines of development in English essays, with one beginning with Chaucer, which was characterized by a casual and intimate style, and the other with Bacon, which was known for its weighty and reasoned style.

Japanese influences, however, are recognized but have so far not received any in-depth examination, even though Kuriyagawa Hakuson is quoted in a large number of studies on modern *xiaopin wen*. The 1935 collection, *Xiaopin wen yu manhua*, for example, contains only superficial discussion of the *manga* tradition in Japan.

Zhou Zuoren, who discerned two kinds of essays in Western literature, proposed the term *meiwen* in 1921. The first was analytical and academic in nature, while the second, narrative and descriptive, was hence artistic. He called the second kind *"meiwen"* (aesthetic writing), describing it as a bridge between poetry and prose. Since the term was ostensibly derived from the Western literary tradition, it is only to be expected that, by this account, *meiwen* writers abounded in the West, and included some of the best-known familiar essayists mentioned above. Zhou Zuoren, however, went on to point out that *meiwen* could be found in classical Chinese literature as well. Traditional forms such as *xu* (prefaces), *ji* (chronicles), and *shuo* (argumentative essays) were early instances of *meiwen*. It was only in the modern period, Zhou maintained, that one looked in vain for similar literary creations. This view helps to explain Zhou's apparent need to draw attention to the flourishing state that this form of writing was enjoying in the West at the time.

Similarly, Wang Tongzhao's *"chun sanwen"* (which he glossed in English as "pure prose") was an importation from the West. Like Zhou, Wang believed there to be a paucity of artistic essays in the Chinese literature of their time, which he attributed to four factors: 1) the lack of precision which characterized Chinese thinking; 2) linguistic and rhetorical inflexibility on the part of most Chinese writers; 3) an overemphasis on rational knowledge, without giving due attention to literary sensibilities in their writings; and 4) the failure of supporters of modern Chinese literature to promote *"chun sanwen."* Leaving aside the possible contradictions among the four factors (especially between the first and third), it should be clear that Wang was attempting here to describe a kind of essay that placed equal emphasis on the impartation of knowledge and the cultivation of pleasurable reading—a twentieth-century reformulation of the age-old charge for literature to instruct and delight.

The defining attributes of the two terms proposed by Zhou and Wang—*mei* (beautiful) and *chun* (pure)—suggest that both writers sought to highlight the belle-lettristic quality of modern Chinese essays. However, without further elaboration, the terms merely beg the question of what constitutes "beauty" on the one hand, and "purity" on the other, and neither Zhou nor Wang ended up convincing their colleagues of the appropriateness of their terms. When Zhou later produced a prodigious body of theoretical writing on the modern Chinese essay, he too would give up the term *meiwen,* and adopt the term *xiaopin wen* in its stead.

If both Zhou Zuoren and Wang Tongzhao were insufficiently specific about the characteristics of their own terms, they had nevertheless succeeded in articulating the ideal for the kind of essay they were advocating. Pedantry, rationality, and argument were to be avoided, whereas flexible language, precise thinking, and a proclivity for description and narration were to be encouraged. They had also taken the first step toward delineating a tradition for the essay. Zhou presented both British and American writers as well as traditional Chinese forms as models, while Wang Tongzhao made special mention of William James and Herbert Spencer, who, in his view, were known for integrating their argumentative writings with aesthetically pleasing language. Admittedly, at this point both Zhou's and Wang's conceptions of the essay tradition were still sketchy and sometimes even self-contradictory.

With the publication of Hu Menghua's and Wu Shuzhen's "Xuyu sanwen" in 1928, however, discussion of the essay had reached such a stage that it was no longer enough for critics to throw out a name for consideration without at the same time elaborating on the aesthetic and cultural implications of the term. In this regard, Hu Menghua and Wu Shuzhen managed to touch on areas not discussed by either Zhou Zuoren or Wang Tongzhao. Hu and Wu began their analysis by pointing out that the name that they had come up with, *xuyu sanwen,* was a translation of the English term, "familiar essay," and *xuyu,* like its English counterpart, described an attitude or a tone. If, on occasion, *xuyu sanwen* wandered into areas of analysis and argumentation, it did so in a detached, impressionistic, and "familiar" way:

> How does a *xuyu sanwen* writer report and comment on a subject of topical reference? Here is an example: Let's say that you come across something in the newspaper or that you come home with news that you've heard somewhere outside. You sit down at the table and tell it in your soft-spoken voice to your kind mother, your loving wife, or your good friend. Let me be even more explicit—[a *xuyu sanwen* is] just like the kind of idle chat you engage in after a cup of tea or wine.
>
> Hu and Wu (1928, 15)

Later in the same article, they continue:

> If you are so good as to go to a teahouse, a bathhouse, or the park to listen to the words of the idle, romantic scholars there and set down their words with your pen, you will end up with a wonderful piece of *xuyu sanwen.*
>
> Hu and Wu (1928, 15)

Later in their article, Hu and Wu tackled another aspect of *xuyu sanwen*, namely its personal quality. Every word in a *xuyu sanwen* had to come from the subjectivity of the writer, they maintained, and it was this very quality that kept a piece of *xuyu sanwen* distinct from "the kind of impersonal, objective writings that criticize, argue, narrate or describe."

While I will return to the familiar qualities of modern Chinese essays at greater length later in this study, it should be pointed out here that the term *xuyu sanwen* is preferable to either *meiwen* or *chun sanwen* not only because it avoids the pitfalls of impressionistic descriptions such as "beautiful" and "pure," but also because it directs the focus of the discussion from language to the relationship between the writer and the reader on the one hand, and the writer and the world around him on the other. Indeed, when Hu Shi praised Zhou Zuoren for disproving the myth that "aesthetic writing cannot be done in the vernacular language," he merely chalked it up as another victory for the vernacular language movement, and said nothing concrete by way of explaining the special appeal of this type of essay. Similarly, Wang Bin argues that *meiwen* as a term came into being because "it served a need" (1988, 2): that is, the need to elevate the position of vernacular language relative to that of classical language. In other words, with Zhou Zuoren's essays as well as his concept of *meiwen* in their arsenal, advocates of the vernacular language could now claim that whatever traditional literature could do with the classical language, modern literature could with the vernacular.[6]

In their enthusiasm over this little victory, they overlooked the more radical aspect of the modern Chinese essay, namely, that it represented an entirely different way of approaching literature and the world.

As it happened, however, the term *xuyu sanwen* did not stick, either, although it continues to be used every now and then to this day. *Meiwen* and *chun sanwen*, on the other hand, have simply vanished from any serious discussion of Chinese essays. The term that gradually won common acceptance and has the widest currency today is *xiaopin wen*. In the same sentence quoted earlier in which he acknowledged the contributions of Zhou Zuoren's term *meiwen*, Hu Shi replaced it with

---

[6]   It is questionable, of course, whether literary language (*wenyan*) and the vernacular *(baihua)* ever exist independently of each other in practice. Even the most ardent supporters of the vernacular movement cannot but write in a combination of the two.

"xiaopin sanwen." Five years later, Zhu Ziqing, in another summation of the accomplishments of the modern essay (1928), followed the same practice. He cited the works of other scholars before him, repeating whatever term a particular scholar might have used, but when he came to his own analysis, the two terms that he used most often were *xiaopin sanwen* and *sanwen.* Thus the term *xiaopin wen* had come gradually and surreptitiously to replace other terms. When Lin Yutang launched his three journals specializing in the publication of essays from 1932 to 1934, he further reinforced the usage of this term in many of his editorial statements. From that point on, his name and his journals have been regarded as something of an emblem of *xiaopin wen.* Other critics, too, seemed relieved to see that discussion of names had ended,[7] as they could now turn to serious argument over the content of the essays. But of this, more later.

Unlike the other terms discussed so far, *xiaopin wen* has historical roots. Zhong Jingwen (1927, 30), quoting *Shishi bian kong jing (Buddhist Interpretation of Emptiness),* pointed out that the term dates back to the Six Dynasties. *Xiaopin,* in this original sense, referred to truncated *(lue)* versions of Buddhist scriptures, as distinct from *dapin,* which signified the full *(xiang)* versions.[8] Zhong, however, believed that the original meaning

---

[7]   See Yu Dafu (1935, 258) where he complained about how critics seemed to play fast and loose with terms, especially imported terms. He pointed out that, for example, some critics maintained that *"xiaopin wen"* and other terms were translated from the English word "essay," which in turn was a translation of the French word *"essais."* Such a process of translation and re-translation led some to consider Chinese writing modeled upon English essays also as *xiaopin wen.* It was one thing to assert that modern *xiaopin wen* was influenced by the Western essay, but quite another to treat the two as the same: "Why should things in China be exactly the same as those in the West? And how can the unique spirit and culture of the West be completely transported to China?" The discussion of terms had indeed reached saturation point by the late 1920s.

[8]   Since then, scholars have come up with other early instances of the term *xiaopin.* See Cao Shujuan for the fullest survey of the use of the term (1988, 17–86). Cao also points out that glossing the term *xiaopin* as a truncated version is not necessarily correct, as that implies that the fuller version precedes the truncated version in time. The fact, however, is that sometimes it is the other way round, with the *dapin* appearing later than the *xiaopin.* Rather than an abbreviation of *dapin,* therefore, it is more correct to say that *xiaopin* is simply different from

of the term *xiaopin* was not relevant to an understanding of modern *xiaopin wen*. When late Ming essayists called their essay collections *xiaopin wen*, he argued, they had already departed from the usage of the Six Dynasties. To the Ming essayists, the term first and foremost described the brevity and casualness of their works. The implied opposite of *xiaopin* in the Ming, as well as in modern times, is no longer *dapin*, but something more akin to analytical and academic writing, so full of high-minded posturing, as Zhou Zuoren pointed out.

The comparisons of late Ming essays with modern ones, however, had been going on for some time even before Zhong's article appeared. On the most superficial level, modern essayists were said to exemplify the style of their Ming predecessors. Accordingly, then, Yu Pingbo and Fei Ming were said to resemble writers of the Jingling School, while Hu Shi, Bing Xin, and Xu Zhimo were likened to those of the Gongan School (Zhou Zuoren 1932, 52).[9] Most of the time, however, comparisons went beyond impressionistic remarks as critics began to consider the similarities of the two periods. Of this group, Zhou Zuoren was most consistent in his efforts, and his theory of the origins of modern Chinese literature, which will be discussed in the next section, came as a result of this line of investigation. Suffice to say at this point that, with the wide adoption of the term *xiaopin*, discussion of the modern Chinese essay veered away from consideration of foreign influences, focusing instead on the continuation of an old tradition in a modern guise.

Before we leave the topic of names, it should be noted that a

---

dapin. These distinctions will all have implications for our discussion in the section "The Essays" below.

[9] It is relevant at this point to refer to an anecdote told by Shi Wei (1941, 47): Yu Pingbo once submitted an essay of his to Zhou Zuoren, Qian Xuantong, and Gu Jiegang without letting on that he was the author. The three were impressed with the essay but were not at all certain about the date of the composition. They decided that the essay, with all its refined language and sensibilities, could not possibly have been written in their own times. At long last, they concluded that it was a product of the early Qing, if not as far back as the late Ming.

I have not been able to verify from other independent sources the truth of this anecdote. My suspicion is that, given its perfect mix of suspense and sur-prise, the anecdote is most likely apocryphal. Be that as it may, it serves to illus-trate very well how deeply facile comparisons between late Ming and modern essayists had taken root in the popular imagination.

broader and more neutral term, *sanwen*, is sometimes used, if only because the term enables one to avoid getting into the kind of controversies that have come to plague other terms. Up to this day, for example, collections of essays are mostly published under titles that clearly display the term *sanwen* rather than others with more specific references. On the literal level, *sanwen* is equivalent to the English word "prose," and is seen in opposition to *yunwen* (verse). In this sense, it encompasses anything that is not marked by a prominent use of rhythm and rhyme.

While it is no doubt correct to name a piece of *xiaopin wen* as a work of *sanwen*, there are many other forms of writing in the vast territory of *sanwen* that do not conform to the specific characteristics of *xiaopin wen*. Therefore, in skirting controversy, critics who use the term *sanwen* have made little contribution to the understanding of *xiaopin wen* per se. Moreover, the two different but overlapping denotations of the term create another problem. On the one hand, it can be used as a complement to *yunwen* to divide all writing into two categories. On the other hand, it also designates a narrower genre of non-fictional prose, more or less equivalent to essays, and as such, allows the domain of literature to be divided into four categories: fiction, drama, poetry, and non-fictional prose. This is precisely why using the term *sanwen* can be problematic. Critics have tended to vacillate between these two conceptions of *sanwen*. In their theoretical discussions, they have tended to use the term *sanwen* in a broad sense to include all forms of prose. Yet, when they deal with particular pieces of work, they have tended for the most part to come up with examples that belong to narrower genres of prose, such as *xiaopin wen*.

The introduction of the term *sanwen* into our discussion of names makes it necessary for us to take a final look at the place the modern Chinese essay occupies in the larger scheme of classification of writing, if only because knowing where it stands relative to other forms of literature will give us a better idea of how it works. Besides, as critics have struggled to square their new understanding of *xiaopin wen* with the tripartite division of literature into fiction, poetry, and drama, a categorization that came from the West, they have also been fond of pointing out the illogicalities and inconsistencies of traditional classifications by people such as Yao Nai, Zeng Guofan, and Chen Tianding. The preceding discussion of the changing domain of *sanwen*, for example, can yield two different trees:

1. Narrow conception of the term *sanwen*
    Poetry
    Drama
    Fiction
    Sanwen (Non-fictional prose): *Xiaopin wen*
                      Other forms of non-fictional prose

2. Broad conception of the term *sanwen*
    Sanwen (Prose):   Drama
                      Fiction
                      Non-fictional prose:
                            Xiaopin wen
                            Other forms of non-fictional prose
    Poetry

These various ways of categorizing literature[10] have combined to sketch a landscape of writing against which I will attempt to position *xiaopin wen*. Rather than coming up with another diagram which is at best cumbersome in representing cross-generic forms such as poetic drama and prose poems, I will lay out below a set of questions that critics cannot avoid asking, if only implicitly, when they are asked to decide whether a piece of work is a *xiaopin wen* or not.

1. Is the work in question a work of prose or poetry?
2. If it is a work of prose, is it fictional or non-fictional?
3. If it is non-fictional,[11] is it creative prose, as opposed to argumentative or analytical prose?
4. Finally, if it is creative, is it personal, meditative prose about everyday experiences, rather than topical and discursive prose of a political and social nature?

If the above four questions seem schematic, they will serve for

---

[10]   I find the following attempts particularly useful: She Shusen (1986), Zheng Mingli (1987), Wang Bin (1988), and Li Ning (1990). Each of these has in turn considered earlier classifications.

[11]   This does not mean that everything in a *xiaopin wen* is to be taken as literal truth. In fact, as Charles Laughlin points out, essayists often create dreamscapes that have no basis in verifiable reality (2008, chapter 5). In a similar way, segments of novels are often read as short essays. What is at issue here is the simulated context in which the essay is read. Even if the essay is fictional, the reader approaches it as if it were not. Please see the section entitled "The Essays" in this Introduction.

now the purpose of leading one, by the process of elimination, to a preliminary understanding of what *xiaopin wen* is.

Disputes

> *What I mean by "A Garden of One's Own" is very flexible in scope, and is by no means restricted to any particular kind of cultivation. It does not matter what a person chooses to grow in it—it could be fruit, vegetables, medicinal herbs, roses, or dandelions. As long as he consciously devotes himself to cultivating the area that he has designated for himself, be it big or small, he has fulfilled his god-given responsibility.*
>
> *Zhou Zuoren (1923, 6)*

Among Chinese writers, the year 1934 was known as the Year of *Xiaopin Wen* (*xiaopin wen nian*). It is unclear who first came up with the name, but in retrospect, the launching in that year of Lin Yutang's *Renjianshi* (*This Human World*), a journal devoted to the publication of *xiaopin wen*, played a major role in popularizing it. From the very beginning, this designation provoked all sorts of reactions from members of various literary circles, ranging from congratulatory applause to sarcastic jeering. The debates over *xiaopin wen* rose to a new level of intensity as a result.

One has to remember that, with the gradual acceptance of the term *xiaopin wen* in the late 1920s and early 1930s, the disputes among critics had by no means abated. For one thing, while most agreed that modern *xiaopin wen* bore remarkable resemblances to essays of the late Ming, arguments still arose as to the precise nature of the similarity: iconoclasm in the face of tradition, or timidity in the face of challenges of the contemporary world? Courageous exploration of the self or willful neglect of the greater collective? An ability to see "the world in a grain of sand" or indulgence in merely gazing at the sand particle itself? The answers one gave to these questions determined whether one was a supporter or detractor of *xiaopin wen*. Secondly, again depending on their answers, different critics might have different notions of what constituted the canons of *xiaopin wen*. For example, should topical essays (*zawen*),[12] for which Lu Xun and other writers were famous, be considered as *xiaopin wen*? Or, should the term be reserved for works that

---

[12] See Scoggin (1997) for a detailed study of *zawen*.

kept a respectful distance from discussion of social and political issues? Framing this particular debate is of course the larger issue of what function literature should perform in a changing society. One might add that this question is by no means settled even today, though the terms of discussion have changed somewhat.[13] A third factor ensuring that the debate would continue was that, even among supporters of *xiaopin wen*, questions arose as to what constituted the *xiaopin wen* tradition. As Zhou Zuoren began his project to rewrite the history of modern Chinese literature, identifying late Ming literature as its immediate precursor, other friendly and unfriendly critics joined in the argument, in turn provoking further thoughts about *xiaopin wen*.

One might begin discussion of the debates over *xiaopin wen* with a comparison of Lu Xun (born Zhou Shuren) and Zhou Zuoren, the two brothers who stood opposite one another on a diverse number of issues in modern Chinese literature.[14] Of the two, Lu Xun was a tireless social gadfly, a fearless voice against injustice, and an icon of the Chinese revolution. His writings are unsentimental and uncompromising, with a somewhat strained style conveying a vision that does not seem to be articulable in any other way. Zhou Zuoren, on the other hand, projected the image of a cultivated recluse, seemingly uncommitted to any cause but in reality uncertain of his role at a time of great political and cultural change. He shied away from the kind of acerbic debates that invigorated Lu Xun, and was content to be left alone to pursue his private interests, or in his words, to cultivate "a garden of his own." His writing is typically serene and aloof. Unlike his brother, who has been hailed as a national hero, Zhou Zuoren was condemned as a traitor during and after World War II and actually served a sentence for treason.

---

[13] Fan Songpei (1993), for example, duly notes the many schools (which he calls tributaries) of essay writing at this time. Yet, he considers the one stream represented by Lu Xun as the "main current" (*zhu chao*), and gives the others, who detract from Lu Xun, such names as "mutation," "counter-current," and "bass."

[14] Comparing the Zhou brothers was a favorite exercise among intellectuals until the 1940s, according to Li Jingbin (1987). After that, with Zhou Zuoren becoming a practical non-person due to his collaboration with the Japanese, the comparison practically stopped. That Lu Xun and Zhou Zuoren represent two different interpretations of *xiaopin wen* has also been frequently commented upon. See, for example, Sun Xizhen (1935), Yu Dafu (1935), and Zhou Muzhai (1935).

Differences in temperament between the two brothers may to some degree account for the fact that they seldom saw eye to eye. Perhaps Zhou Zuoren's reclusive nature, coupled with his aversion to politics, had led him to seek out kindred spirits in the Ming dynasty. In his postscript to Yu Pingbo's *Zaban'er* (1928, 314), he speaks of the "vivacity" of late Ming art and literature, especially that of the Gongan and Jingling schools:

> People of the Gongan school managed to ignore the orthodoxy of classical prose, and proceeded to write with an expressive attitude. Although later critics condemned their writings as superficial, they were in fact expressions of the authentic self. Their achievement is higher than that of the Jingling school. Scholars in the past had a dual approach to writing, but those of the Gongan had a single approach. On this score, they are the same as modern writers....

This "dual approach," Zhou goes on to explain, refers to treating literature both as a way to convey the *dao* (*zaidao*) and as a means of diversion (*xiaoqian*). Here, in a very rudimentary form, is Zhou's theory of the origins of modern literature, which he would flesh out and modify in 1932. For the time being, however, we will focus only on his assertion that modern essays and late Ming essays are alike in combining the didactic and diversional functions into one.

To Lu Xun, such an analysis smacked of wishful thinking, suggesting that Zhou Zuoren simply wanted, as if it were, to have his cake and eat it too; he wanted to be given the freedom to engage in an enjoyable diversion through literature, but, at the same time, to be recognized for having performed some good through his writings. (Note that by 1932, Zhou would emerge from this ambiguity and speak more confidently not only of the existence of but the need for a kind of literature that is non-didactic in nature.) Lu Xun's own view was that, if it were appropriate to speak of literature as having two functions, then the Ming essayists were far from being able to combine the two. One could, in fact, separate writers with a didactic and diversional bent from one another, and that was true not only in the Ming but in the Tang, as well:

> Poetry declined at the end of the Tang, and *xiaopin wen* exuded brilliance. But Luo Yin's "On Slander" is almost full of words of rebellion and anger. Pi Rixiu and Lu Guimeng styled themselves as recluses, and were regarded by others as such, but take a look at the *xiaopin wen* in their *Pizi wen shu* and

Lize cong shu, and you will see that they had not forgotten the affairs of the world.... *Xiaopin wen* at the end of Ming was a bit disengaged from social concerns, but it did not deal exclusively with insignificant topics of the wind and the moon, and one can find in it voices against injustice, satire, criticism, and destruction.

(1933, 70)

Here, Lu Xun is not speaking against *xiaopin wen* as much as those who, out of self-interest, deliberately present a distorted picture of the Chinese literary past. On his own, Lu Xun (1935) even raised a few works of traditional Chinese literature as examples of *xiaopin wen,* but as far as the Gongan and Jingling schools are concerned, he did not have a single favorable word to say.

The most damning remark that Lu Xun (1933, 67–70) made about Zhou Zuoren's kind of *xiaopin wen* is that it was a mere "knickknack" (*xiao baishe*). As a thing of the past, it had no relevance at all to the contemporary world. Although it had a charm of its own,

> at a time when wind and sand keep pelting against our faces, when wolves and tigers gather in droves, who has the leisure to appreciate the beauty of [such things as] amber pendants dangling from paper fans, and jade rings? If we needed beauty at all, we'd prefer enormous edifices that rise in the desert. We'd want something big and strong; it does not have to be very delicate. If we needed something to give us satisfaction, we'd prefer a dagger or a pistol. We'd want something that is sharp and practical; it does not have to be very refined.

Lu Xun's rhetoric escalates and continues in a similar vein until, at the end, he compares people such as Zhou Zuoren to aging prostitutes in Shanghai. The former had to pander the old wares of late Ming essayists when their own stock was losing currency, just as the latter, finding that their declining beauty no longer attracted clients if they remained in their own quarters, now plastered heavy makeup on their faces and began to walk the streets.

The uncharitable analogy to knickknacks and, to a lesser extent, to prostitutes, began to catch on,[15] thanks most probably to its outright viciousness, and late Ming essays and their alleged modern echoes were assigned the same status as objects that served merely a decorative purpose. As for the promoters of the Gongan and Jingling schools, they

---

[15]   See, for example, Mao Dun (1934a, 1934b) and Zhou Muzhai (1935).

were seen to lead, unwittingly or otherwise, to a life out of touch with reality. The caricature of the man of leisure that opened our discussion sets up effectively the contrast between the warmth and peacefulness of his inner sanctum and the inclement weather outside. Only the most insensitive could be satisfied with the cocooned life the man is leading. Significantly, the theme of "knickknacks" remains prominent throughout the caricature, as Qian Gechuan goes one by one through his description of the painting, calligraphy, incense burner, potted plants, snuffbox, and, finally, collection of Ming essays picked at random from the shelf.

It is clear that the focus of the debate had now shifted. Disagreements continued as to what constituted a genuine piece of *xiaopin wen*, but critics were now more concerned with what kind of writing China needed at this particular juncture in history. In the passage just quoted, Lu Xun indicated in figurative terms that what China needed was strong structures that would withstand the onslaught of desert storms, and daggers and pistols that would prove useful in fighting. Yet, he did not rule out completely the need for rest and diversion, if only to better "prepare us for labor and battle" (1933, 70).

By contrast, Lin Yutang's priorities seemed to be just the opposite. Although to some extent he shared Lu Xun's distaste for "knickknacks,"[16]

---

[16] While Lu Xun criticized the "knickknack-style" of *xiaopin wen*, Lin Yutang was quick, perhaps too quick, to point out categorically that modern *xiaopin wen* was not like that at all (1934c, 99): "Modern *xiaopin wen* is different from the kind of traditional knickknack-style writing that dwells on the art of brewing tea or drinking wine, but is also called *xiaopin wen*.... People of the past might withdraw to a '*xiao*' position because they were at odds with the literature of the establishment. The writing that they came up with belonged mostly to the miscellaneous type recording the idle words of recluses, just so that they could avoid writing of a serious and worldly kind. Their behavior can be explained by the fact that literature dealing with affairs of state was usually beset with taboos, and if one simply followed the safe, established formulas, there would not be too many original things one could say. As a result, *biji* literature became the major current in Chinese literature. In staying away from the path of the establishment, modern *xiaopin wen* is the same as *biji*. However, the scope of *xiaopin wen* is much larger, and its usage and forms have also changed. It can no longer be encompassed by the *biji* format." A look at the essays published in the three journals Lin Yutang launched, *Lunyu* (*Analects*), *Renjianshi* (*This Human World*), and *Yuzhou feng* (*Cosmic Wind*), however, will show that some of them belonged squarely to the type that Lu Xun was satirizing.

he was not quite ready to go so far as to choose "daggers and pistols."
The "Inaugural Preface" of *Renjianshi* (*This Human World*) reveals the
kind of writing he was trying to solicit:

> *Xiaopin wen* can be used to advance an argument, to express fully one's
> inner feelings, to depict human ways, to describe social customs, to record
> the trivial, and to discourse on the world at large. Its scope is not fixed,
> yet its core is made of the voice of the self, and its style is leisurely and
> disinterested (*xianshi*).

(1934b, 89)

Later in the same article, he continues to harp on the theme of all-
inclusiveness, adding that *Renjianshi* would entertain submissions touching
on topics "as enormous as the universe, or as small as a fly."

If at this point Lin Yutang appeared to be much more accepting
than Lu Xun of writing different from his own, one has to bear in mind
that he had included a restriction, namely, that essays had to be written
in a leisurely and disinterested style, which is inherently at odds with the
advancement of argument, one of the areas of writing that he seemed
to endorse.[17] By June of the same year, when Lin Yutang published
another article to answer questions arising from his "Inaugural Preface,"
he had made some subtle modifications in his position, toning down the
use of *xiaopin wen* to advance an argument and instead devoting most of
his time to elaborating the nature of a leisurely and disinterested style.
This he described as a kind of liberation, very similar to that afforded
by the use of vernacular language. More precisely, it was a kind of
conversational style, which would work well with any topic.

Meanwhile, one of Lin Yutang's other remarks had given rise to
what was facetiously referred to as "The Debate over the Universe and
the Fly" (Mao Dun 1934a, 112). Like his call for the use of humor
in *Lunyu*, which he had edited two years before, the inclusive gesture
implied in his statement about the universe and the fly did not produce
the result he intended. The quality of the kind of humor that *Lunyu* had
managed to attract was admittedly mixed and, as Mao Dun pointed
out, it was getting more essays in the line of flies than of the universe.
Renjianshi was not doing much better.

Feeling beleaguered, Lin Yutang retreated further in his position,

---

[17]   The restrictiveness of *Lunyu* is further made clear by the submission guidelines
published in the first issue. See Charles Laughlin, 2008, Chapter 4.

while at the same time appearing to take the offensive. Declaring that *Renjianshi* would discuss what non-*xiaopin wen* journals avoided, and avoid what lofty and high-minded writings would discuss (1934c, 100), he had finally positioned himself directly opposite to Lu Xun. While he still occasionally theorized on the extra-literary functions of *xiaopin wen*, he seemed to be more contented with doing what he was good at. As he noted, "What I said about 'advancing an argument' or 'expressing one's emotions' are just matters of style, and have nothing to do with such things as social ideology, or strengthening or losing one's country. That's why I have said before that *Renjianshi* may promote *xiaopin wen* as much as it wants, and our nation will neither be stronger nor weaker because of it. All I want is to run a good magazine, and the most I can do is promote a certain style of prose" (1934b, 102).

Zhou Zuoren had retreated to a similar position earlier in his "A Garden of One's Own" (1923). His strong preference for *xiaopin wen*, however, led him to continue producing an impressive amount of writing on *xiaopin wen*. Among this corpus, his book, *Zhongguo xin wenxue di yuanliu* (*The Origins of Modern Chinese Literature*), deserves special mention not only because it boldly offered an overview of the development of Chinese literature, but because, simplistic and flawed as his arguments may have been, he touched on an important aspect of the *xiaopin* essay often forgotten in the bitter exchanges of the critics.

Zhou's rather elaborate theory was delivered in five lectures at Furen University in 1932. To him, the history of Chinese literature was marked by the alternation of two literary trends: *yanzhi* and *zaidao*. Usually translated as "poetry expressing the heart's wishes" and "literature as a vehicle for the Way (*dao*)," these two trends approximate what are known in the West as the expressive theory and pragmatic theory of literature, respectively. Zhou believed that the domination of one trend over another was closely related to political and cultural conditions of particular historical periods. Hence in the Han, Tang, Song, Ming, and Qing, all deemed stable and politically unified periods of Chinese history by Zhou's account, the pragmatic theory prevailed and literature was summoned to the service of the dominant state ideology of the time. In periods that witnessed major political and social upheavals, however, such as the late Zhou, Six Dynasties, Five Dynasties and Ten Kingdoms, Yuan, and late Ming, the expressive theory raised its head, and imagination was free to roam. The twentieth century, Zhou continued, had so far been a period of instability for China; consequently, its literature bore a striking resemblance to that of the unstable period immediately previous to this one, namely, the late Ming of the late sixteenth and early seventeenth centuries, when various progressive schools of thought had indeed come into being, including the two schools of writing mentioned above, Gongan and Jingling. Zhou's main contention was that essays written in these two periods were similar not only formally, but also in their spirit of rebellion against the stultifying cultural climate that preceded them. What made the modern period different from the late Ming, however, was the presence of the West in the twentieth century, a view that ultimately led Zhou Zuoren to arrive at this equation:

Modern *xiaopin* essays = Essays of the Gongan and Jingling schools + Western progressive ideas and sensibilities.[18]

The attacks on Zhou Zuoren that followed these lectures surprised no one, but it is necessary to separate genuine intellectual disagreement from thinly veiled personal vendettas. Zhou Zuoren had the combined misfortune of having a reclusive nature and Lu Xun as an older brother. Unlike his brother, Zhou Zuoren's real interest was in Chinese and Greek literature, and, after a brief period of total immersion in the May Fourth Movement, he had decided to withdraw to a life of privacy. This apolitical declaration angered many people who interpreted it as an escapist gesture and a betrayal of much of what his brother—and he himself during the heyday of the May Fourth period—had stood for. That Lu Xun himself had come to speak openly against the implications of Zhou's theory only further compromised Zhou's reputation. His effort to establish the link between essays of the late Ming and the modern *xiaopin* essay was seen as just another manifestation of his regressive and anachronistic thinking. Instead of looking forward and outward, his critics charged, Zhou Zuoren would have us look backward. When, in 1937, Zhou Zuoren chose to remain in Beijing rather than flee the Japanese invasion, and later, in 1941, assumed the post of Minister of Education in the occupation government, his critics felt confirmed in their conviction that he was not to be trusted. From this point on, their

---

[18] This, apparently, was Zhou's response to those critics who thought he had not given sufficient credit to Western influences. Zhu Ziqing (1928, 46) says, for example, "The most direct influence on modern prose is, after all, from foreign countries—a point that Zhou Zuoren has not made clear."

attacks on him became all the more vituperative.

Turning to more substantive criticism, there were some who held a different view of history from Zhou. In arguing that periods of unity alternate with those of disorder, Zhou of course was merely reiterating the conventional cyclical view of history. Hence, while the disappearance of an ideological center in the twentieth century had allowed Chinese writers to express themselves freely, Zhou predicted that history would swing back to another period of strict control. This, as he himself admitted, was in direct contradiction to the assumptions that underlay *Baihua wenxue shi* (*A History of Vernacular Literature*), published in 1928 by Hu Shi, who saw the course of Chinese literary history as a slow but unswerving movement toward recognition and then canonization of vernacular literature.

In a somewhat bastardized version of Hu's approach, Chen Zizhan argued that, ever since the May Fourth Movement, Chinese writers had devoted themselves to the mission of propagating new ideas and challenging the tradition, all in a concerted effort to bring China into the modern age (1935, 215). They did not indulge, Chen held, nor would they in the future, in the kind of idle mental introspection characteristic of late Ming writing,[19] but would always work to fulfill the sacrosanct function of literature as a vehicle of social engineering. Even if, for the sake of argument, one were to concede the validity of the two literary trends delineated by Zhou, the twentieth century, according to Chen, had been overwhelmed by the *zaidao* trend. For this reason, Chen, together with others of a similar persuasion, went so far as to contend with Zhou Zuoren for the right to use the term *xiaopin*, which they reserved for short essays with a pronounced social message, such as the topical essay (*zawen*) for which Lu Xun is famous.

It was the next two critics, Qian Zhongshu and Zhu Ziqing, both of whom were respectable *xiaopin* writers in their own right, who managed to detect an underlying theme in this concatenation of voices. Qian Zhongshu (1934), in his review of Zhou's *Zhongguo xin wenxue di yuanliu*, directed his attention to the semantics of the two terms, *yanzhi* and *zaidao*, pointing out that historically, the latter was used in reference

---

[19]   A secondary point of Chen Zizhan's criticism is that the Gongan and Jingling schools are in any case really famous only for poems. Zhou was simply too desperate in his search for early models of *xiaopin wen*, and had overlooked this fundamental point, Chen asserts (see 1935).

to prose and the former, lyrical poetry, and that, therefore, they were literary modes rather than trends. By summoning these two diverse modes of writing to differentiate period styles, Qian believed that Zhou had in effect ignored the restrictions of literary genres under which all writers operate. It was a very common phenomenon in Chinese history, for example, for the same writer to appear an ardent supporter of the pragmatic theory in his prose, but a faithful proponent of the expressive theory in his poetry. In Qian's view, Zhou was being simplistic in describing a historical period as completely dominated by one or the other.

From a different angle, Zhu Ziqing, an admirer of Zhou Zuoren, also questioned the use of *yanzhi*. Tracing the origin of this term to such classical texts as the *Shijing* (*The Book of Songs*), *Liji* (*The Book of Rites*), *Zuo zhuan* (*The Zuo Commentary*), and *Shi da xu* (*The Great Preface to the Book of Poetry*), Zhu duly noted the political use of poetry in antiquity (1947, 29–47). Hence, *yanzhi*, in his view, by no means suggested the expressivism that Zhou had associated with the term, but rather, denoted a state of mind that has more to do with the public domain of diplomacy and political remonstration than with the telling of one's private preoccupations. In this sense, *yanzhi* is in fact not that different from *zaidao*, when the *dao* (the Way) of the latter has been more or less internalized as the *zhi* (the wishes) of the former.[20] Consequently, Zhu held, what Zhou Zuoren called the *yanzhi* tradition of modern *xiaopin wen* should perhaps more appropriately be ascribed to the tradition of *yuanqing* (literature emerging from human feelings) that began in the Six Dynasties period, a time that, significantly, marked the maturation of lyrical aesthetics in China. Zhu's philological excursion should not be taken as mere quibbling over words, for without explicitly saying so, he had extended the genealogy of modern *xiaopin wen* further back than Zhou Zuoren to the Six Dynasties.

Each in his own friendly or hostile way, then, Chen Zizhan, Qian Zhongshu and Zhu Ziqing had led the discussion of what had been regarded up to this point as predominantly a prose form to consideration of the integration of poetic and prose elements in *xiaopin wen*. Zhou Zuoren's own admission that he had indeed merged poetry and prose

---

20   See also Bo Han, who says, "True enough, *xiaopin wen* is a kind of *yanzhi* literature, but within this *zhi*, there is also *dao*. There is no *zhi* without a certain degree of *dao* in it" (1935, 122).

together in his analysis[21] further pointed to a potentially rich area for exploration. This unfortunately produced no further repercussions in the theoretical discussion, and one has to turn to the essays themselves to understand the effect of *xiaopin wen*'s generic mixture of poetry and prose.

The Essays

I have always felt that there are only three kinds of writing in the world. The best kind is writing that comes from speaking to oneself; the second best, from speaking to one person [other than oneself]; and the third, from speaking to many people. The first kind includes poetry and the most pure literature. In this kind of writing, there is an audience, of course, but the writer's first intention is to express what cannot remain unexpressed in his mind.... The second kind includes letters and conversations. Here, one is speaking to bosom friends who fully understand one and whom one fully understands. There is no need to stand on ceremony or strike poses.... The third kind includes all sorts of official correspondences and lecture notes, manifestos and even pieces such as "On the Art of Ruling" and "On Jia Yi." [In this kind of writing] the writer's first intention is to convert his readers to his viewpoint, or even to show off in front of them....

Of the three, I love to read the first kind, but it is beyond me to write it. I produce the third kind every day since I have to come up with notes for my class, but I loathe it. The second kind is the only kind that allows me to appreciate the pleasure of writing. The compositions of which I am most proud are my love letters and then the ordinary correspondence with friends in which I can speak about matters of the heart. In these letters, I write down what comes into

---

[21]   It will be noted here that Zhou Zuoren himself at times did not see *zaidao* and *yanzhi* as exclusive concepts. In his preface to *Zhongguo xin wenxue daxi* (*The Collectanea of Modern Chinese Literature*)—*Prose, Volume I*, he further comments on the way he uses the two terms: "I delineated the two schools of *yanzhi* and *zaidao* merely as a matter of expediency. However, since *yanzhi* traditionally is used to describe poetry and *zaidao* to describe prose, it does appear I have caused some confusion by mixing poetry and prose together in my analysis. Besides, the boundary between *zhi* and *dao* became blurry as a result, leading to further confusion. This is why I have further elaborated my position, saying: To speak of other people's *zhi* is the same as *zaidao*, and to convey one's own *dao* is the same as *yanzhi*" (1935, 250). It is difficult to say whether this annotation serves further to clarify or confuse the issue.

my mind, and what springs from my heart. I am not afraid that somebody else will know of the contents, nor do I care whether the person who reads the letters thinks my writing good or bad, because I know him and he knows me. That, to me, is the most enjoyable thing.

Zhu Guangqian (1936, 291)

As noted in my earlier analysis of the term *xuyu sanwen*, modern Chinese essays are informed by a distinct set of attitudes toward the reader and a particular way of approaching and interpreting the world around us. In the concluding part of this introduction, I will explore these two aspects of *xiaopin wen*, with examples drawn from works included in this anthology.

In 1936, Zhu Guangqian wrote the passage quoted above to decline an invitation from the journal *Tian di ren* (*Heaven, Earth, People*) to submit essays. In his letter, he spoke in the voice of an aficionado of *xiaopin wen* in describing the three types of writing, each of which has its own specific audience. Although he did not state it explicitly, Zhu Guangqian placed *xiaopin wen* in the second kind of writing, ranking it together with letters and conversations. The target audience of this kind of writing, he notes, is one's closest friends, to whom one can freely speak one's mind. There is no need at all for posturing, and one can, to use a term of the *xiaopin* critics, go about one's writing in a leisurely and disinterested *(xianshi)* fashion.

As an illustration of this *xianshi* quality, early discussions of *xiaopin wen* usually alluded to the following passage from Kuriyagawa Hakuson, which, incidentally, also underlines the intimacy between the essayist and his readers:

Sitting in a rocking chair by the stove in winter, or putting on a bathrobe in summer, one drinks tea and chats casually with one's good friends. Put these words directly on paper and you have an *essay*. Go wherever your mood takes you and talk about things that do not give you a headache. You can feel free to express your feelings in ridicule, witticisms, *humor* or *pathos*. The topics may cover, in addition to matters of national import, the petty affairs of the marketplace, opinions on one's readings, news of acquaintances, and memories of the past. Talk about whatever comes to mind, then express it spontaneously with your pen, and you have an essay.[22]

---

[22] Quoted by many including He Yubo (1934, 14) and Li Subo (1932, 48), the passage was first translated into Chinese by, of all people, Lu Xun. The italicized words are in English in his translation.

Taking this passage together with Zhu Guangqian's description of the three circles of readers, one arrives at what can be called the "simulated context"[23] of essays: A person speaking to someone intimate about sundry subjects in an unhurried way. Nothing is considered unworthy of attention, be it a description of the childish antics of a boy servant (Lin Yutang's "Ah Fang"), or an account of being caught in the rain in the mountains (Feng Zikai's "Seeking Shelter from the Rain in the Mountains"), or simply musings upon looking at one's hand (Su Qing's "My Hand"). The other major attributes of *xiaopin wen*—intimacy, naturalness, and artlessness—are in turn seen to evolve directly from this context.

Accordingly, the essayists introduced here took pains to maintain the façade of the simulated context by various rhetorical means. Bing Xin, for example, speaks in her "The Treasure That Will Always Be with Us" of the many personal letters that she lost during the war, many of which, she claims, read like "poetry and essays." Taking the analogy even further, Zhou Zuoren in "Black-Canopied Boats" and Xu Dishan in "Undelivered Letters" simply write their essays in the form of letters. Others, such as Zhu Xiang and Wu Boxiao, pretend to speak to the reader directly, asking for his opinions and inviting him to participate in the world created by their works.

No essay in this anthology, however, is as explicit in maintaining the myth of a frank exchange with readers as Su Xuelin's "In My Moments of Dejection":

> Besides reading, it also cheers me up sometimes to write to friends, because in my letters I can talk about everything under the sun. Although what I say is of no great importance, and for the most part devoid of any structure, there's no need for me to strike unnatural poses or assume affected tones as I would if I were to speak to society at large. I also don't need to follow a carefully worked-out plan as I would in my academic writing. I can say whatever is on my mind—where my thoughts go, so will my pen. This is nothing less than the natural expression of my personality, and an overflow of the truest sounds of my heart. By writing this way, not only do I experience the joy of liberation, but so does my reader.

> Although I do have a few friends, they are all very busy, and when I write

---

[23] The term comes from Patrick Hanan (1973), who uses it in his studies of classical tales and vernacular stories. In many ways, the simulated context of modern essays bears a remarkable resemblance to that of classical tales.

> to them, they are obliged to write back. I feel uneasy about forcing other
> people to sacrifice their precious time to read my letters and then reply,
> just so that I can dispel this feeling of indifference. So, I have thought of
> another way—to write only for myself, and take it as an exchange between
> myself and my own soul.

In the first paragraph, Su Xuelin is still speaking about the joy of
communicating with friends, but in the second, she has actually crossed
the line that separates Zhu Guangqian's first and second groups of
readers. What she proposes to show the second group—the "paintings
of her heart"—should be reserved for herself alone. We are drawn, as it
were, ever closer to her innermost thoughts.

Lest one take this gesture of baring one's soul to one's readers at
face value, however, it bears repeating that all of these rhetorical devices
are but a pretense, and that not all writers felt unabashed enough to
dwell exclusively on private matters in what, in reality, was published
and read by the public. Some even felt the need to justify their passing
over opportunities to comment on topics with social implications. After
talking about, among other things, the poetic pleasures of listening to
the croaking of frogs in a heavy downpour, Zhou Zuoren concludes his
"Bitter Rain" with the following remarks:

> In the villages, the rain this time must have been a disaster for the poor.
> Since I did not witness it, it would be pointless for me to exercise my
> imagination and make a pretense of lamenting their plight. If someone
> were to say that what I have written down here is just my personal business
> and doesn't contribute to human life in general, I'd willingly admit it.
> Talking about my personal affairs is exactly what I set out to do, and I do
> not aspire to any other goal than that. The sun has come out today, and in
> the evening, we can go out to play. I will stop here.

This essay is written in the form of a personal letter to the writer's
friend. As part of a "private letter," the above passage is peculiarly out
of place: Who would find it necessary to apologize for the lack of a
social message in a letter meant only for the recipient? Obviously, then,
Zhou had stepped out of his role as the writer of a personal letter into a
simulated context (with which the rest of the essay conspires); reverting
to Zhou Zuoren the essayist, and perhaps unwittingly revealing that the
supposedly intimate relationship between a writer and his readers is but
part of the simulated context of *xiaopin wen.*

If Zhou is all earnestness in answering the call to contribute to what he calls a "general understanding of life," Yu Pingbo makes a joke out of the whole thing in "Going to the City." Playful and irreverent, Yu draws the reader into collusion with the joke that animates the essay. He begins in an ambulatory manner with a commonplace description of an evening scene—the darkening sky, the continuous stretch of fog, the bumpy ride, and the scenery on the road. If, at this point, the essay seems to wander a bit (which, by the way, seems to be an appropriate analogue to the travel theme of the essay), the title, suggesting a final destination, nevertheless creates an expectation that a denouement will be offered at the end to tie up the loose ends. This, however, fails to materialize, and Yu Pingbo quickly overturns the reader's expectation of a unifying conclusion by raising questions about the very purpose of writing itself. He imagines his reader saying,

> "You know, you really have nothing much to tell about your trip to the city, and yet you're trying to pass this off as an essay? You must be pulling my leg." You never know, though, do you? You, with your wisdom, should be the judge: If indeed there were something to "tell," it would most likely be about a blown-out tire, a break-down by the side of the road, or, worse, a crash into an electric pole, sending the bus and its passengers spilling onto their backs. Even worse still, it could be a shout in the style of the bandits in *Outlaws of the Marsh* that makes even the one in the yellow cotton jacket [i.e., the Emperor] tremble in fear. That would be very messy, wouldn't it? Southerners call incidents like these "unstomachable," and northerners declare them "intolerable." If indeed any of these events had happened, would you really expect me to have the time and peace of mind to toy with my brush and paper and come up with a piece of idle scribbling such as this?

Yu Pingbo's subtle joke, apart from bringing his essay to a conclusion, (albeit not of the kind the title leads us to expect), can by extension be taken as an answer to some of the criticism of *xiaopin wen* discussed earlier. Taken as a general statement about the writing of *xiaopin wen*, his conclusion can be read as an answer to the unrealistic expectations of some critics, who somehow think that the value of writing lies in its advancing certain predetermined social and political goals. However, in areas that demand practical social action, Yu seems to ask, why resort to writing? Who, indeed, "would have the time and peace of mind" to set pen to paper then?

Some writers tried to tread the middle ground and pay lip service to the demand that they provide lessons in their work. In one of his early essays, "Old Men," He Qifang describes three old men who, lonely and more or less neglected, nevertheless inspired the writer as a young boy with their tenacity and rich experiences. Toward the end, he imagines himself reaching a ripe old age:

> Finally, I see that I myself have become an old man, alone and calm, like a tree quietly tucked in the countryside in the winter. I study plants. I live among humble vegetables, tall-standing fruit trees, blooming shrubs. Like them, I follow the cycle of nature's seasons. A hoe is always in my hand, and through it, I get close to the earth. Perhaps I will raise bees under the eaves where there is some sun. Life is too bitter: Let us put a little sugar in our tea. On long nights when sleep is ever shorter, I will sit by the flickering oil lamp and slowly, meticulously, recall and write down the stories of my life.

As far as bringing his reverie to an end and keeping a uniformity of tone is concerned, this would seem to be a fitting conclusion to the essay. Yet, He Qifang is not ready to leave the subject until he provides a word of counsel to the reader:

> But suddenly I awake from deep thought. What a preposterous dream this is! Between my mature years and my old age, there is still a long way to go. What should I fill it with? It should not be dreams but serious work.

Thus ends lamely an essay that would otherwise hold together much more coherently. As one can see from this example, the concluding morals one finds in some of the essays tend to be words of wisdom artificially and perfunctorily attached to the end; while failing to appease the critics, they only succeed in rupturing the aesthetic world that the rest of the essays have conjured up. The ending to Zhu Xiang's "Books" and Liang Yuchun's "On the Road" can be read in a similar way.

When these essays are juxtaposed with Lu Li's "The Water Pestle" and another of He Qifang's essays, "Hunger," the artificiality and superficiality of their attempts to moralize become all the more obvious. Lu Li's essay, in particular, leads the reader imperceptibly but inexorably toward a serious indictment of the inhumanity of society, and for that reason, deserves a closer look here.

"The Water Pestle" opens with a beguilingly innocent question to the reader: "How many of us have heard the monotonous sound of a pestle on the bank of a rushing river at midnight?" This sets up right away what might well have developed into a lyrical description of a pastoral scene. The paragraph that follows continues with more or less the same appealing nature theme: a river bank far from human habitation, a murmuring stream, a lone owl, a ridiculous-looking beaver, and a wild duck flapping its wings on the water. A careful reader may detect a certain jarring note in the mention of wolves howling, but at this point, they are far away in the distant hills, and as such, can easily be excluded from the pastoral world the essay promises to deliver.

Yet, the scene suddenly turns cold and desolate in the next paragraph as the mill by the river is described in terms usually associated with a living hell. The frigid wind and flickering lamp are brought in to emphasize its isolation. Far from the human community it serves, the mill becomes a place of exile for the destitute and unfortunate, fit only for shepherds and wild children. During festivals, the contrast between its solitude and the revelry that takes place around it becomes all the more unmistakable: While families in the nearby village prepare to celebrate the New Year, the old watchman and the child-bride have to work doubly hard by the pestles. The quiet night scene established in the first paragraph now only underscores their lonely, pathetic condition, while some of the images begin to take on sinister implications. The owl, compared to a philosopher in the second paragraph, now appears to resemble human beings in yet another way. Both, apparently, feed on their own kind. Likewise, the game the children play by the water mill, "tiger feeding its cubs," offers a veiled criticism of human cruelty: In contrast to the tiger, who takes care of its young, we human beings prey on the helpless among us.

Finally, Lu Li's essay is largely constructed on the symbolism of sound. At first, the pestles merely sound "monotonous" beside the "murmuring, splashing, flowing water." The howling of wolves is a faint echo, and on the whole, the surroundings are so quiet that one can actually hear the splashing of fish swimming upstream. Other ominous sounds are brought in gradually as one moves further into the essay: the whistling of the northerly wind through the cracks on the mill floor and, more importantly, the magnified sound of the pestles, which have turned into a deafening thud. In the end, their sound tortures the child-bride "like a giant spirit," assaulting her delicate soul day and night. When the news arrives that the child-bride has been drawn into the mortar and reduced to pulp, the writer can only "close the window that opens out to the river and cover [his] head with the comforter to stop the sound of the water mill on the other bank from reaching [his] ears"—the very sound, one will remember, with which the writer begins his essay by inviting the reader to listen.

The effectiveness of "The Water Pestle" can no doubt be attributed predominantly to the meticulous skill with which Lu Li develops his imagery and symbolism, two areas that are more often associated with poetry than with prose. The cross-generic qualities of essays have often been commented on in both China and the West,[24] but when Chinese critics have offered statements to the effect that the essay is a "bridge between prose and poetry" (Zhou Zuoren 1921) or that *xiaopin wen* and lyrical poetry are "a pair of lovely twins, although *xiaopin wen* is much more carefree and mischievous" (Liang Yuchun 1930, 42), they have tended to have in mind matters that go beyond the employment of literary tropes. Rather, they are alluding to a certain kind of suggestiveness in *xiaopin wen* that is reminiscent of lyrical poetry, a quality that enables one to apprehend the significant through the examination of the trivial *(yixiao jianda)*.[25]

---

[24] Western scholarship tends to focus on the boundary between the essay and the short story (Hesse 1989; Gerlach 1989; Ferguson 1982), while Chinese scholarship looks more closely at that between the essay and the poem. An interesting development is observable in Western scholarship: When, as is often the case, an individual text refuses to submit to neat categorization into either essay or story, critics begin to read the text first as an example of one genre, and then of the other, often with highly rewarding results. The strategy employed here is not to label a text as either an essay or a story, but to see what reading it as an essay or as a story will yield. See Hesse, especially. In this connection, one recalls the practice of many Chinese critics, who, in looking for earlier examples of *xiaopin wen*, suggest that portions of long novels such as the preface to *Rulin washi*, or individual biographies in the *Shiji*, can be read as essays. Herein seems to lie some fertile ground for investigation.

[25] The traditional meaning of the term *xiaopin* as the antithesis to *dapin* seems to suggest that what is available in *xiaopin wen* is but a briefer and simpler view of some major truth *(daoli)*, which may have led Lu Xun to make the following sarcastic remark about *xiaopin wen* in general: "Only writing that dwells on minor *daoli*, or simply no *daoli*, and that does not go on at any sustained length—only writing like this can be called *xiaopin wen*" (1935, 287).

Although I share Zhong Jingwen's view (1927) that the traditional meaning of the term *xiaopin* is irrelevant to our study here, Y. K. Kao's observation of the social practice of passing judgment on a person's character during the Six Dynasties may cast light on the *yixiao jianda* quality in *xiaopin wen*. Kao describes the practice in this way: "Judgment was frequently expressed in terms of ranking and classification, but it could also be rendered, more variably, by an epithet and comment. The latter method of delivering a rating partly reflected a new attitude toward judgments: a thorough investigation of the candidate's personal

Yixiao jianda refers first and foremost to a way of making sense of the world and its manifestation in literature, but the phrase has given rise to a variety of interpretations. On the most superficial level, Chen Shuhua (1935, 137) describes the trivial depicted in *xiaopin wen* as "tremendous trifles," a term he borrowed from the title of one of G. K. Chesterton's essay collections. In Chen's relativistic reading of the relationship between the big and the small, the significant and the trivial, the value of any human situation is wholly dependent on the viewer. What appears to be trivial to one can therefore be of tremendous significance to others. Yu Dafu presents another view, referring to the practice of modern essayists of teasing out ethical concerns and human significance from scenes of nature:

> Even the lyrical prose works of the purest of poets always have something to say about the relationship between individual and individual, or between individuals and society, when they are merely speaking about [insignificant things such as] wind and flowers, the snow and the moon.... This is one characteristic of the modern essay: To see the world in a grain of sand, to expound on human ways through the contemplation of half a petal.

> (1935, 258)

While this may be true of individual writers, Yu Dafu, like Chen Shuhua, has overlooked the fact that *yixiao jianda* is a characteristic of the genre rather than of the writers.

In another part of the same article, however, Yu Dafu comes closer to elucidating the poetics of the essay. After pointing out that prose is in general not governed by poetic matters such as tones, meter, parallelism, or antithesis, he nevertheless goes on to say:

> But in an essay, one can find what Wang Yuyang called *shenyun*, or the lingering sense of what Westerners call rhythm, provided that one is not bound inflexibly by tonal rules, and instead considers the broader sense of natural rhythm. The revolution of the seasons, the alternation of *yin* and *yang*, the cycle of day and night, or even the back and forth movement of

---

history was replaced by a cursory but penetrating cameo sketch of character as revealed *at a particular moment*" (1991, 63–64, italics added). Coming from more or less the same time in history, the term *xiaopin* may have carried with it the same cultural associations. As the analysis below will show, that *xiaopin wen* is able to suggest something beyond its literal meanings is ultimately contingent upon its ability to capture a pregnant moment.

our feet as we walk—none of these clash with the rhythms of nature. It is quite possible for essays to convey cadences such as these, but not those generated by language tones.

(1935, 258)

Yu Dafu fails to provide examples, without which it is difficult to ascertain how he sees this broadened sense of rhythm manifesting itself in prose works, but one wonders whether he does not have in mind essays such as Feng Zikai's "A Mean Alleyway," Bing Xin's "The Smile," and He Qifang's "Old Men." There is a sense of poetic repetition in all three essays, where an experience is replayed a number of times, with each successive occasion representing a complication of the earlier ones. One can further argue that, taken by itself, the experience depicted in each of these essays is perhaps of no great importance, but taken together, all of these instances of repetition add up to something larger, allowing the reader as well as the speaker to gain a more complete view not affordable otherwise.

Ultimately, however, *yixiao jianda* has to be understood in connection with the affinity between *xiaopin wen* and lyrical poetry that critics have more than once intimated, especially in the way that *xiaopin wen*, like poetry, is able to capture a singular moment. The following two critics speak about this with varying degrees of explicitness:

> In a matter of several lines, it is possible to portray a character to the fullest, or analyze a political situation to the core.... One cannot expect to find this kind of effect in an argumentative essay. Rather, conversations are like that all the time. Otherwise, why would the ancients have said, "to have a night of conversation is far better than studying for ten years"?... It stimulates one's thinking and leads one to profound thoughts. By revealing the truth in one sentence, one can attain sudden enlightenment. If one follows this method in writing, one will not produce a single bad essay.

(Lin Yutang 1934a, 103)

> In choosing the right material [for a piece of *xiaopin wen*], one has to pick an aspect that best reveals the whole, or compress what one wants to capture in the essay to the most extraordinary moment. Only then does one begin the composition.[26]

(Feng Sanmei 1936, 62)

---

[26] Feng Sanmei uses the word "corner" (*yijiao*), although it is clear from the context that he is referring to a moment in time.

Seize the moment, both Lin and Feng are saying—a moment that is not significant in itself, but constitutes a focal point to which the myriad aspects of the experience being depicted converge; a moment, one might add, that is reminiscent of the lyrical moment in the creation of lyrical poetry.[27]

In this light, Xia Mianzun's "A Memory," Zhang Ailing's "Love," and Fang Lingru's "Home" can be considered records of similar pregnant moments. The latter two essays are especially deserving of comment.

As Zhang's essay is short, I will reproduce it below in its entirety:

This is a true story.

There once lived a beautiful girl from a well-to-do family in a village. Many people came with matchmaking proposals but nothing came of them. She was no more than fifteen or sixteen that year.

One spring evening, she was standing by the back door, her hand resting on a peach tree next to her. She remembered that she had on a moon-white blouse. There was a young man who lived across the road. They had seen each other before, but had never greeted each other. He came over and stopped at a place not too far from her. He said softly, "Oh, you're here too?" She did not say anything in particular. Neither did he. They stood there for a while, and then went about their own business.

That is it.

Later, the girl was abducted by a relative and sold elsewhere as a concubine, after which she was sold three or four more times. She still remembered in her old age the incident that had taken place so long before, though she had lived through a life of numerous terrible upheavals. She often talked about that spring evening... the peach tree by the back door... the young man.

When, among the tens of thousands of people you might have met, you meet the very person you were meant to meet, and when, among the tens

---

[27] Cf. Y. K. Kao, on the lyrical moment: "The moment of the present emerges as the dominant time frame. But this moment is not static, it extends into the past and future in order to accommodate the continual internal evolution of an experience moving from one state to another, and it is in addition a sustaining moment which may last a long time. In other words, the sense of the present is always imminent. Viewed in this light, time is no longer an objective measure, but a subjective quality belonging intimately to experience" (1991, 52).

of thousands of years in the boundless wilderness of time, you arrive at just the right spot at just the right moment, not a step too soon, not a step too late, there is nothing else you can say, but to ask softly, "Oh, you're here, too?"

The highlighted moment—that of the encounter between the young woman and the young man—works subtly in the construction of meaning in Zhang's essay. It draws the reader's attention by virtue of the central position it occupies in the consciousness of the protagonist as well as the physical layout of the essay on the printed page, and therefore is pivotal to one's understanding of the essay. Throughout her account, Zhang stresses the coincidental and, from a storytelling viewpoint, unmotivated aspects of the encounter. Any other possible way of interpreting this experience is thus ruled out. Nothing leads up to it, and nothing, in a sense, comes out of it. "That is it," Zhang writes, peremptorily ending an account that she had just as suddenly started a few lines before. Although in effect the account continues to unfold for yet another paragraph, it is terminated here. A moment is thus established, of which the rest becomes mere extension, and to which the thoughts of the protagonist will always return.

Of these three essays, Fang Lingru's "Home" promises to open up the widest vista for appreciation in its use of the moment. The essay can be read as the chronicle of a discovery. The protagonist has received a writing assignment, presumably from an editor, on the topic of "home." Not knowing where to begin, she frets and complains about the smugness of the editor in somehow thinking that one can "discover the substance of a person's life and the essence of his character from a description of his home life." On the surface it seems very logical, but such a process of inference does not help the protagonist who then, on her own, moves exhaustively from one thought to another, looking for a possible angle to begin her essay:

> What should I write about, then? The situation of the average home? Home life and financial problems? The relationship between culture and family? The influence of home life on the individual? The comforts and sorrows that home life bestows upon a person? Whether everyone does or should have a family? Whether home is something to be cherished or abhorred?

In this state of mental distraction, she goes out to the lake on the night of the Mid-Autumn Festival. Under a dazzling moon and shining stars, her abstractions begin to show signs of breaking down. In their stead, her imagination takes over, as she *imagines* a home scene among primitive people, who bask in comfort and security in the company of their kinfolk. She also *imagines* raising the same question about "home"— a "small question," she emphasizes—to the fishermen living by the water, and decides that they would be just as lost as she is.

Then the moment comes when she hears Cen Shen's poetic lines. If Zhang Ailing has stressed the coincidental and illogical aspects of the moment in the previous essay, Fang Lingru here takes pains to establish the mystery and suddenness of it all. First, a boat comes into view only dimly lit, and the man sitting on the bow, who will prove to be her source of inspiration, is just "a patch of darkness," his face impossible to make out. He is chanting poetry with a sound that transports the listener to a world of dreams and timelessness:

> He chants with a drawn-out sound, the pitch relatively low in the beginning, but rising gradually. After it reaches the peak, it slowly dies down again, until it disappears half in moaning and half in sighing. Listening to the dying cadence, you can imagine a small hill in an ancient painting, half-shrouded in mist. There is a winding stream, too, splashing drops of water as it flows along. The sound of his chanting lingers, trembling all the while, like the shadow of a lone wild goose in the sky gliding in a flash across the water. That, I think, is an appropriate comparison, because the sound itself is *half real, half imaginary*. While half of it is still coming from the person's mouth, half of it has already burrowed its way into our dreams. (Italics added)

Two lines, from Cen Shen's "Feng rujing shi," stand out in the man's chanting: "Meeting by chance on horseback, we lack paper and a writing brush/ Please tell my people at home that I am safe." At this particular moment, things begin to resonate in the protagonist's mind:[28]

> On this night, for these two ancient doleful poetic lines to come bursting from their hearts [i.e., of people who are away from home], their minds

---

[28] Y. K. Kao (1991, 63) argues that resonance rather than causality links man and the world in a lyrical experience. Speaking about early Chinese music, he describes the "principle of interaction" (between man and the world) as suggestive of "the *empathetic resonance that exists between different entities*, particularly between those which share common qualities.... Because these elements are distinct, their joint action is probably due more to *resonance than to causality*" (italics added).

must be filled with longing. Perhaps at this moment, somewhere in a corner concealed in reeds or withering lotus leaves, someone else may also be thinking of home. When he hears the chanting, will he be able to hold back his tears and stop himself from sobbing? Will it take many soothing words from his friend to calm his quivering heart? How can I not think of "home," the topic you gave me, and suddenly come to realize its meaning?

In a manner close to the manifestations of the affective-expressivism expounded by Earl Miner (1990, 84–87) in relation to Asian lyricism, the resonance goes through several stages in this essay: from Cen Shen to the man on the boat, to the imagined person concealed in reeds or lotus leaves, to the protagonist. At each stage, the same powerful yearning for home resonates and is in turn issued forth, until, presumably, it touches the reader as well.

All of this catches the protagonist unaware, and the moment comes to her as a sudden revelation. Throughout the essay, the phrase "at this moment" appears five times and the expressions "suddenly" or "all of a sudden" each appears once. The ending reference to Xin Qiji underscores all too well the unexpectedness of this experience. "*Moran*," which I render "unthinkingly" in my translation to emphasize the intuitiveness by which she obtains "a glimpse of a clear vision," can certainly be translated as "suddenly" as well.

Thus the protagonist's quest comes suddenly to an end at this moment, not thanks to her editor's "cleverness" at inferences or her exhaustive search for possibilities, but by means of a kind of intuitive resonance. Yet, except for one very short line, the protagonist does not tell what the answer to the question is, but devotes the rest of the essay to depicting how the resonance came about. Considering that the title of the essay is "Home," one might fault Fang Lingru for straying from her writing assignment. As an illustration of *yixiao jianda*, however, this piece allows us to recognize the process through which the essay can connect the small with the large, and thereby mean more than it says.

*   *   *   *   *   *   *

In the period covered in this anthology, *xiaopin wen* was always on the defensive. China at the beginning of the century was facing too many pressing challenges, and the writing and reading of *xiaopin wen*, with its open disavowal of subject matter with social and political significance, was a luxury that few critics and writers felt they could afford. In their vehement attacks on *xiaopin wen*, however, they have created distorted views of the genre, many of which are still evident today.

In answering these charges, advocates of *xiaopin wen* can be seen to have adopted several lines of defense. For a while, it was enough just to suggest that *xiaopin wen* resembled or even derived from literary forms from cultures with a strong tradition of individualism and skepticism. When individualism aroused suspicion because of its bourgeois connections, apologists for *xiaopin wen* turned to elaborate on the traditional roots of the form, linking it to the culturally prosperous period of the late Ming. The Ming essayists, moreover, were made out to be iconoclasts. At the same time, others began to go on the offensive and ridicule those who demanded that literature perform a social and political function, calling them "slogan mongers," and their writing, "new eight-legged essays." Each to his own, they said: Writers should be left alone to pursue what they chose, be it a topic, in Lin Yutang's words, "as wide as the universe, or as small as a fly." Zhou Zuoren further provided writers of similar sympathies with a theoretical defense. Arguing that the history of Chinese literature demonstrated an alternation between the *zaidao* and *yanzhi* traditions, he came to the conclusion that the modern period should be marked predominantly by literature that served the intent of the heart. In other words, he implied, it was the detractors of *xiaopin wen* who were out of step with the times.

Beneath the many willful or inadvertent misunderstandings of *xiaopin wen* is perhaps a justified query: How could *xiaopin wen*, celebrating the trivial as it so openly does, expect to be taken seriously? This is where the question of *yixiao jianda* comes in. While, as noted above, the meaning of this phrase was by no means clear to most readers of *xiaopin wen*, it nevertheless lent strength to their defense. No longer did they have to be embarrassed by their narrow focus on things of little import, because *xiaopin wen*, by whatever process critics made it out to be, allowed readers to reach out beyond the world it created.

By the late-1940s, attacks on *xiaopin wen* had begun to soften. Qian Gechuan, who had been so harsh with his caricature of the *xiaopin wen* reader quoted at the beginning of this introduction, paid tribute to Lu Xun and Zhou Zuoren in the same essay (1948, 310). Even Lin Yutang received some words of praise. Similarly, Xia Yan (1954, 314) acknowledged that not everyone had to write "political essays," and that literary essays required "literary cultivation" and "humor"!

Political situations and cultural climates change. More than half a century later, the time is right to review the accomplishments of *xiaopin wen*.

The author is grateful for the support of a Scholarly Editions and Translations Grant from the National Endowment for the Humanities of the USA, which provided teaching relief during the research and the writing of this book.

Essays

❧❧❧

Lu Xun

Lu Xun (1881–1936) was first educated in his hometown of Shaoxing and then in Nanjing, after which he went to Japan for four years. These four years had a profound influence on his intellectual development. Lu Xun went to Japan intending to study medicine, but gave up this plan when he realized that the sickness of the Chinese people lay not so much in body but in mind.

Lu Xun was born Zhou Zhangshou, but took the name Zhou Shuren, by which he was better known, in 1898. Later in life, he published under a number of pen names, among which Lu Xun is the most famous. One of his brothers, Zhou Zuoren, was also a well-known figure in twentieth-century Chinese culture, and three of his essays are featured in this anthology. The Zhou brothers were fellow travelers on the road of modern Chinese literature for a while, sharing many projects in their early careers, but later represented two different literary and political paths.

Lu Xun is considered an icon of modern Chinese literature, and his influence is felt in many areas: translation, cultural and political commentary, short stories, and prose essays. He engaged in extensive polemics in his characteristic acerbic style, which made him a thorn in many people's sides; at the same time, it won him respect and admiration in many quarters.

Lu Xun popularized the genre of *zawen* (the short, satirical topical essay) which he characterized variously as a dagger, a pistol, or a spear—that is, a handy weapon for ideological battle. This he wielded with expert skill, resulting in the *zawen* being forever linked with his name. His shadow can still be seen in many newspaper columns of today.

"The Kite" shows a different side of Lu Xun. Instead of a visionary figure who speaks with moral certainty, this essay projects an image of Lu Xun as a mere mortal filled with regret and self-doubt. Somber, reflective, and ambivalent, it recalls many of his short stories.

The Kite (1925)

Beijing in the winter. There is still snow on the ground. The bare gray and black branches pierce the clear, sunny sky. In the distance, one or two kites float in the air. I am startled and saddened by the sight.

In my hometown, the season for flying kites is the second month of spring. If you hear the rustling of flywheels, look up and you will see a crab kite painted lightly in black or a centipede kite in light blue. There is also the lonely tile kite. With no flywheels, it floats at a low altitude, looking spiritless and pitiable all by itself. But at that time, there are already young shoots on the willow trees and buds on those mountain peaches that have sprouted early in the season, their answer to the decorations children put in the sky. Together, they bring to this world the balmy atmosphere of spring. But where am I now? I am still surrounded by the harshness of deep winter, while floating in the air is the spring scene of my hometown, which I left a long time ago with no thought of ever returning.

But I never liked kite flying, anyway. Not only did I dislike it, I detested it, thinking it a game for losers. My little brother was just the opposite. He was about ten years old, sickly, and so thin that one could not bear looking at him. But kite flying was his passion. Since he could not afford a kite, and I would not have allowed him to fly it anyway, he could only look up at the sky, his jaw dropped in rapture. Sometimes, he would remain like that for half a day. He would exclaim in horror when a distant crab kite took a sudden plunge, and jump in delight when two entangled tile kites unraveled. I found all these antics of his laughable, even despicable.

One day, it suddenly occurred to me that I had not seen him for several days, though I remembered seeing him picking dry bamboo twigs in the backyard. Then something dawned on me, and I immediately went to a deserted shed that was used for storage. I pushed open the door, and sure enough, there he was in the midst of a dusty pile of this and that. He was sitting on a stool, facing a big chair. He stood up, startled; with the color gone from his face, he shrank back. Leaning against the big chair was the bamboo frame of a butterfly kite. The paper had not yet been pasted on it. On the stool was a pair of flywheels, which would become the eyes of the butterfly. He was decorating the flywheels with red paper and had almost finished. Satisfied as I was in discovering his secret, I was also angry that he had tried to hide this from me and had gone to such pains to do something so unworthy. I immediately reached over and broke the frame of one of the butterfly's wings. After throwing the flywheels on the floor, I crushed them under my foot. In age and strength, he was no match for me, so of course my victory was complete. I proudly walked out of the shed, leaving him behind with his misery. As for how he felt later, I did not know, nor did I care to find out.

Yet, my punishment came eventually, a long time after we went our separate ways in life. I was already middle-aged, and happened unfortunately to come across a foreign book about children. I realized only then that playing is the most normal behavior for children, and that toys are their angels. Thereupon, this episode of spiritual murder I had committed in my younger days, to which I had not given a thought in twenty years, suddenly appeared before my eyes. My heart seemed all at once to have turned into lead and sank heavily, hanging on as if on a string.

But my heart did not sink so far that the string broke. It just sank and sank, heavily.

I thought of ways to repair my mistake: to give him a kite, to allow him to fly it, to encourage him to fly it, to go out with him to fly it. We would shout, run, and laugh... but by then, he was already like me, an aged man with a beard.

I also knew of another way to repair my mistake: I would go and beg his forgiveness. When he said, "But I never blamed you," my heart would be unburdened. This was a feasible way. When we met one day, long after life had carved line after line of hardship on our faces, my heart was very heavy. Gradually, our conversation turned to our childhood, and I related that incident to him, reproaching myself for the ignorance of my youth. I thought he was about to say, "But I never blamed you"; I would be immediately forgiven, and a weight thus lifted from my heart.

"Did that really happen?" he laughed, astonished, as if he were listening to somebody else's story. He had forgotten all about it.

Completely forgotten—no grudge whatsoever. Where then to find forgiveness? Forgiveness without a single trace of resentment? Just a pack of lies.

What else could I ask for? My heart will continue to hang heavily.

And now, a spring scene from my hometown has appeared in the sky of this strange land, bringing back to me childhood memories of long ago, and intangible sorrow as well. I'd better hide in the austerity of a harsh winter.… The truth is, though, that I am already surrounded by the harsh winter, which is at this very moment inflicting upon me its stern air and piercing cold.

Xia Mianzun

By all accounts, Xia Mianzun (1886–1946) is a kind, fair-minded, and disciplined man. He is remembered mostly for the contributions he made to literature and education.

Xia received a traditional education at a young age and earned a *xiucai* degree under the old civil examination system in 1901. Inspired by the intellectual climate of the rest of the world, he continued his studies in Japan for two years, where he gained such a degree of mastery of the Japanese language that he became a prolific translator of Japanese books.

His teaching career began soon after his return to China in 1908. Throughout his life, he taught in a number of schools, the most important of which is the Chunhui Middle School in White Horse Lake, where he attracted a group of like-minded educators to the teaching staff. The writers among them would later be loosely grouped together by critics as the "White Horse Lake School." Zhu Ziqing, Ye Shengtao, and Feng Zikai, whose works are included in this anthology, are regarded as core members of this school of writing.

As a teacher, Xia was tireless in promoting the appreciation of the Chinese language among middle school students by editing literary journals and co-authoring literature guides, such as *Wenzhang zuofa* and *Wenxin*. These endeavors contributed indirectly to the development of Chinese literature. The journals provided venues for the publication of many contemporary literary works while the literary guides and manuals nurtured a generation of discriminating readers.

Xia's writing style is plain and unadorned and his essays are held up as models of mildness and subtlety. "A Memory" relates his narrow brush with death, an incident of potential high drama. Yet, Xia characteristically adopts a subdued tone in the essay, giving more attention to what happens before and after the incident of his near drowning rather than to the incident itself. "Winter at White Horse Lake" captures his fond memories of his residence at the Chunhui Middle School, where he spent two productive and meaningful years.

A Memory (1934)

This happened four or five years ago.

In the middle of the Qiantang River, there suddenly emerged a long sandbar. It was about three or four *li* wide, dividing the river in two. People traveling between Hangzhou and Xixing had to take two ferries, the first to the sandbar, where they had to walk or ride in rickshaws for three or four *li*.[1] When they reached the other side of the sandbar, they then had to catch another ferry to reach the other shore. This went on for the major part of a year. People said that such an unusual phenomenon had not been seen for a hundred years.

I will never forget that day: It was the eighteenth day of the ninth month by the old calendar.[2] I was on my way to Shanghai from White Horse Lake. As I had some business to take care of in Hangzhou, I decided not to go by way of Ningbo, but through Hangzhou instead. On the long journey from Cao E to Xixing, I could already hear people talking about the sandbar in the Qiantang River, saying things such as, "The world just isn't the same anymore! West Lake has moved into the city,[3] and now there are two Qiantang Rivers!" Or, "Just before the Taiping Rebellion,[4] a sandbar also rose up from the river, but it didn't remain for as long as this one. No wonder the world is in such turmoil again!" I had not crossed the Qiantang River for some time, and was fascinated by what I heard.

When I got to the Xixing side of the river, it was about four o'clock in the afternoon, and sure enough, I saw a sandbar above the water in the middle of the river, and a lot of people and rickshaws going back and forth on it. After I got on the ferry, I suddenly remembered that it was the eighteenth day of the ninth month, and, judging by the custom people had of coming on the eighteenth day of the eighth month to watch the tide come in on the river, the tide would probably come in at

---

[1]   *Li*, a measurement of length, about one-third of a mile.

[2]   "Old calendar" refers to the lunar calendar.

[3]   The reference is unclear. This may be a general remark on the expansion of Hangzhou city. Whereas, in the past, West Lake lay outside the city limits, now, as the city grew, West Lake had become part of the city itself.

[4]   A revolt that took place in the mid-nineteenth century led by Hong Xiuquan, a frustrated scholar who suffered under the illusion that he was the son of God. The rebels were called "long hairs" because they let their hair grow in defiance of the Manchu rule that required men to shave the tops of their heads.

around four or five o'clock that day. "What if it were just my luck, and it came in while I was walking on the sandbar?" I couldn't help feeling worried. A few of the passengers also spoke of the tide, and we came to an agreement: "Let's wait and see. If the tide comes, we won't step out onto the sandbar, but stay on the ferry instead until the tide recedes."

When the ferry got to the sandbar, dozens of rickshaw pullers came up to us to solicit our business, saying, "The tide will be here soon. Hurry up and get in!" Most of the passengers jumped up onto the sandbar. Even those who had agreed just a short while before to stay behind ended up going away in rickshaws. Besides me, there were only two or three people left in the boat. Four or five rickshaws now came to accost us, the pullers speaking in Xiaoshan dialect. Some said, "There's still time for us to get to the ferry pier," while others said, "Even if the tide comes in, it won't be very high at this time of year. We work here every day—shouldn't we know?" In the end, against our better judgment, the few of us remaining on the ferry also stepped into rickshaws.

Still worried that we might be caught by the tide while aboard the rickshaws, we couldn't wait to get to the ferry pier ahead of us. Who would have guessed that when we were only halfway there, the ferry would have already pulled up the gangplank in preparation for sailing away! The pier in the middle of the river was a temporary one and did not have a receiving lighter, and once the ferry had gone, there was no boat for us to get into. At that moment, the people around us started shouting, "The tide is coming in!" In the distance, all of the unoccupied rickshaws were heading in the direction of the shore, leaving only the three or four on which we were riding on the sandbar. The only thing to do was turn back to the pier from which we had come. Fortunately, the ferry that was there to take passengers from Hangzhou to Xixing had not yet left.

Right around us, all was quiet, and we could hear the thundering of the tide in the distance. The pullers started running and shouting, "Help! Help!" We too shouted, "Help!" and "Let down the gangplank!"

When we jumped onto the gangplank, we could see the head of the tide. The passengers on the ferry put down another plank to widen the gangway, and together they pulled up the rickshaws as well. The tide had reached us by then, and was surprisingly high. The ferry bobbed up and down violently, but at that instant, we had forgotten the danger of the waves and instead felt deeply the joy of being alive and the sympathy of the human world.

After the tide passed, the ferry took off for Xixing. Like students returning home after flunking an examination, our small group found itself once again heading for Hangzhou from Xixing. It was getting dark, and we could vaguely make out the lights on the other side of the river. The tide had covered the sandbar and the Qiantang River had again become one. The ferry could now go directly to the pier in Hangzhou, and there was no need to get rickshaw rides in the middle of the river. When the ferry got to the point where the sandbar had been, one of our fellow sufferers walked to the bow and put a punt into the water to find out the depth of the water. Little did he expect that the punt would go all the way down into the water without touching the bottom.

"That was close!" he exclaimed, putting away the punt and sticking his tongue out. "If we had been caught by the tide, who knows what would have happened to us?"

"Who can tell?" said another comrade-in-suffering. "Best not to think about it!"

I had to agree with them.

Winter at White Horse Lake (1933)

In my life of forty-some years, it was only ten years ago when I first moved to White Horse Lake that I came to appreciate most profoundly what winter was like. Since that time, White Horse Lake has become a small village, but when I first moved there, it was just a wilderness. Chunhui Middle School's new building stood tall on the other side of the lake, and on this side there were several new bungalows at the bottom of the hill, where my family and Mr. Liu Xinru's lived. Apart from us, though, there was no one else within two or three *li*. We moved from busy Hangzhou to this desolate hilly area toward the end of the eleventh month, and for us, that was like casting ourselves into the polar region.

The wind howled there nearly every day, much like the howl of a tiger. The houses, though newly built, were shoddily made, and the wind that came through the gaps in the windows and the door was extraordinarily piercing. Even after we had covered the gaps with layers of paper, the wind would still find its way through the cavities between the hinges and joints. When the wind was particularly strong, we would close the door before it got dark. As soon as we had finished dinner, the whole family would nestle under the quilt and listen in silence to the bellowing of the wind and the roiling of the water in the lake.

The little room against the hill was least exposed to the wind and served as my study. I often pulled my Russian hat farther down over my head and worked there under the kerosene lamp until late at night. The pine trees roared in the wind and the window looked out to the frosty moon, while squeaking rats scurried about on the dusty floor. At moments like this, I felt deeply the poetic sense of bleakness. Unwilling to go to bed, I would sit there all alone poking at the ashes, imagining myself to be a character in a landscape painting indulging in deep and quiet reveries.

Nowadays, there are trees all around White Horse Lake, but in those days, there was not a single tree, and one could get a complete and unobstructed view of the moon and sun from the moment they rose from behind one set of hills to the moment they set behind another. When the sun was out, and as long as there was no wind, it would be so warm that it wasn't like winter at all. We would all sit in the courtyard and bask in the sun, and would even eat lunch outdoors as we would have dinner in the summer. Wherever the sun moved, so would we with our stools and chairs. When the wind struck suddenly, we would grab our chairs and stools and scurry back into the house like refugees, quickly closing the door. On a normal day, the wind would come toward the evening and cease at midnight. When there was a storm, though, the wind would continue day and night, not stopping for two or three days. On the coldest days, the ground would look sickly white like cement, the hills would be frozen into a dull purple, and the lake would be covered with a veneer of dark blue.

I never found snow a nuisance. On snowy days, it would be particularly bright indoors, and there was almost no need to light the lamps at night. The snow would remain on the distant hills for half a month, and all we had to do was raise our eyes and look out the window to take in its beauty. But this was the south, after all, and it only snowed once or twice every winter.

What I remember of winter in White Horse Lake is the wind. Geography explains why it was so windy. On all sides of the lake are hills, except for a gap of half a *li* on the north shore that seems almost like a wide bag opened on purpose to welcome in the wind. The scenery of the lake region is not much different from that of other average scenic places, but its wind is unique. Anyone who has been to White Horse Lake knows just how much wind there is and how strong it is. The wind has always been an important element in our impressions of winter from long past, and the wind of White Horse Lake is all the more out of the ordinary.

And now we have lived as lodgers in Shanghai for a long time. When we occasionally hear the wind late at night, we speak of White Horse Lake, saying, "I wonder how strong the wind is there tonight."

Zhou Zuoren

Zhou Zuoren (1885–1967) is the younger brother of Lu Xun. The two shared the goals of the New Culture Movement, collaborating on a number of projects when they were students in Japan, before parting ways for political and literary reasons. Lu Xun proceeds to exploit the polemical use of literature while Zhou defends the independence of literature from politics. The phrase "A Garden of One's Own," with which this anthology is entitled, comes from an essay of Zhou's of the same title.

Together with Mao Dun, Zheng Zhenduo, Xu Dishan, and Ye Shengtao, Zhou is a founder of the important group Literary Study Society (*Wenxue yanjiu hui*). He also joined Lu Xun, Sun Fuyuan, and Lin Yutang in founding the group *Yusi*.

During the Second World War when the Guomintang evacuated from Beijing, Zhou stayed behind and became the president of Peking University. Later, he also accepted an appointment from the Japanese puppet government as the Librarian of Peking University, for which he was later charged with treason and was subsequently imprisoned.

Zhou stresses the personal side of the essay, to such an extent that it is sometimes difficult to separate the literary persona from the autobiographical writer. The three essays in this anthology therefore have an intimate tone, with two of them written in letter form and the third one as a short piece of reminiscence.

Black-Canopied Boats (1922)

Dear Zirong,

I learned from your letter that you will be visiting my native region and that you want me to give you some pointers. To tell you the truth, what is really memorable about my hometown is not the place itself. But since I was born, grew up, and spent more than ten years there, I do know something about it, and that is why I am writing to acquaint you with the place.

What I want to tell you about has nothing to do with the local customs of the area, of which there are too many to relate in a single letter. In any case, they will be immediately obvious once you are there to see for yourself, and there is no need for me to dwell on them here. What I would rather tell you about is a very interesting thing: boats. In your own hometown, you travel most of the time in rickshaws, trams, or cars, but where I come from, these are not to be found. Except in the city or up in the mountains, where people ride in sedan chairs, people generally use boats to get around. There are two kinds of boats: ordinary black-canopied ones and white-canopied boats, which for the most part travel long distances. There is also the "night boat" to Xinling, which has its own charm but which you would probably find unsuitable, and hence I won't say anything about it.

The large black-canopied boats are called "four-transparent-tiles,"[1] while the small ones are pedaled by foot and are simply called "small boats." But the ones most suitable for traveling are medium-sized "three-pieces" or "three-transparent-tiles." The canopies on these boats are in the shape of a half-circle and are made of bamboo strips and leaves woven together and painted black. Between the two "fixed canopies" is a pane that provides shade from the sun. The pane is also semi-circular in shape, with a wooden frame covered with layers of large fish scales. These scales are about an inch in diameter and nearly transparent. They are like glass, which are quite durable and allow some light to come through, and are therefore called "transparent tiles." The three transparent tiles, which give the boat its name, refer to the two-tiled panes in the middle cabin and the third pane in the back cabin. There are usually two oars in the back and a bamboo punt in the front, which

---

[1] In the original, Zhou indicates the pronunciation of these three words as "sy-menngoa."

is used to steady the boat. On the bow is painted a set of eyes and eyebrows that look like those of a tiger, but it seems to be smiling and looks rather comical and not scary at all.

The white canopies have somewhat different features. The canopy of a "three pieces" is high enough for a person to stand up under, and the cabin is wide enough for a square table, which can seat four people in a game of mah-jongg—you must have learned this game already? The small version is truly as flat as a leaf, and when you sit on a mat placed on the bottom of the boat, your head is only two or three inches from the top of the canopy. You can rest your hands on the bulwark on both sides, or even outside the boat. Sitting on this kind of boat is like sitting right on the water, and when the boat nears the shore, the earth is close to your eyes and nose. If you run into strong winds and large waves, or if you are just a bit careless, the boat could easily capsize, which can be dangerous indeed. However, it can also be rather fun, and is a unique feature of life in this watery region. Just the same, there's no need to try it out yourself, and it's best to take one of the "three-pieces."

When you go out on a boat, you cannot be as impatient as if you were taking a tram, expecting the boat to get you to your destination right away. If you want to go into the city, it is about thirty to forty *li* (there, a *li* is very short, about one third of a mile), and you should be prepared to give a whole day to getting there and coming back. While on board, you should adopt the attitude of a person sightseeing in the mountains. Look at the scenery around you. You will see hills everywhere, the tallow trees on the banks, the red smartweed and white duckweed by the shore, and the fishing huts and bridges of all styles and designs. Should you grow tired, you can lie down in the cabin and pick up a book of informal essays to read, or make a bowl of green tea to drink.

My favorite haunts are places around the Jian Lake area outside the side gate of the city wall, as well as those in the Hejia Pond and Hushang regions. Or you can hire a donkey and visit the Orchid Pavilion on Lougong Town, though I suggest you walk, since riding a donkey might not suit you. When dusk descends upon you, you can return by way of the east gate, which is covered in climbing fig. This can be rather charming. If there's trouble on the road, you can take the afternoon boat to Hangzhou. The scenery is best toward evening, and it's too bad I don't remember the names of the places there.

It's rather delightful to listen to the sounds of the water as you lie in the boat at night—the rowing, the greetings between boats, and the barking of dogs and crowing of roosters in the villages. Hiring a boat to go down to the villages for their ritual dramas can also be a good way to appreciate traditional Chinese theater. In a boat, you can move around freely, watching the performance when you want, sleeping when you want, drinking wine when you want. To me, it is the ideal way to have a bit of amusement. It's a pity that ever since people began to talk about modernization, this kind of performance and ritual parade has been banned. The mediocre middle class has set up Shanghai-style theaters in such places as the "Textile Guild Hall," and people have to buy tickets just to watch some cheap third-rate production from Shanghai. Don't even bother going to such places.

I'm afraid you don't know anybody in my hometown, and am sorry and sad that because of my teaching, I cannot keep you company and chat with you on the night boat. Chuandao and his wife are staying at the bottom of Mount Cheng and I could introduce you to them, but I'm afraid that by the time you get there, they will have left. With the first winter chill upon us, do take good care of yourself! There is more than I could say.

Beijing, November 18, at night

First Love (1922)

I was fourteen then. She was about thirteen. I was living at the time in the Hua Pai Lou in Hangzhou at the home of my grandfather's concubine, Song. Living next door was a family by the name of Yao, and she was their daughter. Her original surname was Yang, and her home was at the Qingbo Gate. Probably because she was the third child, she was known to everybody as Third Daughter. The Yaos, an elderly couple, had no children of their own, and they took her in as their foster daughter. She would come to stay with them some twenty days out of the month.

Song was on very good terms with the daughter-in-law of the lamb butcher in the neighborhood, Shi, but was far from friendly with old Mrs. Yao, and the two never talked to each other. That, however, did not seem to concern Third Daughter, who would often push open our door nonchalantly to come in and play. Usually, she would go upstairs to talk to Song for a while first, then come downstairs, where, with the big cat Sanhua in her arms, she would stand beside the table used by my servant Ran Sheng, and watch me as I practiced my calligraphy by tracing Lu Runxiang from rubbings of wood carvings.

I did not talk to her, not even once, nor did I ever have a good look at her face or carriage. I was probably already very short-sighted then, though there was another reason, as well: Although unconsciously I felt drawn to her, I also must have been almost overwhelmed by her radiance, and was unable to open my eyes to look at her closely. When I think back now, I seem to see her as a young girl with a pointed chin, glistening eyes, a slight build, and a pair of small, slender feet. There was nothing spectacular about her, and yet she was the first person in my romantic life, and she made me direct my love for the first time to someone other than myself. Even before I had any understanding of romance, she was the first member of the opposite sex to arouse my yearning.

I was of course just an ugly duckling then, and I knew that perfectly well myself. But that did not detract from my passion for her. Whenever she came with the cat in her arms to watch me write, I would unknowingly rouse myself up and write with a seriousness not found at other times, feeling in the meantime a vague sense of satisfaction so complete that I had no need of anything else. I did not ask whether she loved me. Perhaps I did not even know that I loved her. But I felt joyous in her presence, and was willing to do my best on her behalf. This was my state of mind at the time, and it was really a gift from her. She had no idea about this at all. Probably my own feeling was merely a faint kind of yearning, and I never saw it in sexual terms.

One evening, after suddenly bursting into anger at the Yaos, Song said, "That Third Daughter of theirs is nothing to brag about, either. One of these days, she will become a prostitute at the Gong Chen Bridge."

I did not quite understand what becoming a prostitute meant. But when I heard that, I thought to myself, "If indeed she becomes that one day, I will definitely go and rescue her."

In this way, about half a year went by. In the seventh or eighth month of that year, my mother fell ill and I had to leave Hangzhou for home. A month later, when Ran Sheng went home on leave, he stopped by our place and told us the news from Hua Pai Lou. He said, "The Third Daughter of the Yangs died of cholera."

I was disturbed by the news, trying to imagine the pain she must have been in, but at the same time, there seemed to be a certain calm within me, as if a huge rock had been lifted from my heart.

Bitter Rain (1924)

Dear Fuyuan,

There has been a lot of rain in Beijing in recent days. I wonder whether you also ran into rain on your way to Chang'an. If so, it may have made your trip even more enjoyable.

Traveling in rainy weather is not necessarily a pleasure, I know. I often used to encounter it on the Hangzhou-Shanghai line, and was always bothered by it. That's why I find I can rarely appreciate the rain when I'm on a train. However, lying in the cabin of a black-canopied boat listening to the rain pattering on the canopy, the oars squeaking and the oarsman shouting, "Move to the bank! Move over!" is like finding oneself in a dream-like world of poetry. The truly intrepid can travel on the kind of boat the boatmen pedal with their feet. Lying down in the cabin of such a boat as it scoots along on a rainy night is a sure way to experience the way of life of people who live on the water. It is a bit dangerous, though, for a clumsy flip in one's sleep can cause the boat to turn upside down.

More than twenty years ago, when I went to Dongpu for my father's nanny's funeral, I ran into a storm on my way back. The small boat rolled through Da Shu Xiang amid billows of waves the color of a white goose, making my trip as full of danger as of excitement. I am by temperament like a fish—or at least like my early ancestors, who cut short their hair and tattooed their bodies—and feel drawn to the water.[2] But I am disappointed by those so-called "seas" in Beijing that are barely bigger than mud puddles. It would be no great loss to be without them.

It looks as if you will spend several days in a virtual desert on your way to Shaanxi, and I expect it might be a relief to have some wind and rain. I imagine you there in the vast desert, sitting decorously in the mule cart sipping a soft drink from a bottle, moving along unhurriedly in the torrential rain. That should be one of life's rare joys. But all of this is only a fantasy on my part, as unreliable as a poet's imagination. Who knows? The rain may have brought you such difficulties that at this moment you are in your mule cart, raising cries of anguish to the

---

[2] According to the *Zuo Commentary*, the people of the Wu Yue area (modern day Zhejiang) customarily cut their hair short and tattooed their bodies before getting into water. It was believed that by doing so, they would ward off serpents and other dangerous animals living in the water.

heavens. I will simply have to ask you about it when you return to the capital.

As for myself, the rain in Beijing these past few days has made life difficult for me. It does not rain that often in Beijing, and not only is the rain gear here far from perfect, even the houses are made without giving enough thought to rain. Except for the very rich, few people use solid bricks and mortar for their houses, most making do instead with mud and lime. The recent changes in the weather—with severe cold in the south and ceaseless rain in the north—have brought out the architectural shortcomings of houses everywhere. A week ago, the west wall of our backyard collapsed under the heavy rain, and the next day, thieves came to fiddle with the wire net on the windows in the north rooms. I immediately hired several workers the following day to rebuild the wall from the ground up, and in two days, they were close to finishing. Just when I thought I would have some worry-free sleep, rain came again the night before last and washed away some ten yards of the south wall just beyond the front door. This time, however, "them folks"[3] (Chuandao and his family), and not I, are the ones with worries, because if the thieves come again, they will hide under "them's" window to wait for a good opportunity. Just to allay "them's" fears, we shall have some major renovations done once the weather improves, but I hope we won't have to wait too long. For the time being, we'll just have to trouble Chuandao's younger brother to serve as our security guard.

It rained through the night two nights ago, and I woke up who knows how many times. In Beijing, except on occasions when people set off firecrackers for the fun of it, it is usually rather quiet at night. I've grown unaccustomed to the sound of rain splashing down right by my ear, which is why I was awakened so many times. Even when I managed to stay asleep, it felt as if my ears were stuck to something soft— something like noodles, perhaps—and my sleep was far from deep. And there's another thing: The children were saying at night how the water had risen to less than one inch from the porch in the front yard. As I listened to the rain in my sleep, I kept thinking in my half-conscious state that the rain had come up to the porch and was at that very moment flowing into the study on the west side of the house. After what seemed

---

[3]　Chuandao refers to Zhang Maochen. In the original, Zhou uses a non-standard word for "they," apparently an attempt to make fun of Chuandao's Zhejiang accent.

like a very long time, the clock finally struck five o'clock, and I opened an umbrella and dashed over to the west chamber in my bare feet. Sure enough, the whole room was flooded. I sighed in relief—for suppose I had rushed over with such anticipation only to find that there was no water in the room! I can't say I wouldn't have felt some disappointment; certainly, I would not be feeling as satisfied as I am now. Fortunately, the books were not touched by the water. Although there is nothing valuable in my study, it would have made a sorrowful sight to have paper soaked into piles like cakes. The water has gone now, but it has left behind a foul smell, the kind that lingers after a flood. It is of course impossible to receive guests there, and even I myself cannot bear to do my writing there. That is why I am writing this letter on the table on my *kang*.[4]

Only two kinds of creatures have found pleasure in the rain this time. The first are small children. They like water, but it is extremely rare for them to have a chance to play in it. Now that the yard has become a river, they have been "wading across the river" in crowds. In truth, the weather is a bit cold to step into water in bare feet, but the children don't seem to mind, and now that they are in there, they won't come out. Seeing how much fun they've been having, even one or two grown-ups went to join their ranks yesterday, but the outcome was rather sad. Three people slid and fell, two of whom were grown-ups, my brother and Chuandao.

Then there are the frogs, which also enjoy rain. Some time ago, I took my children to Gaoliang Bridge to fish, but we didn't catch anything but frogs, some green and others with stripes. When we got home, we set them free in the yard. Ordinarily, they only croak from time to time, but in the past few days they haven't stopped once. Some people take the croaking of frogs as an omen of famine in years to come, but it certainly also conjures up in one's mind a feeling, an image of the country.

Some people with sensitive hearing abhor any sort of noise. Anything that might interfere with their slumber, such as the noises made by sparrows, cicadas, or frogs, becomes a target of their hatred, and there is nothing they would like to do more before taking their afternoon nap than exterminate these creatures. I myself do not think that their sound is as bad as all that; in fact, it is rather fun to have it

---

[4]   *Kang*, a bed usually made of bricks and heated from below that is also used as a
       sitting area during the day.

around and allow it to drift into your ears. I am not referring only to the sounds of insects and animals—which, after all, can become a source of poetic inspiration once you listen to them long enough—but other kinds of sounds as well. When you listen to frogs croaking in the fields in the quiet of the night, you can hear a certain metallic ring, a very unusual sound indeed. And sometimes the croaking is like the sound of a dog; indeed, when the ancients described the sound of frogs as "barking," this could well be the result of empirical observation.

The only kind of frogs we have in our yard now are those with stripes. Their sound is even less appealing: They can only go *gak, gak, gak*, or perhaps it sounds more like *ge, ge, ge*. They croak once, twice, or three times in a single breath, but normally no more than that. Only on rainy mornings do they let out a stream of twelve or thirteen croaks. Clearly, they relish the rain.

In the villages, the rain this time must have been a disaster for the poor. Since I did not witness it, it would be pointless for me to exercise my imagination and make a pretense of lamenting their plight. If someone were to say that what I have written down here is just my personal business and doesn't contribute to human life in general, I'd willingly admit it. Talking about my personal affairs is exactly what I set out to do, and I do not aspire to any other goal than that. The sun has come out today, and in the evening, we can go out to play. I will stop here.

I have been wanting to read about your travels in Qin,[5] but instead I have written something for you to read. This is something of a surprise, wouldn't you say?

---

[5]   Qin, an early name for the Shaanxi region.

Xu Dishan

Xu Dishan (1894–1941) was a native of Tainan, Taiwan, but his family moved to Fujian when he was a child. He received his education from Yenching University, Columbia University, and Oxford University. Trained in literature and religious studies, he later became a writer, an educator, and a folklorist. In 1936, he went to Hong Kong and headed the School of Chinese at The University of Hong Kong, and died six years later of a heart attack.

Xu's literary interest is somewhat different from the other writers anthologized here. His sensibilities are distinctly southern, giving his writings an exotic air even to Chinese readers. His teaching experience at Myanmar and his study and translation of Indian literature also set him apart. "Undelivered Letters" consists of a group of short essays written in the form of letters, three of which are translated in the following pages. In these letters, the reader encounters characters who find themselves in emotional turmoil. The letter writers attempt to give advice to the intended addressee, but the letters are in the end undeliverable, making their messages all the more poignant.

Undelivered Letters (Three Selections) (1923)

To Zhen Rui

Reason for non-delivery: The addressee has left Guangzhou.

Ever since we parted at the Zou Ma Camp, I had not heard any news of you. Knowing that the life you're leading is like that of an itinerant monk, I didn't think I'd have any news for you to read that would relieve you of the sorrow of your travels. Yesterday, I heard from Geng Xiang about your latest comings and goings. I also learned that you are staying at this address, and I couldn't resist writing a few lines to you.

My friend, do you think that sweet flag flowers can grow in the icy oceans of the North Pole, or that flowers like royal water lilies can come into bloom by the Nile? Go home, I say! You left behind a restful, tranquil life to roam about searching for that heartless "heart's desire" of yours. Why bring this punishment upon yourself? You may say that you offended him at one time and have to look him up to apologize to him, but you have already admitted that you were at fault. How can you expect that the old affection, gentle yet firm like jade, could be restored to its blemish-free state?

My friend, I often think of a writing brush that I once used. One day, I accidentally burned the tip of the brush—I was learning seal script at the time, and had heard that a singed brush tip would be easier to write with—and it could not be used anymore. I loved that brush, and tried different ways to mend it but wasn't able to salvage it. Even when I took it to a brush-maker, he couldn't come up with any ideas, except to suggest I use another one. Although I couldn't bear to throw away that precious little object that had been with me day after day, there was nothing I could do but put it away in my brush bag. Human emotions cannot be put away like that, but if, having this knowledge, you nevertheless pretend that they can, you'll end up feeling much better.

You are ready to sacrifice your future, but he does not intend to let you have your wish. Why do you want to do it, then? Go on home! Your fresh young face has left its reflection in the mirror, and the dark shadow lurking behind you is threatening to get inside you, chasing away all your youthful vigor and snatching from you your glamorous outer shell.

Let me once again entreat you. Even if you find your heartless "heart's desire," he will only add to your distress. It's no use at all.

Reply to Lao Yun

Reason for non-delivery: Lao Yun has entered Jin Guang Ming Temple in the mountains. Letter cannot be delivered.

I awoke in the middle of the night when the moon was still in the sky. A thirsty mouse had stolen onto the table to drink the ink in the bowl I used for washing brushes. I got up, and he ran away in fright. He had awakened me, and I had scared him—that made us even. I walked up to the window and sat down there without lighting the lamp. I remembered that on the same night last year, we had a chat in Liaoyin's garden. You said that we were like chirping insects in the grass beneath thousands and thousands of plantain trees. Tonight, the insects must still be chirping in the grass in that garden, but what about us? I thought of going out for a walk by myself, but the yard was full of ghostly shadows. Besides, I had no companion, so I gave up the idea. Since I couldn't sleep, I yearned for some tea. Walking to the back room, I found the young maid sound asleep. I would have hated to liberate her from her slumber, so I gave up the idea of drinking tea as well. I came back to the window and sat down. Feeling aimlessly around the window lattice, my fingers quite accidentally touched the letter you sent me a month ago. I read the letter again in the moonlight. Fortunately, your handwriting is larger than mine, and it was not too difficult to read it in the dim light. Now is the time to reply to your letter.

Lao Yun, I once said to Liaoyin: May all the desolate mountains in the world line up circle upon circle to form one big prison. The beasts will be the guards, the ancient trees will be the fence, the mist and clouds will be handcuffs and fetters, and the vines and ivy will be the chains. There, with a light hand, we will sequester you, the poet criminal who stirs up sorrow in other people! It never occurred to us that you would turn yourself in! You might as well have, but I'm afraid that once you get there, it will no longer be a prison of poetry, but will become a kingdom of poetry instead.

You might want to know why I call you the poet criminal. I do not know why myself. I think that although your poetry is very good, what comes from your pen does not match what is in your heart. How much more wonderful it would be if you were to throw out your pen and go to the poetry prison where only poetry comprehensible to the heart is allowed!

Scenes that inspire poetry can be found all over this world, which is why it's easy to be a poet. Whatever they encounter in their lives, poets can never hold their peace, and are not satisfied until they come out with a few sorrowful lines. The whole thing is incomprehensible! Take tonight, for example. If you were around, you would tease and needle everything here in the yard, not resting until they wept. That is your crime, and that's why I call you a poet criminal—and hope you are one, too!

It is too tiring to hold a flashlight in one hand and write with the other, so I won't write anymore. I didn't wake up tonight because I wanted to reply to your letter, yet this has already taken half an hour of my time without my even noticing it. It is again due to your crimes that I cannot silently talk to the moon.

The sound of the insects in the yard is like the howling of ghosts, causing my hair to stand on end. I'd better put my head under the pillow and let the little mouse drink to his heart's content.

To Jing Ran, the Third Cousin

Reason for non-delivery: No one known as the Third Cousin lives at this address.

I came to look for you, but not because I didn't know you were married. Why didn't you come out and talk with me about old times? Do I need to know your "master"[1] before you'll see me? We are separated by twelve years and three thousand *li* of oceans and mountains. Every hour, month, and year I was here, I prayed to see you again. As soon as I stepped inside your door, my heart started to oscillate like a swing, so much so that one of my arteries was almost torn apart. Who would have expected that I would sit there waiting for a long time and still you would not come? When finally you appeared, you sat down behind me as soon as you were done making pleasantries. Quite a number of people wanted to speak to me just then, so how could I turn around and look at you?

To women, nuptial wine is the tea of forgetfulness: One sip and they lose all memory of their youthful entanglements. This is why when

---

[1] The original uses the word *tian* (sky), which may be interpreted in two ways: i) the woman's husband is compared to the sky, thereby emphasizing the supreme position he holds, and ii) the word *tian* (sky), written 天 is a visual pun on the word *fu* (husband), written 夫.

you saw me, you acted first as if we knew each other, then as if we did not, and you were afraid other people might find out that we did. You wavered, thus putting aside all the kind things you had once said to me.

At the height of autumn that year, we went to Chang Hua Pavilion to look at the withering lotus. Inadvertently, my hand touched the cactus plant by the bamboo fence and would not stop bleeding. You took out some tissue from your compact, and pulled out two strands of your soft, fragrant black hair to dress my wound. Do you remember what you said then? You said, "Although my hair is not as sturdy as a bowstring, it is quite adequate to dress a wound. It might even do to bind the heart of my love." Your bashful words indeed bound my heart that day, but your memory of it, like my wound, has long since faded away.

In the autumn of another year, we were flying a heart-shaped kite on the roof. You put your hand on my shoulder and watched me let the string out all the way. The kite was flying quite high, and because the wind was strong, the string was in danger of breaking. Do you remember what you said then? You said, "This is not the 'red string,'[2] let it go ahead and break." I said, "Do you want me to let go of this 'heart' I made in my spare time? Red string or no red string, I won't let it drift away." You said, "Let the false heart go! We still have our true hearts." You snatched the white string from my hand and let it go. The kite immediately turned a series of somersaults in the air. It flew away with its broken string and was caught at the top of the pagoda at Huang Jia Temple. That broken heart-shaped frame might still be on the pagoda even now, but your memory of it, like the wind that day, is long gone without a trace.

On one occasion, we were listening to partridges on the Liu Hua Bridge, and the sap of jimsonweed growing on the roadside stained your white socks. I asked you to take them off so I could wash them for you. Do you remember what you said then? You said, "Aren't you afraid people might laugh at you—a man washing socks for a woman? Have you forgotten that I once wrote my name on your palm with gardenia stamens? If you were to put your hand in the water to wash my sock, wouldn't it wash away my name from your hand? Could you bear to let that happen?" Alas, now your memory of all this has disappeared like the name you wrote on my palm!

---

[2]   A couple destined to be husband and wife are believed to be tied to one another by an invisible red string.

Nuptial wine truly is the tea of forgetfulness for women: One sip and they lose all memory of their youthful entanglements. But everything remains in my heart like the strands of thread on an abandoned loom. They are woven together, and cannot be broken for a long while. I know that you are very happy now, surrounded by your children. Whenever I think of you, I am as happy as you are when you are with them.

Ye Shengtao

Like Xia Mianzun featured earlier in this anthology, Ye Shengtao (also Ye Shaojun, 1894–1988) is a dedicated teacher, editor, and writer. In addition to many professional and family ties (Xia's daughter was married to Ye's son), these two distinguished writers also collaborated in the writing of *Wenxin* and *Wenzhang jianghua*.

Ye was a founding member of the Literary Study Society (Wenxue yanjiu hui), which promoted the credo that literature exists for the sake of life. Accordingly, Ye emphasizes that it is important for a writer to have direct experiences with what he chooses to write about. In like fashion, he questions the usefulness of "artistic" language at the expense of practicability and readability. "Worthy content," he argues, can only be expressed by "worthy language."

The two selections of "Random Reminiscences" reveal Ye as earthly and yet urbane. He has little tolerance for the kind of backbiting that occurs even in educational circles, or the sentimentality of young people in love who show no regard for the world of hardship around them.

Random Reminiscences (Two Selections)
(1930, published in 1931)

I

I graduated from high school in 1911, and did not have plans to pursue my studies any further. The reason was simple: There was no money at home to support my education. Of course, high school graduates also faced an "employment problem"[1] then, but since there were not many social critics or journal editors in those days, the problem never generated the kind of clamorous discussion found today. Fortuitously, I became a primary school teacher, and began to keep company with a group of second-grade pupils. Thus, I have never had the chance to find out what it is like to pull out all the stops in search of work.

This is fortunate, by all accounts. Later in life, I had a friend who, upon graduating from high school, found himself face to face with so-called "society." He was deeply perplexed by the many roads open to him and did not know which to choose. One day, when he was visiting a park, he happened to notice a pond with water as clear as a mirror. All of a sudden, a feeling of despair overcame him, and a strong desire grew inside him to simply throw himself into the water and end his life right there. I was never as "sentimental"[2] as this young man. It is a worthy profession to be a primary school teacher, so why shouldn't I have given it a try? From a pragmatic point of view, this is another reason that I should be considered fortuitous.

I worked as a primary school teacher for ten years, changing schools twice during this time. At the last two schools where I taught, I was class master of the higher grades, but also taught kindergarten part-time. The children at this level were not old enough for Grade 1, but they had not been as systematically trained as the younger kindergarten children. It was an ill-conceived level. The teaching profession, however, was growing more and more interesting for me, because in those few years, I had begun to hear about foreign educational theories and methods, and

---

[1]   Here and in other places of the essay, Ye Shengtao put certain phrases and expressions in quotation marks, probably because they were considered to be newfangled terms at the time. There is no indication that he was quoting from any particular source, or that he meant them in an ironic way.

[2]   This appears as "sentimental" in Chinese transliteration in the original.

also gained some insight into education on my own, all of which I put into practice. Besides, a few colleagues were old friends. At that time, I looked with disdain upon other teachers who were merely serving time, and assumed they must have moral blemishes on their characters. If only we could erase those blemishes, I thought, it would be a glorious day for the field of education.

After summer vacation in 1921, I began teaching high school. The reason I was invited to do so was a laughable one: I had written some short stories, which were published in magazines. Many people believe that those who can write stories can write well, and that those who can write well can of course teach language. Thus, it seemed appropriate for me to teach Chinese. Even now, this sort of arrangement is still very much the norm. People who have written stories are often appointed as Chinese teachers, and the differences between writers and teachers are seldom noted. As for why I gave up teaching in a primary school for a high school, the reasons are self-evident.

Up to this year, I have taught in five high schools and three universities. In all of these places, I have taught Chinese, and most of these appointments have been part-time. My primary occupation for the last seven years has been as an editor in a publishing house. I often lack the courage to teach at universities: I know how ignorant I am, and how a university teacher should teach. The truth is that I dare not presume when I compare myself with the ideal university teacher. But people tell me, "Universities nowadays are only universities in name. Why should you feel bound by such trivial concerns?" This is of course so, I think, but if "the value of any action is in being true to one's heart," I cannot very well allow myself to be a university teacher only in name simply because universities nowadays are not true universities. Regrettably, there have been times when I, out of weakness, have failed to abide by my beliefs, and have ended up violating my own principles for the sake of friendship. For example, I was teaching "Selected Prose from Former Dynasties" at a certain university this year. On the day after International Labor Day,[3] I received a letter of warning, signed "L." in red pencil, that said in brief that the antiquated

---

[3]   Although it originated in Chicago, International Labor Day is not to be confused with the Labor Day observed in the United States of America. International Labor Day is on May 1, and is celebrated in many countries throughout the world.

writings I was teaching only served to abet reactionary forces and did nothing to benefit students. I was told to resign right away in order to save myself embarrassment. This note made me quite angry. If the charge had been that I was not knowledgeable enough to teach at the university, I would have admitted it. But this letter was attacking me for promoting reactionary forces, my hatred of which I suspect was actually more genuine than Mr. L's. If, on the other hand, it was his belief that the mere act of teaching ancient literature was proof enough of my sympathy with these elements, there being no need to inquire into the ideology of individual pieces of literature, then he should have demanded that the university change the syllabus, and should not have come to criticize me. I found out only later that this incident was a spin-off of some political turmoil at the university. Other faculty members in the same department also received letters of warning from Mr. L., in much harsher terms than those he threw my way. Only then did I laugh, just as people do when they see the ugly face of a clown. I thereby resigned from my post and hoped that I could remain faithful to my principles "forever after."

Given all that I know and my playful, active, youthful frame of mind, I believe it is not inappropriate for me to be a primary school or high school teacher. By saying this, I naturally have not reached the root of the matter. If we want to get to do this, we must ask: What is the true meaning of—as opposed to popularly held beliefs about—education to society? What basic scientific knowledge is relevant to the goals of education? On the technical side, what are the areas that require training to become an educator? Like many teachers, I know only too little about these questions.

IV

My marriage to my wife was arranged. Before our wedding, we had neither met nor written to each other. But after we were married, we found we were quite compatible. At the time, we were both teachers, but taught in two different places. As our letters went back and forth between us, they would cross each other on their way, and sending and receiving mail became two important things in our minds. Forty years have gone by, and we are still very fond of each other. We would be hard pressed to put in words what is so good about the other person. We just feel that we are very suitable for each other, and cannot imagine anyone more suitable. That's all.

To be married in this fashion—like playing the lottery—is of course very dangerous. That my wife and I have ended up loving each other is a matter of chance. To put it in superstitious terms, one can say that we have had the blessings of the old man who used to sit under the moon in the White Cloud Temple by West Lake.[4] Yet, there seemed to be an extra advantage for me in having my marriage arranged. I have never languished in my sleep or had my peace of mind disturbed on account of the search for a mate. Nor have I ever been mired in thoughts of love, or been assaulted in turn by various feelings of hope, despair, envy and bitterness. Of course, it is difficult to say whether it is worth the risk of playing the marriage lottery in order to enjoy this extra advantage, but at least I have directed to other matters the amount of energy and time usually devoted to love.

It is obvious that many people would rather not risk treating marriage as a lottery, and going through courtship before getting married has become an article of common faith. I do not belittle this faith; there are, as they say, "inevitable" reasons why it has become so popular. People who have elevated love to such a supreme position can think only of baring their hearts to each other when they are in love, writing letters, composing poetry, watching movies, and touring famous sights together. When they are out of love, they can only think of crying, writing poetry (with lots of exclamation points), claiming to be the only unfortunate souls in the world, or even going to such extremes as contemplating throwing themselves in the Huangpu River. I only wish to say that to give up one's life for love like this is something that should be questioned. Such love is affordable only to the young capitalist masters and the young mistresses of "eminent families," who have at their disposal the wealth that their fathers and grandfathers have amassed through exploitation. Their status in society has long been decided before they even enter their mothers' wombs, and the world to them is a peaceful, problem-free place. They have so much free time on their hands that they find it hard to take, and end up turning to the matter of love, from which they manufacture a few scenes of happiness and

---

[4] A story in *Xu you guai lu* (*More Tales of the Mysterious and the Strange*) tells of a deity appearing as an old man who is in charge of marriage in the human world. He has a bag of red strings, which he uses to tie together the ankles of those who are destined to be husband and wife.

sorrow. This gives them a few lines to write into their empty book of life. For young people who lack such leisure and entertain some thought of improving themselves, to love like this would only deplete their energy and create obstacles on their way up.

As long as the human race continues to exist, love will persist. But love can appear in different shapes and forms. The game of love played by the young masters and mistresses—let it fade away!

Moon-watching (1933)

People who live in so-called "alleyway houses" are not much concerned with the waxing and waning and coming and going of the moon. Their so-called "courtyard" is no bigger than one square *zhang*,[5] and at night, it is always lit up by a lightbulb of some sixteen candela. Circumstances do not allow them the convenience of noticing the moon. When one is out on the street, a whole string of street lamps comes on even before it gets dark, and having the moon in the sky is merely like having an extra street lamp. When there is no moon, it's as if one of the street lamps is broken and hence has failed to light up. Who would notice the difference?

I said last summer that I rarely heard the sound of cicadas anymore. Now as I talk about the moon, I feel as if I have not seen it for some time. I only recall that on one occasion when I woke up in the middle of the night, I found that the radio in the room across the window from ours had been turned down, and the mah-jongg game next door had also ended. The lamps in the neighborhood had all been turned off. A beam of white, tooth-colored light came in through the south window, casting a shadow of lattice on my bedding. I was slightly astounded by the sight, but realized immediately that it was moonlight. My curiosity aroused, I looked out the window, trying to find the moon. But in a moment, it was obscured by clouds.

People from Beiping often wonder how anyone can "hang on" in a place like Shanghai: Everything is so tense here; the air is so dirty; and when you go out, there's hardly a tree to be seen. Apart from these, they're able to come up with a host of other such reasons. I think the "disappearance" of the moon might be included as one of their reasons why Shanghai is not a good place for "hanging on." If indeed this is regarded as one of the reasons, I cannot agree. There is no reason to regard the need for moon-viewing as one of the many conditions of living, and a broad mind and lofty imagination are not necessarily nurtured by looking at the moon. If we can withdraw our up-turned eyes and redirect them to the ground, we can reap the same or perhaps even more down-to-earth benefits in the cultivation of our character. But I do not object to viewing the moon. All I am saying is that it does not matter if we don't get to look at it.

---

[5]   A measurement of length, slightly more than ten feet.

Once I saw an ideal view of the moon. I was in the rural area of Fuzhou at the time, at the corner where the Min River curves around. One night, I was looking out by the banister of a building, and saw the waves coming in on the river. Under the moonlight, they became like a torrent of mercury. The mountains on the shore were lightly covered with mist, and looked different from the way they appeared at other times. The moon was high in the sky, motionless and self-contented. Stretching all the way from the shore to the building where I was staying was a wide expanse of sandy beach, white with a slightly blue tint in the moonlight. The fragrance of white lilies came from somewhere— perhaps that is the fragrance of the moon, I thought to myself. No distracting thoughts came to my mind. I remained like that for fifteen minutes before turning around. I saw my shadow cast on the oyster-powdered wall,[6] and once again, I became conscious of myself.

It would of course be an enjoyable thing to be able to appreciate such a view of the moon a few more times in one's life, although, as I said earlier, it doesn't really matter if one doesn't get the chance to see it.

---

[6]   In the coastal areas, people scrape off a substance secreted by oysters from rocks on the beaches and use it for whitewashing walls.

Lin Yutang

Lin Yutang (1895–1976) was born to a Christian family in Fujian and received his education in Shanghai, the United States, and Germany. In addition to writing, he was also a scholar of Chinese linguistics, and as such, devised a method of romanizing and categorizing Chinese characters, invented a Chinese typewriter, and compiled a Chinese dictionary.

Lin is one of the few Chinese writers who successfully published in both Chinese and English. In the West, he is perhaps best known as the author of such books as *The Importance of Living*, *The Wisdom of Laotse*, and *The Gay Genius*, in which he interpreted classical Chinese literature and the Chinese approach to living for Western readers. Many of these titles were first published in English before being translated into Chinese, and they continue to command a solid secondary reading public audience among Chinese readers.

From 1932 to 1934, Lin launched three magazines, *Lunyu*, *Renjianshi*, and *Yuzhou feng*, all of which were devoted to essay writing. In these publications, he tirelessly promoted his idea of humor, for which he coined the term *youmo* in order to capture the sound and sense of the English word. He glossed *you* as "hidden" and *mo* as "silent," thus distinguishing humor from the kind of crude and uncharitable laughter of some Chinese jokes. In the rancorous literary debates that marked the 1930s, however, Lin's brand of humor was sometimes misunderstood as frivolous, supercilious, and, worse, lacking social consciousness.

The two essays "Ah Fang" and "Buying Birds" included here illustrate this subtlety of *youmo* very well. The gentle laughter comes not so much from the inherent nature of the events narrated, but from Lin's rendition of them, reflecting a detached but fond view of human life with all its foibles.

Ah Fang (1932)

I have a boy servant at home, whom I'll call Ah Fang for now, though that isn't his real name. He is an extremely clever child. When I hired him from a money changer, he was merely fifteen—sixteen at the most. He is about seventeen or eighteen now, and his voice is beginning to change, sometimes sounding like the crowing of a young rooster. But he is still a small child inside, and this, combined with his extreme cleverness, both make him impervious to our efforts to impose some discipline and undermine our resolve to fire him. As a result, all of our house rules have fallen by the wayside, and it is no longer easy for me to maintain the respect due to me as the master of the house.

Ah Fang's intelligence is indeed superior to that of ordinary people: He can do what others cannot, and indeed there are many things we cannot do without him. But he discharges his duties much like a poet relying on inspiration. In confusion, haste, forgetfulness, and general topsy-turviness, he is without peer in this world. The number of cups and plates he breaks in a week roughly equals those broken by the rest of the servants in half a year. But he has a sunny disposition, and when you reproach him for anything, he simply hangs his head and thinks about his mistakes. He is, moreover, like a king in the kitchen, and the few senior servants have all yielded to him without even realizing it, perhaps because they all feel that his talents place him well above the rank of servant. All you need to do is listen to the way he berates people who have dialed the wrong number, and you will see that he was born to be a young master.

I should first explain why I have allowed Ah Fang to cause such upheaval in our household, and why he is permitted to go scot-free for doing what other servants would not dare do. Before Ah Fang came, miscellaneous tasks such as repairing the doorbell, grounding the electrical wires, hanging pictures, and fixing the ball in the water-tank of the toilet all fell to me. These tasks have now been taken over by Ah Fang, and I can read Plato's *Republic* in peace. I no longer need to put away my book upon being summoned to fix the toilet; nor do I have to put aside my writing just when inspiration strikes to respond to a call of "Hey, the pipes are leaking!" from the kitchen. That I am no longer bothered with matters such as these more than makes up for the losses incurred by Ah Fang.

Ah Fang has special talents and is capable of doing any sort of menial job. When a piece of furniture is broken, he comes up with some ingenious way—by patching and stuffing, yanking and tinkering—of making it work again. When he has nothing to do, he tells stories such as "The Burning of the Red Lotus Temple" to the other children, and it is unclear who has more fun—the child telling the story or those listening. There is one particular thing about him that I especially admire: Ever since coming to our home, he has had his eye on my English typewriter. In the morning when I am still in bed, he is in my study doing a two-hour cleaning job; in fact, he is playing with my typewriter. It is probably the first typewriter he has ever seen in his life, and it fascinates him. When he is cleaning my study, mysterious noises always come from the room. One day, for no reason, the typewriter broke down, and I spent two hours trying to fix it without success. I scolded him for playing with the machine, and that afternoon, when I came back from my walk, Ah Fang said to me, "Sir, the machine is fixed." From that point on, I have had to recognize him as a clever and worthy compatriot.

There are many other things that we cannot do without Ah Fang. He can curse on the phone in English, Mandarin, Shanghainese, and Anhui and Xiamen dialects. (Any outsider has to be a genius to learn Xiamen dialect, and people of mere normal intelligence always keep their distance from it.) He learned somewhere to speak English beautifully, a phenomenon so odd that it can be attributable only to God, the dispenser of intelligence. You only have to teach him something once and he learns it immediately. He can say "waiterminit" rather than "wait-a-meenyoot"[1] as the average college student tends to say. I suggested he go to night school to study English and offered to pay two-thirds of the fee, but he wouldn't do it. Like all geniuses, he is temperamentally ill-disposed to schools.

This is probably sufficient to explain why Ah Fang is allowed to have his way at my home, but getting him to do anything is a different matter altogether. For example, if you ask him to go out to buy a box of matches, he will be gone for two hours and come back with a new pair of cloth shoes and a grasshopper to give to the children—but no matches. Fortunately, he has not lost his innocence and thus does not understand the difference between work and play in this world. It takes him three hours to clean the bedroom because he spends at least

---

[1]   The two words "waiterminit" and "wait-a-meenyoot" appear in English in the original.

an hour feeding the bird or joking with the new maid in the kitchen. "Ah Fang, you are eighteen years old now. You have to be a bit more serious about your work!" my wife says. But what's the use? We still end up watching him smash cups and plates, burn knives in the oven (one of his ingenious innovations is to dry them there after they have been washed), place the dustbin on the table, leave the broom in the clothes closet—he does all these things just so that he can go to the garden to catch grasshoppers for the children. I don't have a single complete set of teacups anymore. When the time comes for him to prepare breakfast, the kitchen is filled with a din of clanging and banging, because he believes that one should be speedy with one's work. Preparing breakfast used to be the duty of the cook, but now it has somehow become Ah Fang's monopoly, perhaps because he enjoys scrambling eggs, and because the cook is a woman. Since Ah Fang looks down on women, she has had to bend to his wishes.

Three weeks ago, we hired another maid to do the laundry, and since then, there has been another game in the kitchen. This maid, though we call her "Old Maid" by custom, is in fact not old at all, only twenty-one, and you will remember that Ah Fang is eighteen. As a result, the kitchen soon became a stage for fun and games. The work slackened all the more, while the sounds of merriment grew louder by the day. The time it took to clean a room jumped from two hours to three, and Ah Fang even forgot his daily task of polishing my shoes. At long last, I was left with no other choice but to issue a serious warning: If he did not polish my shoes and leave them outside my bedroom by six-thirty the next morning, he would be fired. That day, I put on a straight face and did not talk to him at all, determined to reassert some discipline at home. After all, as master of the house, I had my respect to maintain! That night, I called all the servants together and reiterated my warning, and there was fear on everyone's face, especially the two maids responsible for cooking and laundry. Then I went to bed in peace, assured that order at home had been restored.

The next morning, I woke up at six o'clock, and listened quietly to what was happening outside my room. At six-twenty, the young laundry maid left my shoes outside the door. This is unfair, I thought.

"I told Ah Fang to bring my shoes here. Why did you do it for him?" I asked.

"I had to come upstairs anyway," the maid answered respectfully and politely. "That's why I brought them up for him."

"Couldn't he do that himself? Did he ask you to help him, or did you take it upon yourself to bring the shoes upstairs?"

"He didn't ask me," she said. "I did it on my own."

I knew she was lying, because Ah Fang's soul was still wandering somewhere in his dreams. But the circumspect manner in which the young maid defended Ah Fang made me feel embarrassed, and I felt I would rather just give in and forget about restoring order at home. Now, no matter how topsy-turvy the kitchen becomes, I no longer have the right to interfere.

(I finished this essay two years ago. Ah Fang later had an affair with the new maid, and the two engaged in thievery on the outside and were eventually sent to prison. He was released in June of this year, and I have yet to see him.)

Buying Birds (1934)

I like birds and hate dogs. This is by no means due to my personal perversity; rather, it is because I am Chinese. This inclination comes naturally to me as to all Chinese, because all Chinese like birds. However, if you talk to us about some people's love for dogs, you will hear us ask, "What are you talking about?" I will never understand how anybody could befriend the beast, hugging and patting it. Only once did I suddenly come to appreciate this kind of feeling for dogs, and that was when I was reading *The Story of San Michele* by Axel Munthe. In a certain part of the story, Munthe narrates how he challenges a Frenchman to a duel for kicking his dog. I was really moved when I came to that part. It was really only then that I understood the sentiment, and I almost wished that at that instant I had a hunting dog to curl up by my side. But I was only momentarily under the mesmerizing sway of Munthe's language. Now, almost two years after I first read his book, the lofty and noble sentiments I fleetingly felt for dogs have turned to ashes.

The most odious time I have ever spent in my life was in the living room of an American friend. A St. Bernard—a magnificent and alert dog originally bred in the St. Bernard's Hospice in Switzerland, hence its name—insisted on licking my fingers and arm to show its affection. Even more unbearable was the interminable narrative on the part of the hostess about the dog's genealogy. I believe I must have seemed a heretic on that occasion. Staring at her, I looked around in vain for an appropriate thing to say.

"A Swiss friend of mine brought him over directly from Zurich," my hostess said.

"Is that so, Mrs. Pierce?"

"His maternal grandfather once saved a child from an avalanche in the Alps. His great-grand-uncle was a prize-winner in the International Dog Exhibition in 1856."

"I see!"

I did not mean to be rude, but I am afraid I was.

I understand the British like dogs, but, for that matter, the British like everything, including big tomcats. I once debated this with a British friend.

"All this jabbering about making friends with dogs is nonsense," I said. "You people pretend to like animals. It's a good lie, because you goad these beasts into chasing down a poor fox. Why don't you go and caress the fox, and call it 'my deary, my baby'?"

"I think I can explain," my friend answered. "Dogs are amazingly sensitive. They understand you and are loyal to you...."

"Just a minute!" I interrupted. "The reason that I loathe dogs is precisely that they are so sensitive. By nature, I love animals, as evidenced by the fact that I would never deliberately kill even a fly. But I detest those beasts that pretend to be your friend, and come up to you and scratch you all over. I like animals that do not cross my path and know their place. I'd rather love a donkey.... Love a dog? Sure, I suppose it's possible, but why pat it and hug it to boot?"

"Oh, forget it!" my British friend said. "I didn't think I'd be able to convince you." Thereupon, we switched to other topics.

Later, my family circumstances became such that I ended up keeping a dog. I took good care to find someone to feed it, bathe it, and let it sleep in a nice doghouse, but I forbade it to scratch me or show me any affection or loyalty. Truly, I would rather have died than walk it on the street as many fashionable young women do. One time, I saw a maid from northern Jiangsu walking with her unbound feet in a pair of high heels. Obviously, she was a servant in some foreigner's household. She had a walking stick in one hand, and was pulling a little hunting dog with the other. Now, that was a sight! I wouldn't want to make such a weird spectacle of myself. Let the British go and walk their dogs—the two are fated to be together. But not with me! When I go out for a walk, I want to be myself.

But I am here to talk about birds, especially my experience of buying birds the day before yesterday. I have a cage of small birds at home. I don't know what they're called, but they are slightly smaller than sparrows, and the males have white spots on their scarlet chests. Last winter, for one reason or another, several birds died, and for some time I had been thinking of buying a few more to keep the survivors company. The Mid-Autumn Festival fell on that day, and everybody at home had gone out to a tea party, leaving my youngest daughter and me at home. So, I suggested to her that we go to the city to buy birds, and she agreed.

People living in Shanghai know what the bird market at the Temple of the City God is like, and there's no need for me to elaborate. With my little girl in my arms, I walked through the streets congested with pedestrians. The place was like heaven for animal lovers, because there were not only birds, but also frogs, white mice, squirrels, crickets, turtles with some kind of water plant growing on their backs, goldfish, sparrows, centipedes, iguanas, and all sorts of other strange things. Before you make any pronouncements as to whether Chinese people love animals or not, you would be well-advised to go take a look at the cricket seller squatting on the ground in the middle of the road and all the children gathering around him. I walked into a bird store run by someone from Shandong and bought three pairs of birds. Since I had bought the same kind of bird before, I knew the price, and was able to make my purchase without any difficulty. The price was exactly two dollars and ten cents.

The store was on the corner of the street, and there were about forty such birds in a cage. After we settled on a price, the man started to pick out three pairs for me. The commotion in the cage set off a cloud of dust, and I stood back a little. By the time he had picked out three birds, there was already a big crowd of people gathered in front of the store. Idlers on the street are always like that, and there was really nothing unusual about it. After I paid for the birds and picked up my small cage, I became the center of attention and the target of everyone's envy. There was a tremor of joy floating in the air. "What kind of bird is that?" a middle-aged man asked me. "You have to ask at the store," I said. "Do they sing?" another man asked. "How much did you pay for them?" a third one asked. I answered them casually and walked away like some sort of aristocrat, because to the Chinese masses, I was now a proud owner of birds. Something had brought the crowd together, some kind of natural, instinctive common joy that released our collective wish for a harmonious world and shattered the usual wall of silence that exists between strangers. Of course, they had every right to ask me whatever they wanted about the birds, just as they would have had the right to ask me about the first prize of the Aviation Lottery if I were to win it before their very eyes.

I picked up my daughter with one hand and the birdcage with the other, and people on the street turned around to look at us. If I were the child's mother, I would have felt sure that they were admiring my child. But since I am a man, I knew that they were admiring the birds in the cage. Are these birds that unusual? I thought to myself. No, my admirers were just afflicted with the common disorder of loving birds to the point of obsession.

I walked up to a snack shop. It was still early, just past noon, and the upstairs room was empty.

"Give me a bowl of wontons, please," I said.

"What kind of birds are those?" a waiter with a towel on his shoulder asked.

"Give me a bowl of wontons and a dish of boiled chicken," I said.

"Sure, sure. Do they sing or not?"

"They don't sing. Would you make it snappy? I'm hungry."

"Yeah, yeah, yeah. A bowl of wontons! A dish of boiled chicken!" He shouted—or rather, sang—to the kitchen downstairs. "These must be imported birds."

"Oh?" I said, making polite noises.

"This kind of bird lives in the mountains, you know, the mountains, really high mountains. Hey, *Zhanggui*, what kind of birds are these?"

Zhanggui are people who wear glasses and keep the accounts. This one, like his fellow accountants, could read and write. Apart from copper coins and paper money, one didn't expect him to be interested in children's playthings or anything else. But, as soon as he heard about the birds, he not only answered right away, but surprised me greatly by moving his feet around in search of his slippers. He left the counter and slowly came up to my table. As he got close to the birdcage, his frosty look began to melt and he became guileless and talkative, completely at odds with his appearance. He then looked up at the ceiling, his belly protruding from under his short vest, and pronounced his judgment.

"This kind of bird doesn't sing," he observed with authority. "They're just cute little birds, just good enough for little children to play with."

Then he returned to his tall counter, and soon afterward I finished that bowl of wontons.

It was the same on my way back home. People on the street all bent down to see what was inside the cage. I walked into a used bookstore.

"Do you have any Ming editions?" I asked.

"What's in your cage?" the middle-aged shop-owner asked. Three or four customers immediately turned their attention to the birdcage in my hand. There was quite a commotion—I mean outside the cage.

"May I take a look?" an apprentice asked, and he proceeded to snatch the birdcage from my hand.

"Take it and look to your heart's content," I said. "Do you have any Ming editions?" But I no longer had their ear, so I went to browse the shelves by myself. I could not find a single book I wanted, so I picked up the birdcage and walked out of the shop. Again, I immediately became the center of attention. Some people on the street smiled at the birds, and some smiled at me, all because I was the owner of the birds.

Later, I called a Yunfei cab at the Second Yangjing Bridge to go home. I remembered clearly that the last time I had come back from the Temple of the City God with a cage of birds, the clerk at the station had deliberately come out to look at them. This time, he did not see me, and I did not want to draw his attention. But when I stepped into the cab, the driver caught sight of the cage in my hand. Sure enough, his face relaxed at once. Indeed, he practically turned into a small child, just as my driver had the last time. He was very friendly with me and chattered away, our conversation ranging far and wide. By the time we arrived at my home, not only had he taught me the secrets of raising birds and making them sing, he had also divulged to me all the secrets of the Yunfei Taxi Company: the number of cars they had, the bonus the drivers got, his whole childhood, and the possible reason for his getting married.

Now, I understand: If one day, I was called to appear before an impassioned Chinese mob who hated me to the bone and would not rest until they had me at their disposal, I would know precisely what to do. All I would need to do to dissipate their anger was produce my birdcage and show them a beautiful swallow or a musical lark. See, that would be more effective than either a fire hose or tear gas, and more powerful than a speech by Demosthenes! Moreover, in the end, we might even become sworn brothers.

Zhang Henshui

Zhang Henshui (1895–1967) was a prolific and well-known artist of a form of traditional Chinese fiction known as the linked-chapter novel *(zhanghui xiaoshuo)*. A journalist by profession, Zhang picked up novel writing initially as a hobby, but it soon came to absorb all of his creative energy. In a successful writing career that spanned fifty years, he produced more than one hundred such novels, making him one of the most popular writers of the twentieth century.

At first, Zhang did not receive any serious critical attention because he was regarded as a writer of the Mandarin Ducks and Butterflies School, which was condemned by the more politically minded as a pastime of the leisure class. In time, however, Zhang's novels received recognition for both their artistry and function as social documents of his time. His books were a wide canvas depicting a cross-section of Chinese society from the 1920s to the 1940s, characterized by realistic dialogues and his propensity to incorporate current events into their plots.

Zhang also tried his hand at writing essays, which, like his novels, appeared in newspapers before they were published in monographs. "Checkers" was written during wartime in Chongqing. Unlike other pieces in this anthology, it was written in classical Chinese *(wenyan)*, which allowed Zhang to work classical references and allusions seamlessly into his prose. The subject of the essay is a mundane everyday object, but it serves as a vehicle for him to explore changes in human relationships in times of war.

Checkers (1934)

I have never been good at chess, and when forced to play, I can seldom manage to finish a game. The only exception is foreign checkers,[1] of which I can occasionally play a few games. When my wife and I were married more than ten years ago, she was as happy as Xiao Qiao[2] in the early days of her marriage, and our joy was not limited to "painting eyebrows."[3] Even so, she could not possibly pass her time doing nothing but enjoying our conjugal bliss. Hence, I suggested she read Tang poetry, take up freehand flower painting, and practice Zhao and Liu-style calligraphy.[4] She might have shown some interest in the first two lessons, but from the third day on, she ignored my persistent summons. When I showed her the checkers set, however, she was ecstatic.

On wintry nights in Beiping, the northerly wind howled outside and the snowflakes were as big as the palm of one's hand. Inside, the electric lamp brightened up the room, and the fire in the stove made it as warm as spring. We lowered the curtain and sat across from each other, and the potted plum was in bloom. There we would sit with the stove between us, eating oranges as we chatted and feeling so satisfied that we did not need any other entertainment. When we got tired of sitting, we would have a game of checkers across the table. We agreed that if I lost, I would take her to the theater the following day, and that if I won, she would go to the kitchen and prepare a few good dishes for me. Since I tended to lose seven or eight games out of ten, she was only too happy to agree to the wager. I never quite understood how she could beat me when I was the one who had taught her the game in the first place. We have spent half our lives together, going through thick and thin, and this is still a standing joke between us.

The Arts Supply Store of Chongqing recently had some checkers for sale. The boards were made of paper rather than wood, and the

---

[1]   The game referred to here is what is known erroneously in the West as "Chinese checkers." In Zhang's essay, this game is identified as having been imported from a foreign country.

[2]   Xiao Qiao, the younger of two sisters well known for their beauty during the Three Kingdoms period (220–280 AD).

[3]   "Painting eyebrows" refers to the many intimate joys shared by loving couples. See "Biography of Zhang Chang" in *Hanshu* (*The History of Han*).

[4]   Zhao Mengfu (1254–1322) and Liu Gongquan (778–865) are two famous calligraphers.

pieces were small. I bought a set and the events of fifteen years before came rushing back to me. I took it home and showed my wife, saying, "Do you still remember this little game that we used to play?" She let out a gentle sigh, and said, "The jade looks the same, but the horse has grown in age!"[5] I felt dejected at her words and fell silent.

It rained in the mountains that night, and a chilly wind invaded our room. The tea in the pot was cold, and the lamp on my desk had grown dim. I put on my glasses and sat down to work on my novel in the faint light. The sound of my pen moving quickly across the page was like silkworms munching on mulberry leaves. My wife sat next to me, sharing the same lamp as she mended our child's old woolen sweater. We worked in silence. It was completely dark outside, and the bamboo swayed in the wind. There was not a sound apart from dogs barking in the distance. I stopped writing, raised my head, and let out a deep sigh. She immediately got up and took away my pen and paper, and asked me, "If you're not sleepy, shall we have a game of checkers?" I laughed and said, "I could never find a better companion than you! Only you can read my mind." Then we moved the lamp and got ready to play. We played three games in all, but the tables had turned, and I won all three games. I laughed and said, "Is it because I have improved, or is your mind not on the game?" She stood up abruptly to trim the lamp and said, "I forgot to buy oil today. We might not have enough to let the lamp go on like this. Let's put the light out and go to bed so there will be some oil for the lamp when the little boy goes to the bathroom in the middle of the night." I inadvertently touched her hand, and found it cold as ice. I said, sighing, "If trees can change so much, how much more so we mortals!"[6]

That night, I dreamed of Beiping, three times altogether, and woke up three times.

---

[5]   A reference to an incident recorded in the *Guliang Commentary*, "The Second Year of the Duke of Xi." The Duke of Xiang from Jin obtained passage through Yu to attack the Guo state by offering a piece of jade and a horse. Five years later, Jin waged war against Yu and won. When Xun Xi brought back to the Duke of Xiang the horse and the jade that had once been presented to Yu for the right of passage, the former uttered the line quoted in this essay. Here, Zhang Henshui's wife was commenting on the passage of her youth.

[6]   During his northern expedition in 369 AD, Huan Wen passed by Jincheng and saw that the willows he had planted some twenty years before had grown to ten double spans. Upon seeing them, he uttered the line quoted in this essay.

Mao Dun

Mao Dun (1896–1981) is a writer, a critic, and a journalist. His education was spotty. Before he had the chance to complete his university education, he entered full-time employment with the Commercial Press. As an editor there, he had a hand in shaping the direction of such publications as *Xuesheng zazhi* and *Xiaoshuo yuebao*. Mao Dun produced a number of novels that together paint a wide canvass of China under transformation. The most famous of these is probably *Midnight.* He was the Minister of Culture between 1949 and 1965.

The minute details of the quiet but stultifying atmosphere depicted in "Before the Storm" can on the one hand be seen as the trademark of a naturalist writer, as Mao Dun tends to see himself. Yet, it is not difficult to subject the essay to a symbolic reading that reveals a political message underlying the description of the weather on the surface. The storm is approaching, during which strong wind, heavy rain, thunder and lightning will clear the fetid air that envelops China like a shroud. The call for political action and the impatience for the arrival of a better time are unmistakable.

Before the Storm (1934)

Early in the morning, as soon as I got up, I walked to that little stone bridge. I felt the stones and was surprised that there still seemed to be a trace of heat in them. There had not been as much as a wisp of a breeze the whole day before. There had been peals of dry thunder toward evening but no wind, and the night was even more stifling than the day. Toward dawn, there were still two or three people lying on the bridge. Perhaps their bodies had warmed the stones again.

The whole sky was covered by a gray curtain. The sun was out of sight, but its power seemed to have penetrated that gray curtain and was closing above one's head.

There was not a single drop of water in the river, and the cracks in the riverbed looked like lines on a turtle's back. As for the fields, countless ditches had opened up—they were two feet wide, so one surely could call them ditches. The soil was white and almost as hard as cement, as if the whole night was not long enough for it to release all the heat it had absorbed during the day. Now, there seemed to be something like white smoke wafting from those long, narrow openings.

People standing on the bridge felt as if all of the pores on their bodies were blocked. Their stomachs bubbled, as if they were about to heave something up.

Throughout the morning, the gray curtain remained stretched across the sky. It lacked even the smallest hole, and remained completely motionless. There might have been some wind outside the curtain, but we were all wrapped up inside. Had you thrown a chicken feather from the bridge, you would not have seen it flutter and drift its way down. It was like living in a big barrel with the air sucked out. One could open one's arms wide and take a deep breath, but what went inside one's lungs was a whiff of scorching, stifling air.

Sweat kept pushing its way out, just kept pushing, but it was like glue, making you uncomfortable all over, and it dried up to form a shell over you.

At about three o'clock in the afternoon, we felt as if we had turned into fish, our mouths wide open, about to die for lack of water. All of a sudden, a slit appeared in the gray curtain in the sky—yes, a slit, no more and no less!—as if a sharp knife had just cut across the curtain! But then, after the knife ran its course, the curtain closed up again, and it was no different from before the knife had made its cut. No wind came in. After a while, there was a flash in the sky, and again the gray curtain was slit open. But what was the use?

There seemed to be a giant outside holding a gleaming sword in his hand, trying to flick open that gray curtain. He must have been filled with anger, his howling growing more and more urgent. Over and over again, the sword flashed across the sky. *Grrr... grrr!....* His growling had come inside the curtain from outside.

Abruptly, the flashing and growling stopped. It was again an impenetrable gray curtain!

The air was twice as stifling as before! The curtain was twice as thick! The sky was twice as dark!

Perhaps you might have supposed that the giant was now wiping his sweat and catching his breath outside the curtain. You might have been sure that he would attack again. So, you waited anxiously, waiting for the flashing of the sword to pierce through the curtain, and the *grrr... grrr...* of his growling.

But you waited and waited, and instead the flies came. They flew out buzzing from the filthy corners and flew around you, stinging your skin that now seemed covered by a coat of glue. They had just come from a feast at the outhouse, wearing red tops like important officials, and of all places, they chose to squat on your nose.

The mosquitoes came too, humming like old monks chanting their sutras or old scholars reciting ancient prose. The flies could pass contagious diseases, but the mosquitoes just went about sucking your blood.

You jumped up, and swung your cattail leaf fan around, but as soon as you chased away a swarm of them, another swarm seized the opportunity to attack from another side. You screamed at them, but they simply responded by humming and buzzing.

The cicadas on the tree tops outside were singing loudly, "*Szzz.... You're done for!.... Szzzz.... You're done for!....*"

You had no more sweat inside you, and your mouth was dry enough to burn up. Your arms and legs had turned to jelly. You felt that even the end of the world could not be as bad as this!

However, all of a sudden, lightning flashed, and the light lit up the corner of the house. At one stroke, the giant outside ripped the gray curtain to pieces! "*Grrr... uhh! Grr... uhh!*" he cried out triumphantly. *Hoo-weee... hoo-weee... hoo-weee....* The wind that had been blocked outside the curtain for two whole days now hurled itself forward with extraordinary speed! The cicadas grew quiet, the flies escaped, and the mosquitoes hid away. We felt refreshed, as if shedding a shell from our bodies. *Crrack-kack!* The gleaming of the giant's sword flew and danced in the open sky. *Grrr... uhh! Grr... uhh!* Let's have some more of it—and louder still!

Let the heavy storm wash the world until it is clean and cool!

Xu Zhimo

Among the many Chinese literary stars in the twentieth century, Xu Zhimo (1897–1931) probably cuts the most romantic figure. Many people have heard of his turbulent love affairs and his untimely death at thirty-four. His short but remarkable life provides raw material for many films and TV dramas.

Readers of modern Chinese literature, on the other hand, know him as an active proponent of pro-Western aesthetics, mostly derivative of English romantic poetry, which he translated and adapted in his own poetry and prose. Hu Shi described his life as a continuous pursuit of love, liberty, and beauty, the ideals of which are evident in his creative work. "Idle Talk About Life in the Mountains of Florence" can certainly be read in this context.

Similarly, the image of birds circling in the air and flying higher and higher in the sky in "Thoughts of Flying" brings to mind many English antecedents. Yet, one also finds disturbing phrases that are more in tune with the situation of contemporary China. The mention of the august eagles preying on young chickens in the middle of the essay and the concluding image of a "bird-shaped machine" that drops what appears to be a bomb remain as jarring notes that make it difficult to regard this essay merely as a eulogy on flying.

Idle Talk About Life in the Mountains of Florence (1925)

Going out for a walk here on a clear May evening, whether up or down the hill, is like attending a feast of beauty. It is like going to an orchard where fruit imbued with poetry hangs in abundance on every tree. If you are not satisfied with merely standing there to look, all you need to do is reach up and pick it from the trees, and you can savor to your heart's content its freshness, enough to inebriate your soul. The sunlight is balmy, and never too warm. The wind is gentle and soothing; since it frequently comes from the woods brimming with flowers, it brings with it a faint and distant fragrance and a nourishing dampness. It caresses your face and wraps itself gently around your shoulders and waist. The mere act of breathing is an inexhaustible happiness in itself! The air is always clean—there is no smoke in the valley nearby and no mist in the distant hills. The beautiful scenery displays itself without reservation for your leisurely enjoyment, like a picture before your eyes.

The beauty of living in the mountains is, above all, that you never have to fuss over your clothes and appearance. You can feel free to let loose the weeds of hair on your head, and allow that moss of stubble to grow on your cheeks. You can wear whatever clothes you like, be they those of a cowherd, a fisherman, a farmer, a roaming gypsy, or a hunter. You don't have to worry about adjusting your tie—in fact, you can forget about wearing one altogether, and allow your neck and chest half a day of freedom. You can wrap a colorful bandanna around your head and pretend to be a foot soldier of the Taiping troops,[1] or take after Byron with his Egyptian costumes. Most important of all, however, put on the very oldest of your old shoes. Never mind that they look shabby—they are your most loveable friends. They support your weight, allowing you to forget that you still have a pair of feet beneath you.

It's best not to have a companion when you go out like that. I would even strictly forbid it. You should go by yourself, because a companion would only distract you in some way, particularly a young woman, who is the most dangerous and tyrannical of companions. You should avoid her like a beautiful colored snake in the grass.

Usually, when we leave our own homes to go to a friend's house or our place of work, we are merely moving from one cell to another in one big prison. Restraint follows us all the time, and freedom can

---

[1]   Taipings, see the third note of "A Memory."

never find us. But if you have the opportunity to saunter all by yourself among the lovely mountains and villages in these days between spring and summer, then the star of luck is truly shining on you. This is the time when you can appreciate and savor firsthand complete freedom and comfort, when your body and soul act in unison. Dear friends, with every year added to our age, the weight of the cangue around our neck increases and the chains around our ankles tighten. Don't we all look with envy at children rolling and playing in the sand and shallow water, or little cats chasing their own tails? But our cangue and chains are the masters that restrict our movements. That is why, only when you run all by yourself into the embrace of nature, like a naked child throwing itself into the lap of its mother, can you understand what it is like to be happy in the soul, to revel in the mere acts of living, breathing, walking, looking, and listening. For that reason, you have to act strictly for yourself, to be extremely selfish, and to allow only you, your body and soul, to beat at the same pulse with nature, to rise and fall in the same sound wave, to realize yourself in the same wonderful universe. Our untainted innocence is as gentle and frail as mimosa. Once it is touched by a companion, it recoils; but in the clear, quiet sunlight and gentle wind, its posture is natural, its life uninhibited.

When you go roaming by yourself, you will sit, lie, or even roll around on the grass because its warmth and color will naturally awaken the vivaciousness of the child within you. On a quiet path, you will dance wildly despite yourself and watch the grotesque transformation of your shadows, because the languorous movement of the shadows of the trees communicates to you the joy of dancing. You will also spontaneously burst into song, occasionally remembering some broken snatches of music and improvising tunes of your own, because the birds in the woods tell you that this spring scene deserves our praise. It goes without saying, moreover, that your mind will expand naturally with the long mountain paths, and your heart will grow calm as you look at the clear blue sky. Your thoughts will harmonize with the sound of water in the valley and the spring that flows out over the rocks. Sometimes, it runs so clear that you can see through the water to the bottom, and sometimes it whisks itself into a symphony of waves, and flows and flows through the cool olive woods, into the alluring Arno River....

Not only is a traveling companion superfluous, you need not bring even a book with you on short walks such as this. A book is ordinarily the perfect companion, but it is only good on a train or in your own living room, not when you are taking a walk by yourself. What profound inspirations and lucid, beautiful thoughts cannot find their roots in the music of the wind, the hue of the clouds, the rise and fall of mountains and land, the color and fragrance of flowers and grass? Nature is the greatest book of all. Goethe said that we can read the most profound message in its every page and word. Moreover, this book of nature is written in a language comprehensible to all. The Alps and the Wu Lao Peak, Sicily and the Putuo Mountain, the Rhine and the Yangtze, Lake Leman and West Lake, orchid and hortensia, the snow on the reefs on the West Stream in Hangzhou and the red clouds in the sunset at Venice, the lark and the nightingale, to say nothing of the yellow color of wheat, the purple of wisteria, the green of the grass—they all grow together on the land, and wave together in the wind; the symbol they use will forever be the same, and their meaning will always be transparent. As long as your soul is not covered with scars, your eyes not blind and your ears not stopped, this invisible supreme lesson will be yours, and this most precious tonic will be free to you forever. As long as you know this book, you will not be lonely though alone in the world, nor will you be poor though poverty-stricken. You will find consolation when troubled, encouragement when frustrated, inspiration when weak, and a compass when lost.

Thoughts of Flying (1926)

Imagine that it is now snowing outside the window—the street, the city wall, and the rooftops are all covered with it. A policeman in a black cap huddles under the eaves of the house at the corner of the alleyway. His sleepy eyes half open, he is watching the snow frolicking about like tufts of cotton in the air.... Suppose it is very deep into the night, so deep that even the hands of the clock on the wall cannot count it, deep like a mountain cave that spirals downward into the mountain....

Now suppose that I own such a deep night, its bottomless eeriness making the hair on my body stand on end. And then suppose that I am in possession of the snow fluttering down outside the window, muffling the sounds of the city far and near, covering the tortuous wheel tracks on the muddy road, and screening out the uncompromising stream of thoughts going on in my brain....

I long for that kind of depth and that kind of quiet. The nighthawk hiding under the foliage over there will not risk opening its eyes before the sun comes out. I think to myself: Even it has to wait.

In the blue sky there is a dark spot. With the sun shining in your eyes, you can't really see what it is. So you raise your hand to shield your eyes and try to look through the gap between two branches. Yes, it is black, almost the size of a yew nut—no, it's as big as a peach now. There, it has gone west.

*   *   *   *   *   *   *

After lunch, we go to the beach. (This is the southernmost tip of Cornwall in England, which opens up to the Atlantic ocean on three sides.) A twittering sound rises evenly from the bottoms of our feet, slightly trembling, reaches our waists, then our shoulders, passes over our heads, and penetrates the clouds and beyond. Oh, can your imagination turn the vibrating musical notes into a sheet of bright rain, falling from the blue sky to the green earth below? No, the rain is like little dancing feet, the feet of angels. The skylarks have also had their lunch, and leave their humble nests on the ground to fly up to the sky to do their work. God has given them work, and that's whom they are working for. Look, here is one, and there are two over there! Once off the ground, they fly straight up to the highest reaches of the sky, their wings flapping so enthusiastically, so perfectly, so free of hesitation. They are friends with the sky, and they start to sing just as soon as they begin to fly. Their throats are actively at work, music flowing from them like strings of pearls, shiny and tinkling, singing praises of the sky. Look how high they fly! They seem at first as large as beans—no, sesame seeds—but now they are just a patch of black dots, slightly shifting as they fly straight up into the sky. And then you can't see them anymore, not even a shadow, but the shiny fine drizzle still falls incessantly....

*   *   *   *   *   *   *

It is a rare thing indeed to fly with "wings like clouds that stretch down from the sky... and a back that supports the blue sky, and nothing that can stand in the way."[2]... Outside the eastern gate of our town is a yellow earthen mound, on top of which is a seven-storied pagoda, its tip pointing straight up to the sky. Bells are frequently rung from the yard of the pagoda, and most often when the sun is shining from the west. The colorful clouds above the earthen mound are matched by the dazzling bough of red flowers right by West Hill—when the bells are rung, there are one, two, three, four, or even five or six "hungry eagles" circling the top of the pagoda, brushing by the roof and weaving in and out of the clouds above. Their claws curled and their wide grayish wings stretched out, they gaze down at the earth. There in the evening wind, they float in mid-air, totally free of worries, as if there to practice waltzing to the rhythm of the bells.

Those were the mythic *peng* birds of my childhood. On a fine day when there was not a single cloud in the sky, I could tell that the "hungry eagles" of the pagoda were out looking for food just by the sound of their rasping cries in the air. As soon as we thought of them, those bald, round-eyed heroes up in the sky, feathers—jagged like the bristles of a steel brush—seemed to burst forth from our shoulder blades. They waved in the wind, gently rustling. With just a slight flap, we were out the study door, racing our way to frolic in the white clouds that seemed lined with tortoiseshell. Who had the patience to stand at the teacher's desk, shifting from side to side, reciting those impossible books that we'd tried to memorize in the morning? Oh, to fly! Not like sparrows that hippity-hop from branch to branch; or bats that dart around for a feast of mosquitoes under cover of evening darkness; or swallows that build nests under the eaves, their tails drooping and voices fragile. If we are to fly, let's fly all over the sky, let's launch a flight that wind cannot stop nor

---

[2]   *Zhuangzi*, "Xiaoyao you" (Free and Easy Wandering).

clouds impede, a flight that carries us over hills with a single flap of our wings, while our shadows spread shade over twenty *mou*[3] of land below. And then in the evening, when we're tired, we'll ride the wind and circle the sky, dreaming....

I have heard that those eagles prey on young chickens.

*   *   *   *   *   *   *

Yes, to fly! Each human being at one time *could* fly. Angels have wings, and they fly, and we, too, had wings in the beginning, and could fly. When each of us first arrived in the world, we came here by flight, and some among us will fly back when our time in this world is up. These people can only be envied. Most people, however, have forgotten how to fly. Some of us have lost the feathers on our wings, which never grow back, or our wings are now glued together and we can't open them anymore, or our feathers have been clipped and we can only hop about on the ground. And some of us have taken our wings off to the pawnshop to exchange for money, and the date for redemption has long since passed.... Indeed, once we have passed our childhood days, we immediately lose our ability to fly. It is a terrible thing to lose one's wings or be unable to use them because they are in disrepair. Unable to fly back to the sky, you are forced to squat on the ground and gaze helplessly at its unreachable heights, looking on as other blessed souls carouse to and fro in the blue clouds. How pathetic!

Wings on your shoulders are not the same as shoes on your feet: When shoes grow worn, you can always ask your mother for another pair, but not so with wings. A feather broken is a feather lost, and there's no way to replace it. What's more, merely having wings does not alone guarantee that one will be able to fly. If you have carelessly allowed yourself to get fat, your wings may become too weak to pull you up. Now, that would be a problem, wouldn't it? How ludicrous it would be for a small pair of wings to fail at carrying a flabby belly! The moment would come for people to call out to you, "My friend, let's go back, while a purplish hue is still there in the sky!" You would hear their wings fluttering in the air, and see how the spring clouds seem to jump over to support their shoulders as they set their eyes toward that glorious

---

[3]   A land measure that varies from place to place, but is generally regarded as the equivalent of one-sixth of an acre. The variance may indicate differences in productivity.

place they came from. Then they would fade from your vision like mist wafting and drifting, leaving, just like the skylark, only a shower of glittering rain—"Thou art unseen, but yet I hear thy shrill delight"[4]—at that moment, you would be left floundering on earth. How insufferable, how regrettable, how humiliating! Take good care of your wings, my friend, before it is too late.

*　*　*　*　*　*　*

There is not a single human being who does not wish to fly. How aggravating it is to be crawling about on earth all the time, to say nothing of other tribulations! Let us fly away from it all, from it all! Head for the clouds, for the clouds! Which of us does not think about that hundreds and thousands of times a day? Let us fly up to the sky and float around up there, looking at the way our planet rolls about like a tiny ball in the universe. Our gaze will wander from the land to the ocean and then from the ocean back to the land. Let us take a good look in mid-air—only then will we experience the joy of being human, the power of being human, the responsibility of being human. If this mortal vessel of ours is too heavy, let us discard it. If we can, let us fly away from it all, from it all!

*　*　*　*　*　*　*

When human beings first discovered stoneware, they already were wishing for a pair of wings to fly. The mythical animal found on the walls of the caves of primitive people has wings on its back. When they depicted themselves chasing other animals with bows and arrows, they also equipped themselves with wings on their backs. Cupid has a pair of soft, supple wings, and Icarus was the first hero—and the first victim—in the history of flying. The most important sign of angels (idealized human beings that they are) is their wings, which aid them in flight. These wings changed over the years, too, as one can see from Western art. In the beginning, angel wings were like miniature flags, resting on the backs of angels like butterflies. They did no work, although they had all the appearance of true wings. Gradually, the wings grew larger, their position more stable, and their feathers fuller. On the backs of angels now appeared what could be conceived of as real wings. For the first time, the human race had brought the concept of wings to reality, and

---

[4]   P. B. Shelley, "To a Skylark."

understood fully the meaning of flying. The immortal soul of Icarus returns again and again, making it the greatest mission of human beings to make wings, and their greatest success, to fly. We thus reach the limit of ideals, and the extremes of imagination; in doing so, we transform ourselves into gods. Poetry grows forth from wings, and philosophy circles in the air. To fly! Flying transcends everything, encompasses everything, sweeps aside everything, devours everything.

*   *   *   *   *   *   *

Try to climb up that peak over there. If you can't make it all the way, you will fall down the precipice that drops for miles and find yourself buried there! "This human-shaped bird will one day try out his first flight. He will astonish the whole world, making himself the object of all praise and bringing glory to the eternal resting place from which he came." Oh, da Vinci!

But really, to fly? Isn't it true that since Icarus, it has become the task of human beings to make wings? And could this pair of wings actually take off, carrying as they do the weight of civilization? All of us came here by flight, but will we really be able to fly back? Clamped, welded, crushed—will there ever be a day when this human-shaped bird will truly experiment with flight?....

*   *   *   *   *   *   *

All the while, that dark spot has been getting closer and is now above my head. It turns out to be a bird-shaped machine. Suddenly, it swerves to one side and a ball of light falls downward, and *bang!* explodes— my dream of flying is shattered, and a few clouds, broken in pieces, are added to the sky.[5]

---

[5]   The reference of this passage is unclear. One critic interprets it as the explosion of sunspots, although on a more literal level, a description of a bombing is a more likely interpretation. Perhaps, given the flights of imagination in which the author is indulging, this passage should best be taken surrealistically. The main point, at any rate, is that the author is awakened from his reverie by the sound of an explosion.

Yu Dafu

Yu Dafu (1896–1945) received a traditional Chinese education from different schools in Hangzhou in his youth. After he was expelled from Hangzhou University for participating in a student movement, he went to Tokyo University to study economics. It is during this time that he penned "Sinking," for which he is most famous. He also befriended other Chinese intellectuals who were in Japan at the same time, including Guo Moro, Zhang Ziping, and Tian Han, with whom he founded the Creation Society, an important literary group in early twentieth-century China. When he returned to China, Yu served as the editor of the Society's journal and became an active voice in the development of modern Chinese literature.

Yu spent his time during the Second World War in various places in Southeast Asia. It is believed that the Japanese executed him toward the end of the war.

"My Humble Shelter from Wind and Rain: A Chronicle" is a playful account of the process through which Yu acquired his home in Hangzhou. Its whimsical tone is a far cry from the somberness of his other works, which are better known for characters ridden with self-doubt and angst.

My Humble Shelter from Wind and Rain:
A Chronicle (1936)

The wish to own a house has been on my mind for a number of years. Although I understand fully that the desire to create is good, whereas the urge to possess is bad, when it comes to one's own self-interest, I have always felt that possession of the minimum implements of life's four major needs—clothing, food, lodging, and movement—should not be left unsecured. I don't wish to be clothed in brocade and am quite content to eat the coarsest kind of food. But when it is a question of having a house for lodging and a rickshaw—or at least a pair of socks and shoes—for movement, I feel as if one is not even qualified to have a say on anything unless one is equipped with them. A friend of mine also once advised me that as soon as one is born into this world, one cannot do without a piece of land. When one is alive, one needs the space, if for no other reason than to hang around, sleep, or sit in it. Then, when one dies, one needs to have a hole dug some place for burial. That, of course, was the case before the introduction of cremation and the existence of public cemeteries.

Thanks to my friends, after I moved to Hangzhou, I quite unexpectedly came into possession of a piece of land, and the problem of my burial was thus taken care of. As for living, however, I am still living in somebody else's house. Last spring, I wrote in a short composition that I only wished to have a little place of my own. The essay was a light piece written for a particular occasion, and I did not expect anything to come of it. However, a response came soon after it was published. First, an architect friend of mine came to say, "If you want to build a house, we will be at your complete disposal." A friend of some means also said, "If you are not asking for too much, perhaps I can think of a way." With help from all sides, the plan to build a shed that would provide me with a shelter from wind and rain was thus eighty percent realized. People who didn't know me thought that I must have grown rich; those who did said that I was taking a risk. Be it rich or risky, what had started as a mere joke had by twists and turns become a reality by autumn. The pounding began next to my present residence, and the construction of the house was underway. The whole thing may well be a result of my own *folly*,[1] or of my friends' overconfidence in

---

[1]   "Folly" appears in English in the original.

me. In any case, from now on, my tattered books, army cot, old night-stool, and other such things will not have to take after the wandering Confucius and travel from place to place. In these ways, there is something to be said for the desire to possess, after all!

Since I came into this project with nothing but my bare hands, of course I knew better than to entertain unrealistic hopes. Initially, I only planned to use hay where tiles were called for, and mud for the wall. I envisioned five rooms that were neither too big nor too small, all lined up in a row, just so that my yearning for my own place of residence could be satisfied. However, a chance conversation at a relative's home opened up new possibilities. My relative said, "When you build a house, you should at least pick a good day, and check out the bearings of the site. There is a lot to be said for the ancient art of the *I Ching*[2] and the modern study of cosmology and geography." He then proceeded to relate to me a number of verifiable examples of the efficacy of geomancy, and the few friends present also gave their assent upon their honor. More interestingly, the person they recommended, a worker of miracles equipped with the power to divine heavenly wishes, was just like us—a graduate of a modern institution of higher education who had learned his ABCs and studied algebra and geometry.

Following my friend's introduction and my conversion to the mystical arts, the original building plan was changed. The thatched cottage now became a house with a tiled roof, and the five rooms that were originally arranged in a row like army barracks were now split up and put into two small houses with two rooms in one and three in the other. Connecting the two houses was a wall, from which a hole was carved out to serve as an entrance. Moreover, on the two sides on these two houses were added a number of small rooms whose functions were yet to be determined. These changes of course added considerable space to what I had originally planned, but at the same time, my debts were piling higher than the firewall. The person who laid the foundation of my debt is Mr. Guo Xiangjing, who even now is giving me advice, saying, "The dragon claw position on the northeast corner is still too vacant. As a remedy, I suggest you build a south-facing archway, and on top of that a cement terrace. Only then will it work."

By coincidence, what he said happened to touch upon a sore point

---

[2]   Often called *Book of Changes* in English, the *I Ching* is a treatise of mathematics and philosophy, often used for divination.

in my subconscious: All along, I had hoped to build something of a tower at that empty corner, the name of which I had come up with some fifteen or sixteen years before—"The Sunset Tower." Although this tower has not yet been built, the cottage that I hoped would provide me with a mere shed from wind and rain has now taken on a layer of red paint, while its walls are now made of cement. It has even begun to look like those houses in the poorest ghettoes in foreign countries. Although I do not know anything about geomancy, when I think about Mr. Guo's recommendations on misty days or on mornings when the sunlight is not all that strong, I can see that there is nothing mysterious in his proposal that cannot stand the test of modern science. The reason that I have to consider the plan when the light is not strong is that, after all, I am still somewhat faint-hearted about the whole thing, and dare not appear so self-assured as to use the best materials for my humble abode. This consideration is not all that important, however; what *is* a bit troublesome is that the elegant name I had thought of—"Humble Shelter from Rain and Wind"—does not describe the reality anymore. My brow furrowed in thought for a few days, and I came to realize that so-called mountain recluses probably do not actually live in the mountains; I also saw that when we call our sons "little dogs," we are not referring to members of the canine family. Things like this have been done before, and my harmless little lie surely will not bring down upon me the most severe punishment, the death sentence. Besides, there by the West Lake stand lofty mansions the size of the warehouses of big companies like Sincere and Wing On. These are also called "Such-and-Such Cottage," and I have never heard of anyone coming forward to intervene. Best not to think too much about it! I might as well hold to my original idea, keep the old name that I came up with, and call this house my humble shed. The placard bearing the name was written by Mr. Ma Junwu on my behalf. Taking advantage of his recent trip to Hangzhou, I imposed my request upon him, ignoring the searing pain he was suffering in his right hand at the time.

❧❦❧

Su Xuelin

Su Xuelin (1897–1999) was born to a late Qing bureaucrat who held the view that a virtuous woman should be uneducated. Thus, from very early on, Su had to fight for the right to be educated. After threatening to drown herself in a river if her wish were not granted, Su gained permission to attend school. She first entered the Anhwei Provincial First Normal School for Girls, then went on to Beijing Women's Normal College in 1919, and concluded her formal education with three years of study at Institut Franco-Chinois de Lyon. She was called back to China by her mother and married the man that her family had arranged for her before she had a chance to finish her schooling.

Su began her career as a creative writer, and later became a literary scholar. In her late years as a teacher in Taiwan, she published studies of Chinese literature of various periods. She was known as a staunch critic of the Communist Party and its cultural icon, Lu Xun.

As an essayist, Su is adept in manipulating the casualness of the essay form. "In My Moments of Dejection" takes on a personal tone with the reader; she suggests that an essay should be as spontaneous as a letter to a close friend or careless doodling of one's reading notes. The subject matter is similarly pedestrian. Through contact with two ordinary objects, wool and pears, Su contemplates two significant incidents of her past. This associational technique—beginning with a moment and ending with an account through memory—represents a common structural device in *xiaopin wen*.

In My Moments of Dejection (Two Selections) (1929)

I don't know why, but for the past several years, whenever I've written to friends about my recent activities, I've always included this line: "I've felt dejected of late, as if a large poisonous snake were coiled around me." The source of this line seems to be the preface to Mr. Lu Xun's *Outcry.* I enjoy quoting it because I feel that there is something extraordinarily spellbinding about dejection. Who knows where it comes from, but once it attaches itself to a person, there's no way to shake it off. It's like one of those large poisonous snakes in the forests of India regarded as both sacred and demonic.

The scenery in the place where I now live is not bad at all. When you look through the lush forest, you can see the golden shimmering surface of the Huangpu River under the bright sun. There are often boats passing by on the water, their white sails floating on the glimmering water like clouds blown by the wind across a silvery stream. The sound of waves crashing on the rocks reverberates, carried by the wind through the open window. The universe is quiet, but also pulsates to the rhythm of eternal life, singing its praises. The natural scene that stretches itself in front of me is so solemn, so beautiful and lovely. But when I am dejected, this scenery becomes an expanse of grayness. I feel nothing but indifference to it.

I have experienced the sweetness, the bitterness, and all the flavors of life. When I think back on the last several years, I find they are indeed too painful to dwell on. But when my soul is being corroded by this feeling of indifference, I would rather return to those painful years, which, by contrast, invigorated my spirit. But since I do not have the courage of Akutagawa[1] to kill myself, and cannot allow this feeling of indifference to continue eating away at my soul, I must think of some way to distract myself from it.

Lonely by nature, I am not too interested in all the entertainment that one finds in society. Living in the suburbs isolated from the city, I do not have friends with whom I can associate. Apart from taking walks by myself among the fields, I also like to sit at home with pen in hand, jotting down on paper whatever comes to mind, or pulling down from

---

[1]   Akutagawa Ryūnosuke (1892–1927) is a Japanese novelist famous for his overwrought writing style. He drank poison at the age of thirty-five, ending his short but productive life. Before killing himself, he published an article in which he discussed at great length the significance of suicide.

the shelf and reading whatever book comes to hand. Whenever I come across things that speak to my heart, I copy them down in a notebook, which I then open and read at leisure. These can be regarded as my reading notes.

Besides reading, it also cheers me up sometimes to write to friends, because in my letters I can talk about everything under the sun. Although what I say is of no great importance, and for the most part devoid of any structure, there's no need for me to strike unnatural poses or assume affected tones as I would if I were to speak to society at large. I also don't need to follow a carefully worked-out plan as I would in my academic writing. I can say whatever is on my mind—where my thoughts go, so will my pen. This is nothing less than the natural expression of my personality, and an overflow of the truest sounds of my heart. By writing this way, not only do I experience the joy of liberation, but so does my reader.

Although I do have a few friends, they are all very busy, and when I write to them, they are obliged to write back. I feel uneasy about forcing other people to sacrifice their precious time to read my letters and then reply, just so that I can dispel this feeling of indifference. So, I have thought of another way—to write only for myself, and take it as an exchange between myself and my own soul.

I remember several years ago making the acquaintance of a woman writer when I was studying in Lyon, France. Her husband was the chairman of the architecture department at the l'Académie Nationale des Beaux Arts in Lyon, and had designed the famous Basilique de Notre-Dame de Fourvière. I often visited her, and learned that all of the landscape paintings on the walls of her home were the works of her husband. Because painting was not his specialty, they were naturally not all that good. But his style was extremely simple and forceful, and was permeated with a certain freshness and originality. There was a copper tag on the frames of two of the pictures, on which were engraved the words, "In My Moments of Dejection."

Although I would complain every now and then of dejection, I did not truly appreciate its reality then. After I got to know the architect and saw his paintings and the words on the picture frames, I was mystified. Was it possible that a great architect, whose white beard commanded respect and whose mind was so expansive as to encompass that lofty, towering cathedral, could at times be assailed by dejection? He had gone so far as to frame these paintings with such care, and hang them in the living room and the study, as though in perpetual memory of the occasion. Why?

After I returned to China, I was not in touch with the woman writer for some time. I heard that her husband had passed away, but those pictures, casually painted in light blue and red, and the words engraved upon them left a deep impression in my memory. That was the first time that the word "dejection" had caught my attention.

My random reading notes and the communications with my friends or with my own soul recorded below might be regarded as "paintings of my heart" derived from my casual doodling. In order to show what a deep impression they have left in my mind, I will copy, though out of context, the words the architect etched onto his paintings and use them as the title of these "paintings of my heart."

Buying Yarn

I once went out with Kang for a stroll on the street. Whenever we came across things we liked, we bought some. We looked around as we walked. Dazzling electric lights shone from behind glass windows, and the merchandise, whatever it might be, caught our eye, so lovely it all appeared in the glittering light. All of a sudden, I turned around and could not find Kang. I looked for him, and when I found him, he was buying socks at a stall about twenty feet away from me. I did not want to walk back to him, and instead waited for him at a dry goods store.

There was a girl of about sixteen or seventeen in the store. She wore a traditional sheath dress made of simple patterned cloth, and her hair, as shiny as a black cloud, was cut short. Her black eyes, lustrous and vivacious, were set off by her round, tender, light-complexioned face. Though a somewhat ordinary girl, she was quite attractive. Standing shoulder to shoulder with her was an old woman, wan and gaunt. She was haggling with the shopkeeper at the counter over the price of a bundle of yarn. She was undoubtedly the young girl's mother.

Failing to reach an agreeable price, the old woman did not want to buy the yarn. The young woman whispered something in her ear, probably something to the effect that it would be difficult to find yarn of the same color elsewhere and that they shouldn't miss this chance. The old woman was left with no choice but to reach inside her pocket for money....

A most ordinary incident, but as I witnessed it, it brought back a memory of ten years before:

One year in early autumn, my mother and I came to the provincial capital, Anqing, from our home village. I accompanied her one day on an errand to buy some fabric. I saw in the cloth store a glass medallion, of which set inside was an extremely beautiful picture of a snowy scene. I wanted to get it and use it as a paperweight when I drew pictures, so I asked my mother to buy it. The asking price was forty-five cents, which my mother found too expensive. I began to whine, insisting that she buy it. All the people in the store laughed, and said to my mother:

"Madam, take it! It's just the right thing for the little girl to play with."

I was embarrassed. At the time, though not that tall, I was in fact eighteen years old. To my mother, however, I was still an eight-year-old, so no wonder the shopkeepers thought I was a little girl.

With an indulgent smile, my mother protested, "This will get broken if you're not careful. Oh, what's the use of it?—you never listen to me!" Nevertheless, when we left the store, I had the lovely medallion in my pocket.

As I watched this mother and her daughter buying yarn that evening, I remembered that incident between my mother and me. As if in a dream, I stood at the store, dazed.

After getting his socks, Kang caught up with me. He noticed that there were tearstains on my face and that my voice was a bit strained. Surprised, he asked, "Why are you crying here on the street, when everything is fine? Did anybody upset you?"

"Who's crying? There was a gust of wind, and some sand from the road got into my eyes."

With some effort, I came up with this ordinary explanation. I could not think of anything else to say, so I left the yarn store with Kang and continued on our walk.

Xiao Xi and the Huizhou Pears

In Huizhou, not far away from our hometown, grows a kind of white-skinned pear. We call them snow pears. They are as refreshingly cool as ice and as sweet as honey, far superior to ordinary pears. Even the famous Tianjin pear cannot compare with them. They are Anhui's best product, and it's a pity that the underdeveloped transportation system in China makes it impossible to ship them out. The honor of being the best fruit thus goes unchallenged to the arbutus and loquat of Zhejiang, the lychee of southern Guangdong, and the grapes of the north.

Recently, however, this kind of pear has come to Shanghai. Just the other day, I saw several baskets of real Huizhou snow pears for sale at Hu Kaiwen's Writing Brush Store on North Sichuan Road. The store is run by people from Huizhou. Perhaps the shopkeepers had brought the snow pears to Shanghai on returning from their hometown, and that was why there were not too many of them for sale.

Having seen the Huizhou snow pears during the day, I dreamed of them at night. In my dream, I saw a big pear tree with a trunk so thick that only a grown-up could have stretched his arms all the way around it. Its leaves were luxuriant and the branches were richly studded with fruit. Xiao Xi was holding a bamboo pole and was beating the top branches with it, making pears fall down like rain. I picked up a large white pear and was about to put it in my mouth when I suddenly woke up.

Xiao Xi was my oldest sister-in-law's bond-maid, who had accompanied her when she married into our family. Xiao Xi had died several years before. I never thought of her, and had no idea why she had appeared in my dream about the Huizhou pears.

I thought about it for a while, and finally figured it out. The complex and seamless process by which things come together in dreams is far beyond the reach of our intellect in our waking life. Sometimes, two things may be inherently connected to each other, but on the surface, they often appear unrelated. It never occurs to us that we should pay attention to the way they are tied together, which is why we never think about their relationship. But dreams can find the ties between things and bring them together in an ingenious way, as filaments connect fallen flowers or the spring wind gathers duckweed to one spot. Oh, how clever dreams are!

Xiao Xi was from Shandong, and she was only eight years old when she came to our home. She was by no means beautiful, just an ordinary-looking girl. But her tender white skin, typical of people from the north, and her apple-like cheeks had often won my mother's admiration. I was also a mere child at that time, and liked to play with little boys and girls about my age, including Xiao Xi. She would teach me folk songs from the north, all of them very delightful. I have forgotten many of them, except:

> My First Mistress
> My Second Mistress
> You pull the bellow and I strike the iron

and:

> My father puts on his glass hat
> My mother puts on her *click-clack* shoes
> *Click-clack, click-clack* she goes up
> And *click-clack, click-clack* she comes down.

Even now, I can still recall her limpid voice.

Besides these songs, I also remember one time when we had a fight over my beloved cat. I was older than Xiao Xi by four years, and was stronger than she was, as well. I remember grabbing her hair and trying to pin her to the ground. She raised her foot to kick me, but eventually didn't have the courage to do so. Instead, she only tried to push me off with her hands. In the end, the two of us fell down and rolled around on the ground.... This left me with a very deep impression, which is why I can still remember it clearly. As for other things, I cannot remember them anymore.

I later went to school in the provincial capital, and went home only during summer vacations. Xiao Xi had grown up, her skin had grown coarse, and her figure stocky. Her cheeks, however, remained like apples, red and lovely.

When I got home one year, I heard Xiao Xi had died. How did she die? My oldest sister told me that during spring the previous year, Xiao Xi had suddenly come down with an illness, which left her with a fever day and night. Ah Tong, a tailor working at our home, felt sorry for her. Xiao Xi's bedroom and Ah Tong's workshop faced each other, and when the doors were open, one could see from one room into the other. People from the villages were open with their feelings, and did not give too much thought to social strictures. Ah Tong often went to Xiao Xi's door to enquire about her health, and brought her many large Huizhou pears to quench her thirst. Although he dared not go inside to comfort her, his thoughtfulness over her well-being and his loving and solicitous affection touched Xiao Xi's heart.

After Xiao Xi recovered from her illness, it became clear to other people that the two were in love. When my sister-in-law got wind of this, she became very angry. She was raised in the orthodox way, and would not allow one of her maids to be involved in such a scandalous affair. But Xiao Xi had already reached the marriageable age, and by common understanding, my sister-in-law could no longer keep her. So, she decided to marry Xiao Xi off. Some people suggested she give Xiao Xi to Ah Tong, but she adamantly refused. She was furious that Xiao Xi had caused her embarrassment, and was therefore determined to stand in the way of Xiao Xi's love affair.

When the lovers learned of my sister-in-law's intentions, they eloped. People were dispatched to track them down, and the two went into hiding in the valley. It was in the second month, when the spring weather was still chilly and the valley still filled with ice. They hid in the deep grass by the stream for a day and a night.

When they were brought back, it was feared they might resort to suicide, so nothing was done to them. Ah Tong felt that he had lost the respect of other people, however, and using some excuse, left town and looked for work elsewhere. As for Xiao Xi, she was forced to marry a twenty-some-year-old peasant.

The following year, Xiao Xi gave birth to a little girl, but died from complications of childbirth.

When Ah Tong came back from his wanderings, he learned of Xiao Xi's death. He bought some paper money and food and offered them to her memory at her graveside. Thus their ill-fated affair came to an end.

Later, whenever Ah Tong mentioned Xiao Xi to other people, he would say with tears in his eyes, "If they had married Xiao Xi to me, she never would have died! I'm over thirty years old—I would have known how to take care of her when she fell ill!"

Feng Zikai

Feng Zikai (1898–1975) was a man of many talents. During his long career, he made significant contributions as a writer, a painter, a musician, and most of all, as an educator. In 1922, after returning from an eight-month stay in Japan, where he studied art, music, Japanese, and English, he joined the faculty of the Chunhui Middle School in Zhejiang, an experience that had a lasting effect on him and on other writers of the so-called White Horse Lake School. His writing years span from the 1920s to the 1970s, but beginning from the mid-1940s, he directed his energies to painting (which he called *manhua*, after the Japanese term) and music education.

Underlying all of Feng Zikai's work is a firm belief that adult life is artificial and crippling while childhood is pure and natural. At times, the views he expresses seem to take on a Buddhist shade, further reinforced by his friendship with Li Shutong and Ma Yifu. Feng's philosophy finds echoes both in his subject matter and style. He frequently painted and wrote about the simple joys in life, the greater beauty of nature, and the unpretentiousness of children in a style that can best be described as direct and unassuming.

Feng the humanist comes through clearly in the three essays chosen for this anthology. "Seeking Shelter from the Rain in the Mountains" recounts how music salvages what could have been a disappointing excursion. "Children" spells out his fond adoration for the ways of the young, while "A Mean Alleyway" is a tribute to Ma Yifu, the classicist, whose solemn attitude to life represented an ideal to which Feng aspired.

Children (1928)

I remember that four months ago, for no particular reason at all, I impulsively gathered up my children—the veritable flock of swallows that they are—from our rented house in Shanghai. As if escorting prisoners under guard, I put them on a train and took them back to my home village, where I put them up in a dingy one-story house. I then returned to the international settlement in Shanghai, and lived there by myself for four months. For what purpose did I undertake such an action? And what plan could I have had in mind at the time? On reflection, I can hardly believe it now myself. In fact, both the so-called plan and the purpose were all an illusion that I conjured up just to deceive and worry myself. What practical good did they do? All they did was bring to my life more senseless labor and tribulations, conjure a few rounds of happiness and sorrow, and add to the scars that were already on my soul.

When I got back to Shanghai and walked into the lonely, empty rented house, my mind kept returning to the two lines of the Buddhist canon *Leng Yan*: "The myriad illusions in your heart are like white clouds found in the sky. How much more insignificant is the world itself, a mere illusion within an illusion!"

That night, I cleaned up the place. I gathered together all the extra firewood, all the rice left behind in the baskets, the urns and vessels by the stove, and other miscellaneous daily necessities that I had accumulated in three years of living in the house. I gave them to the son of the neighborhood shopkeeper who used to work at our house part-time. I don't know why, but for some reason I did not give away the four pairs of old, torn children's shoes. These I arranged neatly under my bed. Later, whenever I caught sight of them, I felt a twinge of unnamable happiness. I kept this up until several days later, when my friend from next door came over for a chat. He said that there was something eerie about those shoes under the bed when there were no children to be seen in the house. Only then did I realize how foolish I had been, and I put the shoes away.

My friends often remark that I care a lot for my children. Indeed, I do, and I often think of them, especially now that I am living alone. But in addition to being an instinct, I believe there is something to my concern and thought for my children that goes further. It is because of this particular element that I often disregard my ineptness at writing and painting and endeavor to depict children in my works. Because my sons and daughters are all still little (the oldest is only nine years old), my concern for my own offspring is in part a concern for other children as well, that is, for all the children of the world. I cannot say now how I will feel about my children after they grow up, but I can predict that it will be different from how I feel now, in that this additional element will no longer be there.

When I think about the four leisurely and tranquil months I spent living by myself, I miss the time I had then and I also feel thankful for it. However, as soon as I returned to the single-storied house in my hometown and was surrounded by my children, I could not help feeling a kind of self-pity, because compared with their innocent, healthy, and energetic ways, my way of life—whether sitting in boredom and meditating, or studying and engaging in research, or merely going through the motions of good manners and fulfilling social obligations— is altogether perverse, sick, and maimed.

And so I returned to my hometown one hot summer afternoon. Toward the evening of the following day, I took my four children—nine-year-old Ah Bao, seven-year-old Ruanruan, five-year-old Zhanzhan, and three-year-old Ah Wei—to the ash tree in the yard, and we sat down on the ground under its shade to eat watermelon. The red of the scorching sun was gradually fading and the blue cool of the evening was growing ever more refreshing. The breeze gently ruffled the children's silken hair and the perspiration vanished from our bodies. In the midst of such complete contentment, my children seemed to be almost bursting with the joy of life, so much so that they had to find an outlet for their happiness. The three-year-old expressed it first in music, giggling and rocking himself about in his satisfaction. While he munched on watermelon, he let out a sound—*ngam ngam*—that resembled that of a cat enjoying some food it had just stolen. This musical expression immediately found an echo in five-year-old Zhanzhan, who proceeded to deliver his poem: "Zhanzhan eats watermelon. Sister Bao eats watermelon. Ruanruan eats watermelon. Ah Wei eats watermelon." This poetic recitation in turn aroused a prosaic mathematical response from the seven-year-old and the nine-year-old, who immediately summed up the meaning of Zhanzhan's poetic lines and reported their findings: "Four people are eating four pieces of watermelon."

I silently played the role of adjudicator, evaluating their performances. I found the musical expression of three-year-old Ah Wei most incisive and complete, and most capable of expressing the delight he felt. Five-year-old Zhanzhan had translated this happiness into (his own brand of) poetry at something of a loss, but thanks to the rhythm and melody of his lines, a sense of life's vigor was still allowed to emerge. The prosaic, mathematical, conceptual expression of Ruanruan and Ah Bao was, by contrast, even more superficial. Even then, though, between their attitude and their complete immersion in the act of eating watermelon, what they managed to apprehend with their unclouded minds was still more complete than what adults can achieve. Of all people, only children are capable of the healthiest level of discernment, and only they can appreciate in the most accurate and thorough manner the world's realities. Compared to them, my perceptions have already been hampered and even injured by my worldly intellect, and I have become a pathetic cripple. I should never allow them to call me "father," if that word implies respect.

I set up a desk temporarily by the south window in our single-story building, on top of which I laid down in neat order my drafting paper, envelopes, writing brush, inkstone, ink-bottle and glue, as well as a watch and a tea set. I do not like it when people move my things around; this was something I had developed when I lived alone. I... no, *we* adults are always guarded, careful, circumspect and polite in our behavior and we perform such actions as grinding ink, putting down the writing brush, and pouring tea all quite gingerly. The arrangement of our desktops is thus the same every day so that things do not get damaged or disturbed. In my case, the movements of my feet and arms have been so constrained by their surroundings as to have developed a kind of cautious inertia. But, as soon as the children climb up onto my desk, they proceed to upset its order, mess up its arrangement, and destroy the objects I placed there. They pick up my fountain pen and give it a violent shake, spraying spots of ink on the desk and their clothes, then put the nib into the bottle of glue. Then they yank off the copper cap of the writing brush, knocking over the teapot with the back of their hands and sending the lid crashing to the floor. I am of course irritated when all of this happens, and I cannot restrain myself from screaming at them, taking things away from them, or even slapping them on the cheek. But I come to regret it immediately: My scolding is followed by laughter, what I took from them I return at double the amount, and the hand that went out to slap them goes limp halfway and becomes a hand that caresses. I realize my mistake right away: How absurd it is for me to insist that my children behave as I do! My... no, *our—adults'* behavior is so artificial because the feelings of our bodies and limbs have been oppressed by the world around us to such an extent that they have grown cramped. Children, on the other hand, are still in possession of their god-given bodies and their inborn, active, pristine life force. How can we expect them to be hampered like us? Scraping and bowing, advancing and withdrawing properly, walking and carrying oneself with fastidious precision—these are all the manners of adults. They are like implements of torture, there to maim the healthy body given to us by heaven. As a result, a vivacious person goes numb in the arms and legs, finally becoming paralyzed. How absurd it is for a cripple to insist the healthy behave as he does!

What is my relationship with my children? I feel perplexed and curious because I did not come to this world with the intention of becoming a father. For now, they and I belong to totally different worlds. They are far wiser and healthier than I, but they are my children. What a peculiar relationship! People in this world regard having children as a blessing, and hope that their children will become an extension of themselves. In truth, I do not understand what is in their minds. I believe that of all the relationships in the world, the most natural and reasonable is between friends. Under the most natural and reasonable circumstances, all other bonds—between rulers and subjects, parents and children, brothers and sisters, husbands and wives—are merely friendship in a broader sense. This is why friendship is in reality the foundation of all human relationships. As they say, "Friendship is the bond between members of the same species." Nurtured by the same land, we are friends to each other, and are all children of Nature. Some have forgotten their Greater Parents in Nature, and recognize only their lesser parents in the human world. They think that since parents can give birth to children and, as a corollary, since children are born to parents, they can find the continuation of themselves in their offspring and thus will exist forever. As a result, those without children complain about the blindness of the will of heaven, and those with children of no merit come to pity their own lot and drown their sorrows in the cup. In reality, when does heaven ever show any partiality to its own children, all of whom it begets and nurtures? I really do not understand these people at all.

Recently, my mind has been occupied by four things: the *gods* and stars high above, and children and the arts down below. My own offspring, like a pack of swallows, are the few people in the world who have the strongest bond with me. They occupy the same position in my heart as the arts, the stars, and the gods.

A Mean Alleyway (1933)

In Hangzhou, all the side streets are called alleyways. This is a word not found in my hometown. When I first arrived in Hangzhou as a child, my attention was drawn to this word. In the past, when I had come across the passage in the *Confucian Analects*, "Living in a mean alleyway on a bowlful of rice and a ladleful of water...,"[1] I had no idea what a mean alleyway was like.... In my imagination, it was merely a dirty, narrow lane with a broken wall that, favored by some fortuitous elements, had become the dwelling place of a cultivated person like Yan Hui. In my hometown, there was no shortage of dirty and narrow lanes, but none of them conjured up in my mind the image of a mean alleyway. Only when I got to Hangzhou and learned this word did it confirm in my mind that the so-called alleyway inhabited by Yan Hui probably referred to those narrow lanes in Hangzhou. Whenever I walk by this kind of alleyway, I always suspect that living on the other side of those dilapidated walls may be a latter-day Yan Hui. One lane especially seems to me to represent the typical mean alleyway. At the mention of the words "mean alleyway," images of this particular lane come to my mind. In fact, I have been to this mean alleyway only three times, but each time it left an impression on me so distinct that I can now write about them.

It was almost twenty years ago when I first visited this mean alleyway. I was only seventeen or eighteen at the time, and was studying at the Hangzhou Junior Teacher's College. My art teacher, Mr. L.,[2] must have found the power of the arts inadequate for his spiritual needs. He gave us all of his paintings, music books, tools, and instruments, and went up to the hills to fast for seventeen days. He then came back to study Buddhism and prepare to become a monk. One day, shortly before he joined the order, he took me to this alleyway to visit Mr. M.[3] I followed Mr. L. into an old house in the alleyway. A middle-aged man came out to greet us. He was short and stocky, and his face was covered

---

[1] This line describes Yan Hui, Confucius's favorite student, who is well known for his modest way of life and his ease in the face of hardship.

[2] Li Shutong, 1880–1942, an extraordinary man of many talents with accomplishments in different areas of literature and the arts, was a strong advocate of art and music education. Very much a man of the world, he suddenly converted to Buddhism and became a monk at the age of thirty-nine.

[3] Ma Yifu, 1883–1967, a well-known classics scholar.

with a beard. I bowed to him when I was introduced, and sat down in a chair and listened to the two of them talk. I did not really understand fully what they were saying. All I heard were isolated words such as *lengyan* and *yuanjue*.[4] The English word "philosophy" also appeared in their conversation. I had just learned that word, and found it interesting to hear them use it. But on the whole, I did not quite follow what they said, partly because Mr. L. was speaking in the Tianjin dialect, and Mr. M. used pure Shaoxing dialect when he told the servant to pour tea, but used the dialect with a northern accent when he spoke to us. I didn't understand any of these dialects fully. At the time, I thought to myself, "If you would simply speak to me as you spoke to your servant, I might be able to understand more." However, it would have been awkward for me to say that, so I sat there quietly and pretended to follow their conversation.

In fact, I was silently observing the appearance of this Mr. M. whom I had just met. His head was large and round, and the top, at about the place where the brain is, was especially enormous. Were his body less stout than it was, I thought, it might not be able to support his head. His eyes were not as delicate-looking as Mr. L.'s, but they were large, round, and bright. The upper eyelids arched forcefully, and his dark pupils were set just right underneath. His beard started from his left ear, grew along his face, and reached all the way to his right ear. Its color was as dark as his pupils. At that time, I was devoted to the study of charcoal drawing, and it occurred to me that his portrait would be best done in charcoal, though I would not be able to capture the forceful lines of his eyes.

Just as I was scrutinizing him, he suddenly burst into gales of laughter. I was startled by the resonance and cheerfulness of his laugh, which was so unlike his speaking voice that it could easily have come from a different person. As he laughed, he was also staring at me with his sparkling black eyes. I was making artistic and musical observations about him, and had no idea what he was laughing about. Since I had been pretending to be listening to them, I could not possibly just sit there without responding. At the same time, it would be awkward for me to ask, "What are you laughing at?" and request that he repeat himself. So I forced myself to laugh, and continued to pretend that I understood what they were saying, knowing full well that they would not put me

---

[4]   Names of Buddhist scriptures.

to the test to see how much I really comprehended. Upon reflection, however, I felt rather ashamed. I was ashamed of my deceitfulness, and blamed myself for not knowing their dialects. The more they talked, the more they had to say, the more uproarious Mr. M.'s laughing became, and the more ashamed I felt. From the moment we arrived at his house to the moment we took our leave, I was filled with regret and shame, like a puppet that had been brought to this old house in this mean alleyway against its wish for a few hours of display.

The second time I came to this mean alleyway was the year before last, sixteen years after the first time, when I had behaved like a puppet. In those sixteen or seventeen years, I had been to many places to earn a living. I had married, a group of children had been borne to me, and my mother had also died. As for Mr. M., he had remained the same all those years, living by himself in seclusion in the old house in the mean alleyway. It was on the Qing Ming Festival[5] when I saw him the second time. I was asked by Mr. L. to bring to him two stones for seal carving. I saw that the alleyway remained like the Yan Hui residence I had imagined it to be, and just as before, an ancient aura still pervaded the house. Mr. M.'s demeanor was no different from more than ten years before: He still had his strong, well-defined eyelids, bright pupils, and loud, cheerful laughter. But I, who was there to listen to his laughter, had changed. His dialect was no longer a problem for me, and I could understand completely everything he said. The pain of being a puppet was no more, but in its place was another deeper kind.

That was the period when I had just lost my mother. From the time I was little, my mother had assumed the role of both parents to raise me, and I had never repaid her even in the smallest way. In my extreme sorrow, my heart was filled with anger and perplexity over the inconstancy of life. Since I lacked the power to extricate myself from such anger and perplexity, I sank into a state of depression. I only wanted to wander[6] in the hills and by the rivers with my children, so as to forget my pain temporarily. Most of all, I recoiled from listening to any talk that touched upon the fundamental questions of life. And thus, with my full knowledge, I allowed myself to sink low. I could, however, still hide my degeneration from people in my own social circle.

---

5   A Chinese festival that usually falls in early April, during which people visit their ancestral tombs.

6   Feng Zikai uses the English word "picnic" in place of "wander" in the original.

To earn a living, I only have to read a few pages of a book and write for a few hours every day. I have always abstained from wine and meat, and I neither gamble nor go to the theater. My only hobbies are smoking half a tin of Meili cigarettes a day, allowing myself a few pieces of candy, and playing with my children with the toys that I buy for them. In the eyes of my social associates, someone like me is far from being a sunken soul; rather, I tend to be upheld as an outstanding individual. But, in contrast to the solemnity with which Mr. M. approached life, it was obvious that I had indeed debased myself. He talked to me about an album of my work, *Pictures to Protect Lives*, for which he had written a preface. He encouraged me, and, knowing of the sorrow I felt over the death of my mother, further consoled me by expounding on the meaning of "life's inconstancy." In fact, I did not need to listen to him; all that it took was one look at him, and I felt so ashamed of myself that I wished I could find a place to hide. It was as if there was a ball of tangled thread in my mind—impossible to sever but just as impossible to sort out. And since I could not untangle it, I wrapped the whole thing up like a paper package in my mind. I felt uncomfortable there before him. After sitting with him for an hour or so, I took my leave.

When he saw me to the door, I felt the same kind of joy that had descended upon me at this same place some ten years before when, after playing the puppet for a few hours, I was finally allowed to go. I walked out of the mean alleyway, and saw a rickshaw parked at the corner of the street. Without asking the price, I got in it. I looked up and found that the weather was fine, so I decided to go to Caizhi Zhai, the confectionery, to buy some candy, which I then brought to the Liu He Pagoda and spent my Qing Ming Festival there. When I dragged my tired body back to my hotel at night, however, I thought of my host whom I had visited that morning, and felt a strong, respectful fondness for him. I planned to visit him again the following morning, when I would open my "paper package" in front of him. But when morning came, my heart was again totally taken up by the spring scenery of West Lake.

The third time I went to the mean alleyway was a week ago. This time, I went there on my own accord. Mr. M. was still living by himself like a hermit in the old house in the mean alleyway. His eyes were still forceful and glittering, and his laughter was as cheerful as before. The only thing that surprised me was that his jet-black beard had turned silvery gray and was almost white. I thought of the lines, "White hair spares no one/ It grows on the head of the idler and prime minister alike." At the same time, I regretted that I had not come sooner and more often to befriend him. I also blamed myself for having lived such a degenerate life these three years. My mother has been dead now for more than three years and on the surface, it appears that I have given in to life's inconstancy and am not as grieved and angry as before. At the same time, having emerged from my depression, I want to settle down for a protracted act of defiance against life's inconstancy.

Whenever I come across ancient poetic lines on the subject of life's inconstancy—"The song of merriment dies down in the courtyard/ The lamps come down from the tower," or "The bright moon of the six dynasties is now shining on the Qinhuai River in the clear night," or "The white-haired palace maids still remain, chatting about Emperor Xuanzong"—I always interpret them in pictures, two of which I earlier sent to Mr. M. Recently, I wanted to gather more lines on this topic for my pictures and was preparing to compile *An Album of Inconstancy*. I mentioned this thought to Mr. M., and asked him for advice. He pointed out to me enthusiastically many Buddhist scriptures and literary collections from which I could find such materials, and recited for me many wonderful lines. At last, changing the topic all of a sudden, he said, "Inconstancy is constancy. It is easy to draw inconstancy, but not so with constancy." I had not heard words like these for a long time. No wonder I had felt so despondent! His very words rescued me from the burning house of inconstancy, and I felt an inexhaustible sense of serenity coming over me. At that moment, I thought to myself: After I finish the *Album of Inconstancy*, I will put together an *Album of Constancy*. I would not need to ask him for a preface for that album, because in it, every page, from beginning to end, would be blank.

When I walked out of the mean alleyway that day, it was already dusk. With sleet falling, the street was filled with scenes of the end of the year. I walked on the street alone, disoriented. I recalled the time three years before when I had got in the rickshaw without first finding out the price, and an earlier time twenty years before when I had felt liberated after playing the puppet for several hours. I felt as if I were in a dream.

January 15, 1933 at Shimen Wan

Seeking Shelter from the Rain in the Mountains (1935)

Two days ago, with two little girls in tow, I went sightseeing in the mountains in the area of West Lake. Quite unexpectedly, it began to rain and we scurried for shelter. Ahead of us, we saw a small temple, at the entrance of which were several village houses. One was a teahouse, which sold incense and candles on the side. We dashed toward it as if it were our own home. Though the teahouse was tiny, it charged one full *jiao*[7] for a pot of tea. At that point, though, we would not have found it overpriced even if it had cost double that.

The tea grew weaker and weaker with each refill of water, and the rain grew heavier and heavier with each passing minute. At first, I was rather dismayed at having met with rain on our mountain tour, but then a kind of solitary, somber sensation at having been trapped there in the mountains by the rain started to awaken my interest, and I began to think that this was in fact much better than touring the mountains in fine weather. As the verse goes, "The mountains are tranquil and misty, and the rain wondrous." At this very moment, I came to appreciate that the scene was actually quite exquisite. The two little girls failed to understand, however: Trapped in the teahouse by the rain, they were disgruntled and unceasing in their complaints. I could not explain to them the state of mind I was in, nor did I want them to "be grown up" so that they could appreciate it.

The teahouse owner was playing his *huqin*[8] at the entrance to the store, and this was the only sound we heard besides the rain. He was playing "Plum Blossoms in Three Tunes." Although the notes were a bit off, he was able to keep a good beat. He was apparently playing in lieu of a radio to attract customers as there were only a few of them in the teahouse. Unfortunately, after playing for a while, he stopped, and we were left with only the unrelenting, riotous sound of the rain. In order to appease the two girls, I went over to the owner to borrow his *huqin*. "Would you mind lending me your *huqin*?" I asked. He politely handed it over to me.

I returned inside the teahouse with the instrument in my hand. The two little girls were beside themselves with joy. "Do you know how to play it? Do you?" I proceeded to show them how. In my younger days,

---

[7]   *Jiao*, equivalent to one-tenth of one *yuan*, the standard measure of Chinese currency.

[8]   A two-stringed musical instrument.

I had learned the tune "Plum Blossoms" from Ah Qing, the firewood dealer who lived next door to us, and the basics of *huqin* from the tailor, a big fellow, living across the street. That is why, although I had grown rusty with the *huqin*, I still managed to hit the notes correctly. Ah Qing's teaching method was most unique: He only played the tune but never showed me any musical scores, and it turned out that although he played the tune expertly, he did not read music. I could only look upon him with awe, knowing full well that I would never learn to play as well as he. Later, I found out that the tailor knew music, so I asked him to teach me. He wrote down on a piece of paper the scale positions of the *xiao gong* mode and the *zheng gong* mode, and in this way, I began my practice of *huqin*. That I am still able to play the notes right is partly due to my previous experience with the violin and partly due to what I learned from the tailor.

There in that teahouse in the mountains, then, I sat down at the window with rain pouring right outside and slowly and leisurely—I would have made mistakes otherwise—played a few Western tunes. Like singing girls on the West Lake, the two little girls sang along, drawing people from the houses to come and watch. One of the girls wanted to sing "The Shining Lights of a Fishing Village," and asked me to play along. As I accompanied her on the *huqin*, the young people joined in, all at once bringing warmth to this desolate place in the bitter rain. For seven years, I had earned my living as a music teacher, accompanying a quartet of mixed chorus on the piano and playing Beethoven sonatas, but never in my life had I enjoyed music as much as I did that day.

Two empty rickshaws came by and we decided to take them. I paid for the tea and returned the *huqin*, and we said good-bye to the young people from the village and boarded the rickshaws. The oilcloth was let down in front of my eyes, blocking the rain from view. I thought back to our experience a moment ago, and felt that the *huqin* was indeed a wonderful instrument. A piano is as heavy as a coffin, and a violin costs twenty, thirty, or even as much as a hundred *yuan*. Although they are superbly made, how many people on this earth can afford to enjoy them? A *huqin* costs but a few *jiao*. Although its range is not as wide as the violin's, it is certainly adequate for popular tunes. And although the quality of its sound is not as beautiful, it is not at all intolerable when tuned right. This instrument is very widespread among the Chinese people. You can find it in barbershops and tailor shops, on boats in northern Jiangsu or in small remote villages. If only we could compose a few simple but inspiring pieces of *huqin* music, making them as popular as "The Shining Lights of a Fishing Village," the results would be more profound and widely spread than the music education in our schools.

When we left the village, the young people there, unwilling to see us go, saw us off to the rickshaws. I myself also found it hard to leave. (I humored them, saying, "We will come again next week." In truth, I am afraid chances are we will never go there again to drink tea or play *huqin* in my lifetime.) We met by chance like floating weeds in the water; if not for the *huqin*, what feeling would these young people have had for a passerby like me? And for my part, why would I have had any attachment to them? As an ancient phrase puts it, "Music induces social harmony." I never realized the wisdom of this adage in my seven or eight years as a music teacher. Little did I expect that I would come to appreciate its meaning in that desolate village that day!

❧❧❧❧

Lu Yin

Lu Yin (1898–1934), born Huang Shuyi, had a short but productive life. In her writing career of fourteen years, she left behind an impressive repertoire of novels, stories, essays, and dramatic works.

All accounts of her life, including her autobiography, seem to highlight her unhappy childhood and her two marriages. Lu Yin's superstitious mother believed her to be an ill omen, and sent her away from home to be raised by a wet nurse at an early age. Her experiences at a Protestant missionary school afterwards were unpleasant, and led her to question the motive of the spread of Western religion. It was not until 1919 when she attended the Beijing Women's Normal College before she came into her own. There she befriended Su Xuelin, Feng Yuanjun, and Shi Pingmei, who would become women writers in their own right.

Her two happy but short marriages were sensational news in literary circles. Both were considered "unorthodox." Her first husband was already wedded to another woman by a previous arrangement when he and Lu Yin got married, while her second husband was nine years her junior. Both ended tragically, the first with her husband's death and the second with her own death during childbirth.

These autobiographical facts inevitably affect the reception of Lu Yin's works, which together project a woman narrator that is despondent and yet feistily independent. "Thorns on the Rosebush" excerpted here, however, came from a relatively peaceful period of Lu Yin's life after her second marriage. Even she seemed surprised at her newfound serenity. Yet, the rumblings of restlessness are never too far away as she hankers for a change of scene. Beautiful as it is, life is not without its prickly moments.

Thorns on the Rosebush (1933)

For people who see the world as a stage, the natural tendency is to do one's utmost to embellish the stage and change its scenery. For such a person to settle on one thing or in one place would go against his nature. It may well be an inborn characteristic of mine that makes me dissatisfied with the state in which I find myself; and there is not a single moment when I do not want to assert this trait in different spheres of life. Ever since I was small, I have enjoyed living like floating duckweed. No matter where I am, I always get tired of a place after living there for half a year or so, and always find a way to change the scenery. I was only in my teens when I graduated from high school, yet I had already left behind the warmth and comfort of my home to lead a life of wandering. I remember that whenever I took leave of my mother and the other people at home, carrying my simple luggage and setting out all by myself on the endless road before me, they were always saddened by my departure, while I was full of excitement, ready to take in new stimulation. With only my bag on my shoulder and a breeze blowing about me, I felt totally unfettered. This is why I always want a change of scene at least once or twice a year, except when circumstances prevent me from doing so.

It is a rare occurrence in life when things turn out as one wishes, though. Much as I always long for change, I was recently forced to spend three or four years in the ancient city. The pressures of life had reduced me to living like a beaten dog with my head bowed and my ears folded back. Those three or four years were just too sad to speak of. There was nothing to break the dull routine of breathing in chalk dust, grading students' papers, and going over the same lectures like a gramophone. Days, months, even years went by just like that. I finally got to the point where I simply could not take the extreme boredom anymore, and I decided to break out of this prison and shake off my chains, becoming again the unbridled horse that I had once been. The petty human world is no longer worthy of my attention, and I am no longer servant to its authority. Thus did I come to wander about the four seas this past year—seeing the angry waves of the Pacific, walking the streets of prosperous and congested Tokyo, and lingering around the green waves of West Lake. Of these places, West Lake suits me best, which is why, without the least coercion, I have been staying there for seven months.

But even so, I was not content just to stay in one place, and in the last seven months, I have moved twice. At first, I lived by the lake. The house there was in the Shanghai style—like a cage for pigeons, though people usually call such houses by the pretty name of "foreign-style house." When we first moved there, I would stand in front of the window that overlooked the lake and watch the misty waves hover on the water and the clouds float above the hill. For a while, I was taken in by the wonderful changing scenes before my eyes, but by the time I had been there for three months, I suddenly felt that the color of the lake and the hills had grown dim, and the misty waves had become quite ordinary. Everything was so plain, so mundane. I immediately thought of escaping. Later, I spent two whole days combing through all of the places along the lakeshore, and finally found another foreign-style house, a rather quiet one, in an alleyway off a major street. I have been very satisfied with this new place. In front of the house is a mulberry field as green as jade, and beyond the mulberries flows a river which meanders around several acres of land overgrown with wheat. What a surprise to be able to find such a rustic place in the heart of the bustling city! In this house, I can hear roosters crowing in the morning and dogs barking at night, suggesting to my mind thoughts of a lost paradise.[1]

As soon as you enter the front gate of the compound, a grove of bamboo meets your eyes, green and shadowy, waving and striking poses in the breeze. Colorful garden balsams, cannas, day lilies, morning glories, and hibiscus grow in different parts of the yard. In the midst of the flowers is a cement road with a dozen or so grapevines growing on either side. At the end of the road is the clean, spacious veranda. There are eight such foreign-style houses there. I feel refreshed just looking at the green window screen reflecting the green of the bamboo grove. This is indeed the place for me to rest my soul after the monotonous and cluttered life I have led for the last few years. I am particularly pleased with the two words, "My Cottage," written on the placard above the door. I do not presume to be the genteel type, but now that I have found a place compatible with my temperament, who cares whether it is your "My Cottage," or his "My Cottage"? For now, it doesn't hurt at all to take it as *my* "My Cottage." Isn't it a sign of good luck that I have come to lead the life of a recluse here, if only for a short time?

---

[1]   The crowing of roosters and barking of dogs have long been used to create a scene of peacefulness.

I have stayed in "My Cottage" now for just a month, but during this time, there have been quite a few memorable episodes in my life. These episodes are like thorns that grow on a beautiful and fragrant rosebush, and those who come into contact with them will, of course, feel a certain slight pain.

Zheng Zhenduo

Zheng Zhenduo (1898–1958) was born in Zhejiang and was educated in Beijing. He led an active career as a writer, journalist, archaeologist, and literary scholar. In the wake of the May Fourth period, he played an active role in the literary scene as the editor of a number of literary magazines. After 1949, he became the head of the Archaeological Research Institute of the Chinese Academy of Science. He died in a plane crash in 1958 on his way to Cairo as a representative of a Chinese cultural envoy.

Essay writing is but a small part of his literary activities. He studied and published on Greek and Roman mythology and translated Russian and Indian literature.

Like many writers at the time, Zheng views literature as a mirror of life. In "The Pleasures of Food and Wine," the writer captures the socializing scenes of Shanghai during that period. Most of them take the form of endless dreary social gatherings, where one attends out of a sense of obligation. The essay then turns to other types of drinking and eating, either by oneself or in the company of one's loved ones and friends, where quiet reflection and frank exchanges with one's associates can take place.

The Pleasures of Food and Wine (1932)

Although it was winter, the weather was not too cold. The rain dripped down, and the sky was overcast with gray clouds. The fire in the stove had died out, but on a day so much like autumn, it was too warm to relight it. There was not a single soul at home—they had all gone out to "socialize." I sat by myself in the room and was unable to summon enough interest to read a book. I picked up the morning newspaper from time to time to look at the advertisements. Suddenly, it occurred to me that I could go to see "Merry Widow,"[1] so I got on a tram and alighted at Park Road.

Inside the dark theater, the band played melodiously as the shadows on the white screen sat, stood, hurried, cried, laughed, grieved, raged, loved, despaired, and dueled. It was the same thing all over again, the same story that they had written and rewritten, performed and re-performed time and again.

But at least one line from the film stood out in my memory: "Who knows how many times I have walked away from the dinner table with an empty stomach?"

This is an extremely witty observation, one that can be used to describe accurately this society of ours, where not a single day passes without a dinner party.

Every businessman, every bureaucrat, and everyone who has a somewhat extended social circle can be seen every evening frittering away their time in a restaurant or a hotel. Sometimes, one has to go to three or four parties in one night. In truth, people who have such a busy social schedule live like prostitutes. They arrive at one place, sit for a while, and then leave in a hurry to go to a different place. There they again sit down for a while, before moving on to the next. Their stomachs are never full, I think. There are quite a few of these socialites, who, at the end of their socializing, when the last drop of wine is drunk and the lamp has been dimmed, return home only to fill up on rice gruel they have their servants prepare for them.

Compared to large, prosperous Shanghai, we pretty much amount to provincial country bumpkins. As we live in the country, it is no easy undertaking for us to go to Shanghai. We lead the lives of country people, and it is indeed rare to find us spending more than a few

---

[1]   Appears in English in the original.

evenings a month socializing. Many people may say that we are "high-minded," but that is too lofty a word for us; indeed, we are not like that at all. We are simply not used to a life of wining and dining, and therefore maintain our uncouth rustic ways.

Thanks to the good intentions of our friends, we are invited to parties from time to time. We find at most only three or four familiar faces, and the rest are all strangers. We either wait for the host to introduce us, or ask each other's names and exchange namecards on our own. After we stammer through the pleasantries required in a first meeting, we fall silent, not knowing what else to say. What we manage to come up with sounds vacuous; and not a single word comes straight from the heart. Feeble noises, having slipped through our throats, come out of our mouths, and when we think afterward of the perfunctory way in which we carried on these conversations, we cannot help but laugh. An evening thus can go by among the dazzling lights and senseless exchanges of a party. But what a lifeless evening!

Quite a few times, there have been simply too many strangers at these parties, and I have not known anyone but the host. I have even forgotten the names of people I talked with right after I asked. After a few words with the host, there was nothing I could talk to anyone about. I had no idea what work they did, or what kind of people they were. Even if I had things to say, I would not have dared express my opinions without reserve. During some parties, I have sat on needles throughout the entire evening. Course after course of sumptuous food has been brought to the table, but I could hardly taste them. At last, I have not been able to stand it any longer, and, lying to my host, have said that I was not feeling well, or still had to go to another party, or some such thing. During the last few days, rumors have run amok, and I have had a better excuse: I've been able to say that there might be an early curfew, and that I might not be able to get back to the Chinese settlement.[2] Although this is rude and improper, and although my hosts, as expected, have sincerely tried to make me stay, I have pushed aside all other considerations and insisted on leaving. It is no easy task to survive an evening like this! After I get home, I get myself a bowl of rice gruel, and, even though there may only be a small plate of dried turnips, I find it relaxing and much to my taste to eat like that.

---

[2]   At the time, Shanghai was divided into international and Chinese settlements. Movement across the settlements was sometimes strictly regulated.

For weddings and birthdays, our friends may decide to host an extravagant feast in a certain garden or in the great hall of a certain hotel. We may be unfortunate enough to be invited, and more unfortunately still, they may be such close friends that we cannot decline. It would not do simply to show up, offer our congratulations and good wishes, and, muttering some excuse, make ourselves scarce. Hence, another intolerable evening! Very often, we keep our eyes wide open to search for friends, and when our hard work pays off, we stick closely by them and don't dare lose sight of each other. When the time comes to sit down, the few of us can at least have each other to talk to and we won't have to be loners sitting uncomfortably among a pack of strangers, feeling anxious and abandoned. When the few of us are absorbed into our own conversations, we look up every now and then at the person across the table from us. He sits there forlornly, alone. When we raise our cups, he raises his, too. When the food comes, one of us will say, "Please, please help yourselves," at the same time reaching out our chopsticks to the plate. The man, too, will say, "Please, please help yourselves" and reach out his chopsticks. There is nothing for him to do but eat. When the food is gone, he can only sit there by himself, fidgeting. We cannot help feeling sorry for him when we see that, but he is still obliged to hang around until the feast is finally over and he can stand up to leave.

If the pleasures of dinner parties were nothing more than this, then we should curse the first person who came up with the idea of throwing parties. And if the joy of drinking were merely thus, then we should pull Du Kang[3] and Dionysus down from their exalted positions.

Fortunately, however, some dinner parties are not like these, and there are other circumstances conducive to the pleasure of drinking. It has been said that drinking by oneself is most enjoyable. When I was little, I often saw my grandfather holding a tin decanter and pouring yellow wine into a small white porcelain cup for himself alone. He would lift the cup and take a small sip—just a small sip—and put it down. He would then pick up some food with his chopsticks. In this way, he would slowly enjoy his wine and food. Even after we had put down our bowls and chopsticks and left the table, he would still be raising his cup and taking small sips. His real dinner would not even start until an hour and

---

[3]   Du Kang, an emperor of the Xia dynasty (2205–1766 BC), is also known as the first person in Chinese history to make wine.

a half later. As he drank, his face would turn pink, and he would often call out, "Come, children." We would then come up to him, and he would pick up some morsels of food from the dishes prepared specially for him. He would put them in our mouths, and ask, "Isn't this good?" and we often nodded our heads in reply. Among the grandchildren, he was especially fond of me, and I was summoned to his side most often. He would often kiss my cheek, the stubble above his lips scratching and hurting me. The smell of wine from his mouth and nose was hard to bear.

Day after day, he would pass the afternoon and the evening in this way. I have never had the chance to experience this kind of pleasure, but as I think back now, it seems to me that he was very cheerful then. He was totally drunk with happiness and lived in the midst of joy, as if all of his burdens and worries had been lifted from his heart. This was his whole world, and the whole world was completely his.

There is another kind of pleasure to be found in dinner parties that I have come to appreciate in recent years, namely getting together with a few friends with whom one can talk about anything at all. There are no unfamiliar faces around the table, and we can casually drink and eat. The topics of conversation range from heaven to earth. Sometimes our words are witty and funny, heated like fire or sharp like a sword. Sometimes, we get deep into conversation about scholarship and the arts; at other times, we freely tease each other; at yet other times, we argue with each other until our faces and ears grow flushed and hot. Lofty ideals may come to grace our discussions, and talk of love encounters, family affairs, and personal matters urge us to go on and on. We bare our hearts to each other, and reveal the faces that we would not normally show to the world. We talk and talk, more and more excitedly, and forget what it feels like to be tired. The wine is all gone, so is the food, but we keep the conversation going. Even if the place is noisy or shabby, a place where we normally would not like to spend even one more second, at this particular moment we are oblivious to its shortcomings and go on talking. Nobody is willing to be the first one to stand up and take his leave, and if it were not for the curfew or family injunctions, no one would go. Although idle chats like this might appear to be extremely trivial or meaningless, we have come to appreciate the pleasure of dining together. The truth of the matter is that one could easily find gems of wisdom in our casual conversations, through which we influence, understand, and learn and benefit from each other.

"Let's drink another cup. One more, just one more!"

"No, I can't take any more, and that's the truth."

People who cannot drink are often forced to drink more than they can take. Their faces glow under the light, and they look more robust and radiant than ever.

"Shengtao,[4] let's drink this up," I often say to him, my cup poised. I like to gulp down a whole cup at a time.

"Slow down, don't drink so fast! The pleasure of drinking is found in taking a sip at a time, not in 'bottoms up,'" Shengtao protests, but in the end he also gulps down a whole cup, one after another.

Sometimes we even pressure teetotalers like Yuzhi[5] and Yanbing[6] to drink a cup with us, whereupon everyone roars with laughter, the kind of pure laughter that comes from the heart.

Yet another example is on festivals, when the whole family sits around a table, on top of which are placed some ten pairs of red lacquered chopsticks. Even those who are away from home have a pair, and seats are placed at the table on their behalf. Little children laugh and play rowdily, and gentle smiles can be seen on the faces of the mother and the grandmother. The wife is busy supervising the servants cooking in the kitchen and bringing food out to the living room. Although this is not the same as partying with one's friends, there is a special kind of harmonious feeling to it, envied to no end by people who live alone.

Then there is the pleasure of eating dinner with one's love in a quiet room in a hotel. Or, coming out of the theater with one's wife, one might want to go to a restaurant to have a cup or two. Or, by the fireside in the company of one's grandmother or mother, one can enjoy the leisure of staying up late with a few small dishes of food. All are extremely joyful occasions that can transport the soul of anyone who takes part in them.

The pleasures of food and wine can be so diverse!

---

[4]   Ye Shengtao (1894–1988), writer and language pedagogue. His works "Moon-watching" and "Random Reminiscences" are included in this anthology.

[5]   Hu Yuzhi (1896–1986), a famous journalist.

[6]   Shen Yanbing (1896–1981), better known as Mao Dun. See his piece "Before the Storm," which is included in this anthology.

Zhu Ziqing

Zhu Ziqing (1898–1948) was an accomplished essayist and poet and a noted scholar of classical Chinese literature. He taught Chinese in Qinghua University and many high schools, and in such a capacity, co-edited with other writers and teachers many language textbooks that have had a long-lasting influence on language teaching in China. Many of his essays are considered to be models of modern prose, and as such, have been included in many textbooks and anthologies. He also left behind scholarly treatises on various genres of Chinese literature, especially *shih* poetry.

Zhu's even temper is reflected in his essays, which are marked by an unpretentious air and a natural style. Sun Fuyuan notices accordingly Zhu's tendency to forgo "violent or provocative" language even in his most polemical pieces. More often, his essays deal with the pedestrian goings-on around him—memories of his father or his wife, a walk by the lotus pond, or a trip on the train. All these observations, however, are imbued with the author's profound emotions and his insights into the workings of the human world.

The two essays collected here represent two of the major themes that Zhu Ziqing explores in his works: family relationship and social phenomena. "Looking for a Mate" narrates in an anecdotal way the age-old practice of arranged marriage, while "Random Notes on Sea Travel" describes the service of the "Ningbo gang," which at one point monopolized the attendant profession on passenger boats. Both arranged marriage and the Ningbo gang are something of the past, and for that very reason, Zhu's essays have now become important social documents.

Looking for a Mate (1934)

I am the oldest son in our family, as well as the oldest grandson. This is why, when I was not quite eleven years old, there was discussion about finding me a wife. I was unsure of what this all meant, of course, but before I knew it, a mate had been found for me. The bride was from my great grandmother's maiden family, and she lived in a village in a small county in the northern part of Jiangsu. Our family, probably including me, had also lived there for a long time, but I am too stupid to remember a single thing about the place. My grandmother had often talked about it from her opium couch, and she would mention the name of one or another villager. At first, the things she said seemed to me to be enveloped in a haze of white mist, but as time went by, they became familiar, even intimate. I felt at that time that, apart from the place where we were then living, the most interesting place in the world must be that village, known as "The Garden Manor." That is why, when I heard that my future wife lived there, I found that to be the way things should be, and did not have any objections.

Every year, someone would come from the village to visit. They would be dressed in short blue coats with long-stemmed pipes in their mouths, and would bring with them such things as barley flour and dried sweet potatoes. Sometimes they would also talk to us about the young girl. She was probably four years older than I, rather tall, with small feet. At that time, though, I was actually more excited about the flour and dried potatoes.

I remember that when I was twelve, they sent news from the place that the young mistress had died of consumption. Nobody at home expressed any sorrow, probably because when they had last seen her, she had still been very little, and now that many years had passed, they could not remember what she was like. My father was working as a government official in another province at the time, and my mother, anxious about my marriage, asked the tailor who often came to our home to sew to serve as matchmaker, for tailors frequented many homes and had the chance to see their womenfolk.

The idea seemed to work. The tailor came back one day and told us about the prospects of a particular family: They were wealthy, with two daughters. One had been born to the concubine, while the one with whom he was trying to match me was the older daughter born to the first wife. He said that the other side had suggested that the two families find an occasion to observe their child's prospective mate. My mother agreed and an appointment was set for the tailor to bring me to a teahouse. I remember it being winter, and on that day, my mother made me put on my date-colored robe made of Nanjing silk, a black mandarin jacket of the same material, and my black satin skullcap with the red knot. She also instructed to me conduct myself with care.

In the teahouse, we met with a man sent to observe me. He had a square face and big ears, and was almost the same age as I am now. He was wearing a cloth robe and a cloth mandarin jacket, and looked as if he were in mourning. He was rather kind, and, as he looked me over, asked me what book I was then studying and other such questions. After we got home, the tailor said that the man had examined me very closely, that he thought that the area between my nose and lips was long, and therefore that I would live to a ripe old age. He also observed the way I walked for fear there might be something wrong with my feet. In any event, now that they had observed me, it was our turn to observe her. My mother sent along her trusted old nanny, who came back with the report that the older daughter was bigger than I by a wide margin, filling up a round-backed armchair when she sat down. The second daughter, on the other hand, was rather slender. My mother said that women who were too fat could have trouble conceiving, like so-and-so among our relatives. She then suggested to the tailor that he match me up with the second daughter. The other family was apparently offended by this proposal and would not agree to it. And so the matter came to an end.

Somewhat later, my mother got to know a woman at the mah-jongg table. The woman had a daughter who seemed clever and alert, and my mother's interest was aroused. When she came home, she told us that the young girl was the same age as I, and that, from the way she hopped about, it was obvious that she was still a child. Some time passed, and my mother sent someone to sound out the family. Apparently, the head of the family was also an official, but at a rank even lower than my father's—it was the year before the restoration[1] and people were still concerned about such things—and that is why they were happy with the match. The whole affair had almost come to fruition when, all of a sudden, something went wrong. My mother had somehow found out that a widow employed by a grandmother in our clan knew the family

---

[1] That is, the restoration of rule by Han Chinese in 1911, when Manchu rule was overthrown.

very well. My mother had summoned her for information, and she was evasive in her answers. Finally, however, the truth came out. It turned out that the young girl had been adopted, though the family doted on her as if she were their own flesh and blood. My mother lost heart. Two years later, we heard that the girl had contracted tuberculosis and had become addicted to opium. My mother said thank goodness we had not gone ahead with the match! I was beginning to understand things like this, and had similar thoughts.

In the year of the restoration, my father came down with typhoid fever. We tried many doctors and finally decided on a Mr. Wu, who was to become my future father-in-law. One day, the manservant who was often sent to call for the doctor came back to say that the doctor had a daughter at home. Since my father was lying sick, my mother naturally was all the more worried about my marriage prospects. As soon as she heard the news, she bombarded the servant with questions. Now, the servant was just making offhand remarks and of course could not give satisfactory answers to all my mother's questions. When the doctor came the next time, my mother sent someone to ask one of his sedan carriers whether the young lady had been born to the family. The carrier said yes. My mother then brought the matter up with my father, and asked my uncle to speak to the doctor. I was sitting by my father's sick bed that day and heard every word. After ascertaining that the young lady had not been promised to anybody in marriage, my uncle asked the doctor, "What would you think of a family such as So-and-So's?" The doctor replied, "That would be rather nice." The conversation ended there. What followed was for the two families to observe the two of us. Once again, my mother sent her trusted old nanny. This time the report was favorable, even though she felt that the feet of the young lady were a bit big. So it was decided. My mother conveyed through the sedan carrier the wish that the bride's family could perhaps begin to bind her feet.

After my wife came to our house, she related that when the old nanny had come to observe her, she had already hidden away and the nanny saw another girl who was put in her place. The message delivered by the sedan carrier nonetheless gave rise to a small tempest. My father-in-law said to my mother-in-law, "I've always told you to have her feet bound, but you wouldn't listen to me. See what people are saying about us now!" But my mother-in-law said, "So what? I won't do it! We'll see what they can do about it." In the end, however, she compromised, and my wife's feet were bound until she married into our house.

Random Notes on Sea Travel (1926)

The last time I returned south from Beijing, I took the Tongzhou boat from Tianjin, which had been robbed a year earlier. That incident seems so far away now, but what might still discourage people from taking the boat is its filth, which is truly intolerable. This boat belongs to a British company, and such filth seems to be quite enough to tarnish the colors of the British flag. But the British would say, "What does it matter? The boat is for Chinese passengers, and they have the right to be filthy. What business is it of ours? If we wanted to take the boat, we'd go first class. Do you know what that's like? Since Chinese passengers taking ordinary class or lower are not allowed in, everything is fine there!" No wonder my friends taking the boat with me called this the "imperialism boat." Imperialism boat! But were we indeed oppressed on board? Oh, yes, for sure!

For the moment, let me talk about the attendants.

If there is any group of people whom I detest, it must be attendants from Ningbo. Boats and hotels are their turf. Their solidarity results from combining the cohesiveness of clan society with that of bandits. For this reason, like other "Ningbo gangs," they are not to be dismissed lightly. Their basic duties are to take care of passengers, but the reality is quite the opposite: What passengers actually receive from them amounts to humiliation, threats, and trickery. In the past, Chinese people always complained about "hardship on the road," but that was due to the difficulties of getting from place to place. Nowadays, with all the convenient means of transportation available to us, even experienced travelers still complain. Why is this? The reason, I submit, is that, compared to mere inconveniences of transportation, boat attendants and porters on the dock are even more difficult to deal with. This is why, when people used to lament "hardship on the road," it was a "materialistic" problem; nowadays, the complaints one hears have taken on an "idealistic" ring. Such a change, of course, is connected to a certain extent with the general order and morality in society, and the parties we speak of should not be expected to bear all of the responsibility alone, though surely their intrinsically "malevolent character" also plays an important part.

Since I have taken boat trips quite often, I have endured no small measure of humiliation. Let me for the time being talk just about the boat attendants. If you go to reserve a seat at a time when there are not too many other passengers, the attendants may merely greet you with a frosty look, but if there are a lot of passengers, then you really are out of luck. They may turn their backs and simply ignore you, or they may pack you off with words sharper than knives. For example, they might say, "Just wait for the next boat." They will say it with such nonchalance that it won't concern them at all even if you are hopping about with impatience.

Perhaps travelers are all a bit out of sorts, and impatience often shows on their faces. This the attendants counter with lethargy, and they are only too happy to have some fun with you. They respond to everything with indifference and apathy, and the more impatient you become, the happier they are. They don't bear you any particular grudge: They simply want to toy with you and have a little fun, in much the same way as genteel ladies play with their dogs. That's why you have to keep this in mind: When you go to book a boat ticket, don't be in a hurry to call out to them. While you may want to speak to them as soon as possible, they will have to teach you a lesson first, even if it is merely by muttering things that are ostensibly not intended for you, such as "What's the big deal? All that screaming!" Only after this will they raise their voice to address you, and say, "Yes! Coming! What's up?"

Also remember this: The more slowly you speak and the lower your voice is, the better. Don't be too cordial, but don't be too uncordial, either. If you behave like this, you'll have put your foot in the door and shown that you are well seasoned. They won't necessarily welcome you, but neither will they play tricks on you. They will simply speak to you tersely and coldly, but you have to realize that you will already have been granted a favorable reception, and should actually feel somewhat flustered at having been so honored.

Once you have booked your ticket, you should get on board as late as possible, though of course you do not want to miss the boat altogether. It is best to arrive two or even just one hour before the departure time. By doing so, you will indicate that you have "poise and composure" and are not to be compared with the nervous and anxious "idiots." Besides, you have to understand that the attendants need to go on shore to take care of their personal affairs. If you arrive too early, you will be in their way, and although they could ask their fellow attendants to serve you, it would still be an imposition upon them. To the attendants, it is never worth going to any trouble for a passenger, and for their part, passengers should know that it is really not advisable to create any trouble for the attendants. Thus, passengers who do not take their time getting on the boat will again have to suffer the treatment reserved for "idiots." A boat may leave at ten o'clock in the morning, and you may think that there isn't anything wrong with arriving at ten o'clock the night before. But that is not necessarily so, because the attendants have to play mah-jongg at night. Your presence will only disturb their merrymaking, and they will surely feel put upon. There is in all these considerations and maneuvers a certain "understanding," a certain unwritten "code," a certain "insider's intuition." You have to be an "idiot" a number of times before you get the right feel.

Once the boat has taken off, you may think that the attendants are free, and that it won't hurt to call on them for help. If you really think that, then you should get ready to learn another lesson. During the day, the attendants need to chat and take care of their personal business, and at night, they have to smoke opium and play mah-jongg. Where are they supposed to find time to serve you? They already have to bring you a basin of water for cleaning up in the morning, fetch your meals during the day, hand you a towel after you eat, lay out your bedding when you board the boat, and fold it up when you go ashore. That already is plenty of work and quite enough to ask of them, and any further requests would surely be beyond the call of duty. You will need to go out of your cabin, gently call out for their attention, and gently talk to them, and then they may do as you ask and do nothing to harm you.

Even better, try finding out in advance the names of a couple of attendants, and when you need help, call out their names in a casual way. The result will be outstanding. But you have to be at ease with the whole thing when you call out their names, as if you were very familiar with them—don't show even a trace of timidity. The reason that calling their names is particularly effective is that those who are called will feel that you want to be on good terms with them (which means that you will not be stingy with gratuities.) In addition, the other attendants may think that you are familiar with the people you call and will thus feel a certain degree of respect for you. This is why, when you call out again, others will also come to help you. But even then, you should only call for their help sparingly. If you trouble them all the time, they will find that you are after all a mere "idiot" trying to pass himself off as an insider, and their manner will change immediately.

As for those who shout out "Boy!" without even getting up from their bunk beds, as if they were chanting poetry, well, they may assume the airs of someone in charge, but in the eyes of the attendants, there is no question that they too are members of the "idiot" group. Thereupon, they will answer with annoyance, "What's the big deal, shouting like that?" Even then, however, they will still come to you, but if you persist in calling for them again, they will say, "What's the problem? Shouting like that?... Why don't you go sing a song instead!" Unless you are really oblivious to how you are treated or are really angry at them, chances are that you will not call them again.

"When Confucius entered the temple of the Duke of Zhou, he asked about everything,"[2] for which he is still admired today. But when you get on a boat, best not to ask anything at all. Attendants are by nature lazy and inclined to avoid anything that might cause them trouble. If you ask them anything, they will either say they don't know, or they may deliberately give you a wrong answer just to have some fun with you. Fortunately for them, they are not supposed to bear any responsibility to the passengers besides taking care of the luggage. Perhaps the most common questions that passengers ask concern the time of arrival: "We *will* get there tomorrow, won't we?" "We should be there by the afternoon, I suppose?" The attendants will answer offhandedly, saying, "Don't worry, we'll get there," or simply, "What's the rush!" In short, you will not get a direct answer at all. Their answers always change, in any case, so you won't know what to believe. And since you don't know what to believe, naturally you will not ask again. This is precisely what they want, some peace and quiet.

When the attendants are on board the boat, they always hang around the so-called first class dining room, sitting at tables gabbing. One or two passengers may manage to squeeze their way in, but if the tables are all taken up by passengers, leaving no place for the attendants to sit, they will be offended. At night, they will discourteously turn off the lights, and you will have to grope your way out in the dark. In this way, the dining room becomes their private property. When they sit around a table, a few of them may have something to say, but the others don't say a thing and may simply sit there silently or play mah-jongg. Even I would feel bored just looking at them, but that is how they pass their time. They have on their faces a look of weariness, cynicism, and indifference, as if at one time they had taken great pains to practice it to perfection. It is a most terrible look, a look that keeps people a thousand miles away.

---

2   See *Lunyu*, "Bayi," book III.

At night, the electric lights somehow cover over the torpidity of their expression; this is when they are just beginning to feel alive. They lay down their opium paraphernalia for a smoke, or open the table for a game of mah-jongg. After they smoke their opium, laughter gradually comes to them, and their mah-jongg games usually last through the night, filling the small dining room with the sounds of mah-jongg tiles and their arguments. The passengers, especially the indisposed, get no sleep, but what is that to them? It is each passenger's duty to listen to them. Some of the attendants neither smoke opium nor play mah-jongg, but instead take out their cigarette cards and meticulously look through them one by one with the air of a connoisseur. Such is their "elegant" pastime.

I said earlier that the attendants' solidarity resembles that of clan society and bandit groups, but sometimes there is also antagonism among them. Internal hostilities, however, rarely break out in the open on the boat. What you see instead is a milder manifestation of their disagreements. As *The Book of Documents* has it, "The mouth can either send out good news or give rise to conflicts." What comes out of the attendants' mouths, therefore, seems to deserve attention. All attendants are invariably sharp-tongued, partly by training and partly due to the region whence they come. Perhaps they would rather be "beaten on foot than in words."[3] This is why, even among friends, they can get so angry at each other on account of one or two irrelevant remarks, intended or otherwise, that they drop their usual imperturbable expression and take on a violent, malicious look. But they are "vicious" only in words, and never actually seem to get physical and come to blows with one another. As the saying goes, "A gentleman fights with words, and a vulgar person fights with his fists." In this regard, although the attendants do have their arguments, they never depart from the ways of the gentleman. Some say that this is what makes a southerner a southerner, and I believe there is some truth in it.

When it comes to passengers, however, the attendants not only don't allow themselves to be "beaten in words," they also take on a certain playful attitude, seldom allowing themselves to lose their tempers on account of passengers. If you, on the other hand, lose your temper on account of *them*, then it becomes all the easier for them to toy with you. In their dealings with passengers, they also have the advantage of

---

[3] That is, they would prefer to suffer an actual loss than to lose an argument.

finding strength in numbers. Passengers are always on their own, and though there are always so many of them around, the attendants are not worried that any will fail to submit to them. This is why they do not need to get angry. Even on the slight chance that one of them loses out at the hands of a passenger, there are plenty of others who share the same indignity. Since the shame does not fall on one person alone, why get angry? If the truth be known, the passengers are not even qualified to make them angry. Their own conflicts with each other, however, are of immediate concern to themselves. Each attendant has to fight that battle on his own and cannot rely on some ready force for support. That is why they must make a fuss over even the most trivial arguments.

If an attendant smiles at you, it means that in a few minutes, he will come to collect a tip. Although there is no set amount one should give, there is an unwritten formula, and if you give in accordance with it, you may not receive a word of thanks, but at least no verbal abuse will come your way. If you deviate from the formula too far and give too little, however, they will ridicule you first and then curse you, and in the end, you will end up giving them more. Though one may think there is really no reason for the passengers to pay more after being insulted in this way, in reality the passengers who have been cursed are so intimidated that they always end up giving a higher amount. Even then, one will have to listen to a lot of grumbling before the whole matter can come to an end. On one occasion, a student who was on the same boat as I gave only forty *jiao*[4] when the expected gratuity was one *yuan*. The attendant fought tooth and claw, but to no avail. Tossing the money onto the bunk bed, he said, "Take this back for your bus fare!" and left in a huff. Finally, the student added a little bit more and gave the money to him. Only then did he quietly accept it, his face expressionless like a piece of wood, as if the money were beneath his dignity.

After the matter of the gratuity is settled, it is time to roll up the bedding. But even at this moment, one has to proceed cautiously. If you show any impatience, you will get another lecture, even though you have already paid up. Only after the bedding is packed away does your oppression come to an end. Now it's time to get ready for another round of exploitation from the porters on the dock, not to mention the attendants in your hotel.

---

[4]   See the first note in "Seeking Shelter from the Rain in the Mountains."

I started out by saying that I would write about my trip on the Tongzhou boat, but ended up with a "Condemnation of Attendants." Perhaps I appear to contradict myself—but, no, all crows are black. It would not be too far wrong to apply this saying, with caution, to Ningbo attendants on any boat. Although I have spoken about attendants in general, those on the Tongzhou boat are included in the lot; whether I further specify or not is of no significance.

❧❦

Lao She

Lao She (1899–1966) is a well-known novelist, playwright, and an accomplished amateur actor of different types of regional drama. He also experimented with various forms of popular entertainment such as *shuoshu* and *xiangsheng*. His travels in England and the United States and his wide reading in English literature have left a deep imprint on his works. Steeped in local flavors, mostly due to his adept use of local dialects, his writings are nevertheless imbued with a sense of humor that can be traced to English literature. His novels depict the lives of ordinary people, which earned him the accolade of "The People's Writer." Lao She was cruelly persecuted during the Cultural Revolution and was driven to drown himself. His suicide has since been regarded as symbolic of the suffering that is inflicted upon intellectuals and the complete breakdown of social order during the Cultural Revolution.

"Winter in Jinan" was written at the time when Lao She taught in the Shangdong province. Like many other of his essays, "Winter in Jinan" has been included in Chinese textbooks for its expert use of language.

Winter in Jinan (1934)

For someone like me who has grown used to living in Beiping, it is miraculous not to hear the wind howling in winter. In Jinan, though, you don't feel the wind at all in winter. For someone like me who has just returned from London, it is puzzling to be able to see the sun at all, but in Jinan, the sun is always out in winter. Of course, in tropical areas, the sun is always vicious, and a luminous sky only strikes fear in people's hearts. Yet, to find oneself in the northern part of China, and still be warm and sunny in winter—Jinan is indeed a wonderful place!

If it were only the sunlight, that would not be so unusual. But close your eyes and imagine this: An ancient city, with hills and rivers, lying warm and comfortable under the blue sky, waiting only for the spring wind to awaken it. Now, isn't that just a perfect scene?

A range of small hills forms a circle around Jinan, with only a small opening toward the north. This circle of small hills is especially lovely in winter, when Jinan seems to have been placed in a little cradle, with the hills murmuring peacefully and quietly, "Be at ease, it will certainly be warm here." Indeed, people in Jinan seem to smile all winter long. When they look at the hills, they feel reassured and at ease. As their eyes move from the sky to the hills, the thought naturally comes to them, "I wonder if perhaps spring will be here tomorrow? It's so warm! The grass on the hills will surely turn green by tonight." Even if their fantasy does not materialize, they are in no particular hurry, because with such a benevolent winter, why would anyone wish for anything more?

Jinan is at its most wonderful after a light snow. The short pine trees appear so dark green, while their tops sport a head of white blossoms, making them look like Japanese nurses. Their white peaks give the blue sky a silver border. In some places up on the slope, the snow is a bit thick, but in others, one can still see the color of the grass. With a patch of white here, a patch of light yellow there, the hills seem to have donned a wavy-patterned shirt. As one watches, the whole shirt seems to flap in the wind, and one hopes to catch sight of a bit more of the hill's beautiful complexion. When the sun is about to set, light yellow sunlight shines on the middle of the hill. The thin layer of snow seems to grow bashful and blush a light pink.

But only a bit of snow will do, thank you. Jinan cannot take heavy snow—those little hills are far too delicate.

Ancient Jinan, so cramped inside the city, but so spacious outside!

Lying on the slope of the hills are some small villages, and lying atop the houses there is snow. That's right, this is a small landscape painting, which might well have been the handiwork of some famous painter of the Tang dynasty.

What about the river? Not only does it not freeze, the heat actually seems to hover above the waterweeds. The waterweeds are so green they seem to be giving forth all of the green they have been storing up for an entire year. The brighter the sky, the greener they become. If only out of regard for the greenness of the water plants, the water cannot bear to freeze. Besides, the long branch of the dangling willow still wants to cast its reflection in the water. Look up, by all means, from the clear water in the river, to the sky above, then higher still and all the way up. It is so limpid, so blue! The whole scene, from top to bottom, is a delicate blue crystal. And inside this crystal, you will find red roofs, hills with yellow grass, and grayish trees like clusters of flowers on a rug.

This is winter in Jinan.

❧❧❧

Bing Xin

Bing Xin (1900–1999) is one of the most eminent Chinese women writers of the twentieth century. She was educated at Yenching Univesity, where she wrote for the school newspaper. Later, when she was pursuing an MA in literature at Wellesley University in the US, she incorporated her overseas experiences in her writing in the form of short letters, which she entitled *To the Young Readers*. Thus began her long-standing interest in children's literature even as she continued to write for adults.

The Bing Xin Style, which critics use to describe her distinctive way of writing, is informed by an unwavering sense of optimism and her profound faith in human love. These qualities are evident in the two essays chosen for this anthology. "The Smile" strings together memories of three different smiles in the writer's memory that "melt in the harmony of love, inseparable." "The Treasure That Will Always Be with Us" recalls with forgiveness the damage that the Japanese aggressors inflicted upon China. There is no question that the writer hates the war, but that does little to change her view of human nature, which will always resurface in the end.

The Smile (1936)

The sound of rain has gradually quieted down. Faintly, crisp light comes in from behind the curtain. I push open the window. Ah! The cool clouds have dispersed. Under the moonlight, the lingering drops of rain are twinkling on the leaves like thousands of fireflies. I never thought there could be such a beautiful picture after an evening of bitter rain and loneliness.

I stand by the window for some time, and begin to feel slightly chilly. I turn around, and all of a sudden, the light seems to play tricks on my eyes, and everything in the house appears hidden behind a film of brightness. Only the angel in the picture on the wall is bathed in a sheen of quiet light. This angel, clad in white, is holding a bouquet of flowers. His wings poised, he is smiling at me.

"I seem to have seen this smile somewhere before. When did I...." Unaware, I sit down by the window, thinking—silently thinking.

The curtain of my mind, which has up to now been tightly closed, slowly opens, and an impression from five years ago emerges. On a long abandoned road, the mud under the donkey's feet was still slippery. Water was trickling in the gullies in the field. The green trees in the nearby villages were all enveloped in mist. The crescent moon was like a bow hung on the top of a tree. I was riding along. There seemed to be a little child on the roadside, his arm holding something dazzlingly white. The donkey had already passed him by, and I, without thinking, turned around. He was holding a bouquet of flowers, standing in his bare feet, smiling at me.

"I seem to have seen this smile somewhere before." I was still thinking, silently thinking.

Another curtain appears and then slowly opens. An impression from ten years ago emerges. Drop by drop, rain from the eaves of the thatched roof fell on my clothes. By the steps, water bubbles turned and churned. Cleansed by the rain, the wheat growing in rows and the grape trellises outside the door were splendid and fresh in yellow and green. After a long time, the rain finally stopped, and I quickly went down the slope. Ahead of me, I could see the moon rising from the sea. All of a sudden, I remembered that I had left something behind. I stopped and turned around. The old woman from the cottage—she was leaning against the door. Flowers in her arms, she was smiling at me.

The same mysterious expressions. Like filaments in the air, they drift, slowly converge, and are now mingled together.

At this moment, my mind is bright and quiet, as if I had joined the realm of the immortals, or returned to my home country. Three smiles appear in my eyes, and for an instant they melt in the harmony of love, inseparable.

The Treasure That Will Always Be with Us (1946)

Wenzao came back all smiles. Under his arm was a thick book, *A Collection of Famous Chinese Paintings*, which he had just bought from an old bookstore for 600 *yen*.

I watched him pore over the book under the lamp. I didn't say anything, but instead sat quietly in a corner of the study and looked at him. This lovable, forgetful scholar of mine had forgotten his sorrowful past.

The two of us, especially Wenzao, loved to buy books. When he was studying in the United States, he very often had exhausted his spending money by the end of each month because of his unrestrained purchase of books. He would always cheerfully fill his stomach with bread and cold water, and thought that food for the spirit was more important than that for the body. When we were courting, he didn't give me flowers, candy or anything special, but rather, all sorts of rare books, timeless masterpieces of literature, philosophy, and art.

After we were married, the living room and study of our small new home were indeed covered, as the saying goes, with "gems everywhere." Even the walls were decorated with quite valuable calligraphy and paintings.

Ten years later, the books in our possession had increased in number, including both those we bought ourselves and those given to us by friends. On the average, we added ten or more books every month to our collection, not counting magazines and various academic journals. In our living room, we placed new books on the semi-circular padauk table, and changed them almost every week. When friends and students came to our home, the first thing they did was come stand by the table and flip through our books.

Over those ten years, as we collected books, we traveled to quite a few places, took many artistic pictures, and bought many paintings, a lot of antiques, and other souvenirs. After our friends and we had looked and marveled at them, we would hang these treasures or store them away with great love and care.

On June 29 of the twenty-sixth year of the Republican Era (1937), we came back from Europe on the Siberian Railway. We came through the three provinces in the northeast, entered the Shan Hai Gate, and returned to Beiping. Twenty or so relatives, friends, and students came to the train station to meet us. When we reached our home, they could not wait to help us unpack our luggage, and eagerly looked at the things we had brought back home from distant places.

On July 7, war broke out on the Lugou Bridge.[1] In order to fight for peace and justice, we decided to move to the rear line to give what little we had to the war of resistance. But because our little daughter, Zongli, was soon to be born and we also had to help with the launching of a new school year at Yenching University, we stayed in Beiping for another year. During that year, there wasn't a single day when we weren't preparing to leave Beiping: We took most of the furnishings and objects for display in our home and either gave them away to friends, donated them to public causes, or sold them. Only those things that we treasured the most were left behind. We were unwilling to take the risk of bringing them with us into exile, and therefore carefully put them in boxes and stored them in the rooms above the classrooms at Yenching University. These included the diaries that Wenzao had kept at Tsinghua University, my diaries from my three years in the United States, our complete and lengthy correspondence over the previous six years, and letters from my mother, friends, and many anonymous "young readers." Many read like poetry and essays, and there were also the letters and poetry my father had written to my mother in his younger days in Shanghai. After my mother died, they came to me for safekeeping. Also included were autographed books given to me by other writers, such as Rabindranath Tagore's *The Crescent Moon* and other works by him, *To the Lighthouse* and other works by Virginia Woolf, books by Lu Xun, Zhou Zuoren, Lao She, Ba Jin, Ding Ling, Su Xuelin, Ling Shuhua, and Mao Dun—altogether over one hundred titles. Then there were the large and small photos of the children and our trips, different sorts of rare books, picture albums, letter collections, works of calligraphy and paintings, and many, many other souvenirs of artistic value.... Together, they filled fifteen large wooden crates, and I have not even counted some twenty or thirty cloth binders of lecture notes and teaching materials that Wenzao had compiled over the previous fifteen years.

As we packed these things away, there were always many students there to help us. Some kept a log of our things, others wrapped them up, and still others put them into crates.... We sat on the floor and

---

[1]   Known in the West as the Marco Polo Bridge Incident. On July 7, 1937, Japanese soldiers opened fire at the bridge near Beijing when their request to enter Wan Ping to look for a missing officer was turned down.

worked diligently, and when we grew tired, we also took our rest there on the floor, drinking tea and chatting. How we all hated the war! It was destroying our culture, damaging our works of art, and snatching away our time as scholars to study and write. All of these losses could never be compensated for by material rewards. At any rate, a war of aggression could never bring about any lasting rewards in the first place.

When the young people carried on with their expressions of indignation, I often became quiet on account of fatigue. I would think of the time during the Jurchen invasion of the Song kingdom during the twelfth century, when our great woman poet Li Yi'an and her husband, Zhao Mingcheng, had to flee the war in haste. The bronze and stone pieces, calligraphy, and paintings that they had collected over the years were thus lost. In the epilogue to her *Records of Metal and Stone*, Li Yi'an described how much she and her husband, while still impoverished newlyweds, had been enamored of works of art though they could not afford them, and how they had gradually collected them along with many bronze and stone pieces as their livelihood improved. To safeguard these treasures, they had built a library, which they also decorated with pieces from their collection. The epilogue is redolent of the happiness of their lives together and the joys of peace. Later, the Jurchen invasion, the death of her husband, her loss of the bronze and stoneware, and her destitute old age all serve to convey to the fullest the miserable end of the literati class in times of war.

I do not presume to compare myself with Li Yi'an, but like her, I have a collector for a husband. Where Li Yi'an and I differ is that her experiences only brought her grief and lamentation, while I have always believed that war is temporary, and that justice and truth will prevail in the end. It is still a worthy proposition after all if, in exchange for the tragic loss of cultural artifacts, the highest levels of rationality are awakened in human beings.

* * * * * * *

This notwithstanding, I can never forget the "treasures" I left behind in Beiping. In July of this year, I had the opportunity to return to Beiping for the first time, and I immediately rushed back to the campus of Yenching University. There, I discovered the landscape of the campus had not changed at all; indeed, after half a year of cleaning up, the campus was just as splendid and magnificent as before. The trees were more luxuriant, and the ripples in the lake no different from the past.

I walked to the yard of my old residence, however, and found that the whole canopy of wisteria, whose fragrance used to spread to the neighbors, was no more there. Even the frame had disappeared. Not a single red and white rose in front of the veranda was left. I climbed up to the loft. The walls were bare. Wenzao's twenty or thirty binders of teaching materials and lecture notes had disappeared.

My mind was overtaken by an inexpressible void. I stood there quietly for a while, turned around, and came down.

I ran into a janitor who had worked there before the war. When the subject of our house came up, he said that, following the closure of the university when war had broken out between Japan and the United States, our house had been turned into a barracks for Japanese troops, and Wenzao's study had been used as the place for interrogating professors. As for the binders of notes, the soldiers had taken them away. Where they were now, nobody knew.

Two days later, with trepidation, I walked up to the attic of the big building where I had stored my crates of books. Just as I expected, the door of the little room in the attic was open. I turned on the lights, and all I could see were the bare walls. My diaries, my letters, my books... everything was gone.

The white-haired janitor was standing by the door with the keys in his hand. He observed the wordless silence that had befallen me, and quietly walked up to my side. As if to apologize, he tried to console me, saying, "The day after Pearl Harbor incident, Japanese soldiers came to surround the university. The students were thrown off campus, and we were all locked up, but the next day, we were all thrown out, too. When we came back last August, we found all the buildings bare—the rooms had been so altered and torn up that we couldn't recognize them.... Those things of yours... like everyone else's things, they probably are lost for good.... I'm really happy, though, to see you've been in good health these past few years."

I thanked him. Tears suddenly rolled down my cheeks, and I turned around and went downstairs.

I slowly walked across the green slope and came to the pond. I walked around it twice, looking at the stone boat by the pavilion far away on the small island in the middle of the pond. My mind gradually emerged from a feeling of desolation and loneliness, and a realization and sense of happiness came over me.

Since ancient times, who knows how many people all over the world have had in their possession a treasure hundreds and thousands of times more valuable than what I once owned. Apart from things that have been destroyed, all that has escaped destruction must have changed hands many times. My diaries, letters, and all the other things that captured my experiences and states of mind over those years were of course very precious, but, as the old janitor had said, I am still healthy. I can thus continue to narrate stories, describe the world, and spread my philosophy.

The war has snatched away and destroyed a part of my treasure, but it has increased in me the most precious treasure that cannot be lost—my faith in the human race.

The human race is marching forward. It is noble, and will slowly return to the wide and even road from the numerous wrong and winding paths into which it has strayed. There will be a day when all the schools in the world will be filled with healthy and energetic students, and all of the teachers' studies will be packed with books, where they will be studying, researching, and seeking happiness for the whole human race.

The human race is also forgetful. Several years of tragedy from the war are not enough to eliminate a hobby of several decades. When I travel to the scenic districts on this trip to Japan, I have not been able to get excited about taking pictures and collecting souvenirs. But my bookworm of a husband has already gone far beyond his economic means to begin buying books again.

Yu Pingbo

Yu Pingbo (1900–1990) is a descendant of the famous scholar Yu Yue of the Qing dynasty, and received at home solid training in classical Chinese studies. He studied at Peking University, where he immersed himself in the New Culture Movement, writing essays and vernacular poetry, and founding with colleagues the journal *New Wave*. Later, he turned his attention to the study of history and classical literature, most notably that of *Dream of the Red Chamber*. In 1954, Mao Zedong launched a campaign to criticize the "reactionary" thoughts that Yu Pingbo supposedly propagates in his study of *Dream of the Red Chamber*, with the result that Yu became a literary pariah for many years.

Yu's essays show a close affinity to *meiwen* (see discussion in "Introduction") about which Zhou Zuoren speaks eloquently. Essays of this type are a far cry from the topical polemical essay (*zawen*) popular at the time. In the place of heavy-handed argumentation and rational precision, *meiwen* demonstrates a detached attitude to life and an associational approach to the understanding of human experiences, rendered in simple and familiar wordings. "Going to the City" acknowledges in the conclusion the "pointlessness" of its composition, in effect challenging the very assumption that literature has to be socially useful. "West Lake on the Evening of the Eighteenth Day of the Sixth Month" is similarly lacking in social relevance, but manages to capture the dreamlike quality of a late-night excursion.

West Lake on the Evening of the Eighteenth Day of the Sixth Month (1925)

Let me have a go at writing my own "A Midsummer Night's Dream." Some things of the past feel like a dream when we try to retrieve traces of them. This is not at all unusual. Other things are like a dream even as they happen, no more and no less, and one need not speak of memory at all. What I am writing here is an excellent example of the latter.

Those of us who live in Hangzhou of course remember the festival on the eighteenth of the sixth month by the lunar calendar, which is more remarkable than any of the other festivals, such as Cold Food Day, Cleansing Day, and Double Ninth.[1] This can be clearly seen on West Lake.

People in Hangzhou are always so "stiff and shabby." (Do not take offense—I am no different.) Only on the night of the eighteenth of the sixth month do they seem to go completely insane with enthusiasm. (This is what Mr. Lu Xun says in praise of mosquitoes.) Surely, we must have the blessing of the Buddha to thank for this—even though when the eighteenth of the sixth month began to be celebrated as a festival, the Panchen Lama had yet to come to West Lake.

People say that Hangzhou is the land of Buddha, and if indeed there is a Buddha, I will not deny that the place deserves the name. Take, for example, the eighteenth of the sixth month, which I am talking about now, and which is actually a Buddhist festival. I understand that Guanyin's birthday is on the nineteenth of the sixth month, a date established long ago and which therefore must be true. The eighteenth is the night before that day.

To begin with, San Tian Zhu Temple and Ling Yin Temple are sacred sites south of the Yangtze. On this birthday of the "All Merciful and All Benevolent Guanyin"—I am using a gaudy epithet, what a sacrilege!—it is not surprising that believers should congregate at West Lake. Naturally, in the minds of the pilgrims, the earlier they can offer incense, the more respect they will be able to show and the

---

[1]   Cold Food Day falls in April, a day when no cooking fires are allowed. Cleansing Day falls in late March or early April. Ritual and actual baths are taken on that day. Double Ninth is celebrated on the ninth day of the ninth month. It is the custom to hike to a high place on that day to avoid malevolent elements that are supposed to visit one's home.

more blessings they will receive. This is why it is so important to "burn the first incense." They tacitly accept the formula that the amount of blessings one receives is directly proportional to how early one offers incense. Since one can never have too many blessings, one can never be too early in offering incense. As it has developed, people have tended to go to offer their incense earlier and earlier in the day, so early now that they begin their pilgrimage late on the previous day. (You see how paradoxical it is!) And thus, through no merit of its own, the evening of the eighteenth of the sixth month has come to be observed as a festival.

I have forgotten whose poem it is (and remember only one line of it), from which we can imagine how the scenery of West Lake once looked: "Clouds and mountains on three sides, and a city wall on one." But people who row in West Lake nowadays can never know what that means. The clouds and mountains are as before, but where is the parapet by the lake? When we gaze toward the east, we see only rows and rows of city dwellings during the day, and twinkling lights in the evening. Although this is by no means an unpleasant sight, every now and then I humbly try to imagine the forbidding, labyrinth-like, but dilapidated parapets that used to cast their shadows on the ripples of the lake.

Since there used to be a city, naturally there were city gates, too. From north to south, there were three gates by the lake: the Qingbo, the Yongjin, and the Qiantang. Deep into the night, all three gates would be locked. Because the pilgrims had to get out of the city early, and the earlier the better, they had to think of a way to go through the gates. Their method was not to climb over the wall or imitate the crowing of roosters[2] (to resort to these measures would have been both disgraceful and dangerous), but rather to leave the city the previous night. In those days, it was sheer desolation outside the city wall. You couldn't have found the Lakeside Juying Restaurant then, to say nothing of such places as the West Lake Hotel and Xinxin Inn. The pilgrims were thus left with no choice but to wander the whole night long, and make do with the companionship of the lakes and mountains.

---

2   Lord Meng Chang made his escape from Qin in 299 BC with the help of two retainers who imitated the sound of dogs barking and roosters crowing. On hearing the sound, the guard thought that it was morning and opened the city gates. See *Shiji* (*Records of the Grand Historian*), "Meng Chang Jun liezhuan" (Biography of Lord Meng Chang).

Fortunately, the hot weather and wonderful moon prevented it from becoming too much of an ordeal. As for games such as setting lotus lamps on the river, those were simply entertainments devised by city-dwellers who could not stand the boredom of the night, and are not necessarily the refined pastimes they were later rumored to be. People in Hangzhou lived right by the lake, but they chose to hide within the city during ordinary times, and only came out to wander for one night a year when they were under coercion from two sides—the government (which closed the city gates) and the Buddhist goddess (whose birthday it was.) That was truly "shabby!" Even after the wall was torn down, people still chose to come out of the city only on the eighteenth of the month. I think this was probably a result of inertia, rather than an instance of full-scale insanity.

I lived in Hangzhou for five years, but only once spent the evening of the eighteenth of the sixth month there. I was very often somewhere else during the summer—if not in the United States, then in Beijing. I remember that one year, I was getting ready to go to Beijing on the morning of the eighteenth, and that night, Yinhuai and others hired a weary boatman and bobbed around on the lake for a while. They later told me that the boat had been somewhat broken down, and the tour was less than enjoyable. I was rather surprised to hear about their excursion.

Last year, we lived in the Yu Towers, and had the opportunity to witness the splendor of the celebration. At that time, we were still living with H. and his family. H. is a fun-loving person, so his children looked forward to this festival all the more eagerly. They had lived in the city year after year, and were a bit insulated from the lake and hills. Now, the whole family moved out to the lake and, the day before the celebration, they rushed out to Yue Fei's Grave to reserve a boat. Ordinarily, the fee would be four to five *jiao* for a night of touring, but now it cost no less than three *yuan*. On the afternoon of the eighteenth, we discussed going to the city to get some refreshments for our party that night. The two of us went with Miss Y. and Miss L., and with the sunset behind us, we leisurely rowed our boat to the city.

When the bus got onto the White Sand Causeway on our way back, we found before and behind us all kinds of vehicles and horses traveling on the same road like water flowing in a river. Evening had fallen by then. Ah, the area around the Lake Towers had become a small marketplace! Dazzling gaslights were hung high on Lou Wai Lou restaurant, and diners had already gathered like ants. Up and down the small restaurant and on the roadside in front of it, the area was bustling with noise and excitement. Vendors lined both sides of the road under the trees, and the air whirred with the sound of buying and selling. It was like that all the way to the park, with a continuous flow of pedestrians strolling here and there. We looked out to the west, and the hubbub of people in the lit-up area around Yue Fei's Grave was no different from here, forming a striking contrast to the quiet lake, with its lonely green willows. Involuntarily, I became as excited as a child.

We rushed through dinner, not caring how it tasted, and wanted to get on our boat right away. As luck would have it, a group of women merrymakers arrived. We naturally let them take the boat first and we stayed behind. H. is a quiet soul, and he suggested we sit down by the Xiling Bridge to rest and wait for the moon to come out before getting on the boat. We had to agree—in any case, we did not have the boat just then—but we were all slightly disappointed.

It was still quiet and deserted by the Xiling Bridge. We sat for a while and listened to flutes and drums from afar. The sound of people talking and laughing seemed so muffled and distant, and all of a sudden, a wave of loneliness washed over us, so different from what we had been expecting. Every now and then, two or three lotus lamps on the water floated toward us, and the children all said that the lamps were here. I looked at the lamps bobbing up and down in the water and found them rather pathetic. Later, fleet after fleet of boats advertising the Japanese medicine Jintan came by, bringing with them rows of red lanterns and heavy drums. Like a fire dragon, they wove their way through the inner and outer lake, and seemed to shatter quite a bit of our loneliness. But soon, the red hue shining in the water grew dimmer and moved further away. Because we did not have the boat and could not follow them, their brief visit only made us feel all the more listless. The light yellow moon had already risen in the east, slightly brightening the sky and water, but our boat was still nowhere in sight.

The moon rose higher and higher in the sky, and finally we found it difficult just to sit there. One by one, some of us began to slip back to the Yu Towers. H. was displeased, and also walked home. Close to home there was still plenty of activity. I saw many lanterns and people, and felt as if I had come home after a long absence. Was it my pedestrian soul that prevented me from enjoying this religious festival? I took a bite of the ham that I had just bought myself and found it very salty. How tiresome! Fortunately, the customers before us left soon afterward, and the boat was once again tied under the willow tree. Although it was getting late, we could go to the lake, after all. I tried to drum up interest among the children, saying, "Let's go! Let's hurry!"

Bright red lotus lanterns were floating on the silvery night waves, and our boat followed after them. They had begun to grow sparser by that time, no longer as plentiful as before. Quite a number of lanterns had been set out on the lake, but there were more people there gathering them up. They gathered up the lanterns from the waves, and put them in a conspicuous place on their boats for display, and then proudly moved on. Yet, when the candles had burned down and the lanterns dimmed, their boats returned to their original state, battered and ugly. Thanks to them, however, the lake had been robbed of its beautiful lights. They certainly knew how to spoil the fun! "Let's move on. Take us to 'Three Pools Mirroring the Moon,'" we told the boatman.

The painted pleasure boats on West Lake are usually not as beautiful as those on the Qinhuai River. Only tonight did they come out complete with warm, soothing lights and the resonant sounds of singing. But they had their own kind of splendor as they wove their way about the serene lake, embraced by mountains and the lone moon high up in the sky which imbued everything above and below with a feeling of transparency. These boats are in no way inferior to their sisters elsewhere. To resort to clichés, summer in West Lake is like a "breeze in the woods," and that in the Qinhuai River is like "the beauty of the boudoir." Besides, there is fun and merriment on the Qinhuai River night after night, whereas at West Lake, this happy time comes only once a year. In times of rain or storms, you might even miss it.

Around the pier in the park, boats of all sizes were crowded together. The light of the lanterns and the moon dimmed in the white glow of the gas lamps on the shore, and we figured we might as well move on to another place. When we had first got on the boat, we could hear people on the boats on the other side singing the languid tune "Tired of Painting Eyebrows" in the *nanlu* mode. By the time we rowed over, their song had ended and all was quiet. We found this disappointing, too, and decided to go to a different place. The boat slowly made its way to "Three Pools Mirroring the Moon."

It is difficult to express in words the brilliance of the moon at midnight that night. In the middle of the lake, it was quiet and chilly, but the sound of singing and talking and the frail gleam of the lanterns from the shore formed a shimmering, glowing circle of light that surrounded the lake. Our hearts were thus not altogether subdued, as on other nights when we took a boat out, but we trembled gently inside with a combination of perhaps some excitement and more forlornness. The chimera of the lights, the rippling of the waves, the swift movement of the clouds, the rocking of the boat... all seemed to merge with the images inside our hearts. Feelings of softness and smoothness tended to be the only signs that we had entered into the world of dreams; at that very instant, the outing had become no more and no less a dream.

By the time we arrived at "Three Pools Mirroring the Moon," there were again many songs and lanterns, but we were tired. We stopped there for a while, and proceeded to navigate around the little isle. Gradually, the scene around us turned desolate. Tree roots leaned at an angle on the shore, and old grass was all tangled beside them. The three miniature, cone-shaped stone pagodas and the Lei Feng Pagoda, upright like a bald writing brush, were standing together in the moonlight. There were not too many lights on the south shore, which made the waves seem more chilling and the moon brighter. Our eyes smarted more and more from fatigue until we could hardly keep them open, so we rowed back. We could hear the most popular piece three-six[3] playing from a boat nearby; its soft harmony coming in waves, as if it were unwilling to see us turn back. I remembered that H. had once come up with a line, "Light from distant lamps comes out from behind the tree, as bright as persimmons," and I had completed the couplet with "Tired oars dip into the waves, tardily, as if dipping into syrup." Although on that occasion we did not have in mind what was before our eyes tonight, the two lines could well describe the present scene. We turned around, and rowed to where the lights were.

We went ashore, walking as if in a dream. H. and his wife went back to the Lake Towers, but we lingered on the White Sand Causeway, unwilling to go. The Lou Wai Lou Restaurant was still bright with lamps up and down, and the diners had not yet dispersed. On the road was a continuous flow of sightseers walking in twos and threes. We turned around and once again walked toward the park. Fewer lantern boats were anchored there, but there were still five or six of them. One boat had a welcome banner, and its lights were particularly bright. It sold cold

---

[3]   Three-six, also known as *sanluo*, refers to the popular piece "Meihua sannong" (Three Renditions of the Peach Blossom).

drinks and snacks, so we got on board to have a soft drink. A woman sat in the middle cabin, heavily made up though not at all beautiful. At first glance, we thought she was one of the customers. Later, when we somehow figured out that she was a live signboard to attract customers, we laughed at this realization and left.

No matter how tired and bored we might have been, we still wanted to persist until daybreak before returning to the tall tower to look for our dreams—that was what we were all expecting. But things did not turn out the way we wanted. Not at all easy with the thought that their children were out roaming on the lake in the deep of the night, H. and his wife came out again to bring them home. L., the youngest, grumbled just before he left, "It wasn't much fun at all, tonight!" With his head bent and feet dragging, he nonetheless went home, leaving only us. What could we do with just the few of us? Huan, moreover, could not stand the chill of the night. "Let's all go back, then!"

Upstairs, they had all turned in. My wife and I stood by the cement banister with the simple, widely spaced lattice. The whole corridor was bathed in moonlight. We saw that the boat that had been selling cold drinks a while ago was moving toward the middle of the lake. That live signboard of a woman must still be sitting there, trying hard to keep her sleepy eyes open. Both of us came to this same thought at the same time. Under the moon that was beginning to set in the west, the sound *ding—ding—dang, ding—ding—dong* came to us from the boat. The boat moved farther off, and gradually we could not hear the sound anymore. A night breeze blew by, and once again, *ding—dang, ding—dong*.

Everything got farther away from us. Even my own shadow under the moon looked blurrier than the mist. I turned around to go to bed, and for some reason, skipped a step. The broken dream going by like an arrow stopped for a second, then continued its flight as if shot from a bow. Such a strange "Midsummer Night's Dream!" Even now, I don't know what to make of it. After all, it turned around to give me a glance before going away. How could I hold a grudge against it? Did I like it? No, not at all.

Going to the City (1933)

The bus goes into the city at half-past five in the afternoon.

The old Summer Palace is nothing but mounds of dirt. Beyond, the West Hills are dim and purplish, and above them, the winter sun is enveloped in a thin layer of orange clouds. Winter has just arrived and the days are short in this northern land. The setting sun moves as fast as an arrow, but as soon as the bus turns the corner, leaving the sun behind it, all one can see ahead is dusk.

Hai Dian is so desolate, and so small. There are only two streets altogether, and the bus passes through them in a flash. It then passes Huang Zhuang, and picks up speed until it is going some thirty *li* an hour. Open fields dash by, trees are hurled behind us, village houses come in and out of view.... Who cares? Haven't I traveled this road enough times and had enough of these sights? Who takes the trouble to look out the window? These scattered patches of withering yellow and sickly green are gradually dissolving into a continuous thin stretch of gray fog.

When we first got on the bus, everybody was talking and smiling. As the bus travels farther, the sounds of the motor and the wheels rolling on the ground rattle on relentlessly, and it requires an effort just to talk. Gradually, the conversation dies down. (If a foreign woman were on the bus, it would be different.) We are almost there. Sit tight.

Electric lights shine into our eyes. A slight movement, and we are in the neighborhood of the city gate. Gaoliang Bridge, which is something of a historical site, takes one's breath away. On the street, people are wearing thick cotton jackets. The city gate opens its round mouth, waiting to swallow up the bus. The watchtowers of the city wall, though close to collapsing, still stand solidly enough in the shadow just ahead and are rather imposing.

By the time the bus enters the city, night has fallen. It's a pity that I have forgotten its name, its past, and even a fraction of the sentiment it once induced in me. Now it is merely a rectangle made up of city walls with houses and streets inside.

The door of the bus opens and closes with a bang, and the passengers grow fewer. When it reaches the final stop, usually only two or three of us, not necessarily friends, are left on the bus; sometimes it's only the driver, the conductor and me. I get off mechanically and look around me, my hands hugging and pulling at my baggage.

Sometimes they call out nonchalantly, "Take your time!" or "Mind your head!" Then, not long after, a rickshaw slowly pulls off with me as the passenger and goes away safely.

"You know, you really have nothing much to tell about your trip to the city, and yet you're trying to pass this off as an essay? You must be pulling my leg." You never know, though, do you? You, with your wisdom, should be the judge: If indeed there were something to "tell," it would most likely be about a blown-out tire, a break-down by the side of the road, or, worse, a crash into an electric pole, sending the bus and its passengers spilling onto their backs. Even worse still, it could be a shout in the style of the bandits in *Outlaws of the Marsh* that makes even the one in the yellow cotton jacket tremble in fear.[4] That would be very messy, wouldn't it? Southerners call incidents like these "unstomachable," and northerners declare them "intolerable." If indeed any of these events had happened, would you really expect me to have the time and peace of mind to toy with my brush and paper and come up with a piece of idle scribbling such as this?

Besides, "nothing to tell" really means "is yet to be told." Isn't it the case that in novels one often finds phrases such as "the night passed, with nothing to tell?"

---

[4]   *Outlaws of the Marsh (Shuihu Zhuan)*, a fourteenth-century Chinese novel about the adventures of a group of bandits. The "one in the yellow cotton jacket" probably refers to the Emperor Huizhong, who must have felt threatened by the growing group of bandits.

Fang Lingru

Fang Lingru (1897–1976) grew up in the oppressive atmosphere of a scholar's family. Against the gender bias of the time, she fought to be allowed to be educated. Her uncle forced her into marriage with the son of a local gentry family. While the marriage was far from happy, she was given the chance to further her education when her husband went to the US for study. After returning to China, she divorced her husband and made a living from translating and teaching. During this time, she formed a close association with other writers such as Ba Jin, Liang Shiqiu, and Ding Ling, and maintained a long-lasting friendship with them.

Fang's first literary attempt was in 1929, when she began writing poetry. She has since been regarded as one of the few women poets of the Crescent Moon Society. Her prose, with its plain and straightforward language, nevertheless reads like poetry. "Home," for example, is built upon a heightened moment, where a line of poetry from the Tang poet Cen Shen triggers in her a host of complex feelings that one comes to associate with home. One observes the same kind of creative process at work in many other essays in this anthology as well.

Home (1936)

"Home," the topic you assigned me, has been on my mind for a long time, and it wouldn't hurt to tell you, I think, that this assignment from you has actually become a heavy burden to me. Every day, I mull over the best way to approach it. You were right when you said that I stayed at home "from morning till night," but don't be too pleased with your own cleverness! Do you think you can get a glimpse of a person's true demeanor from a mirror alone? Do you think you can discover the substance of a person's life and the essence of his character from a description of his home life? What a pity it is that I don't even like looking at myself in the mirror, and that, though you know that I stay at home "from morning till night," you will never know what I do, what food I eat, and what clothes I wear when I am at home!

What should I write about, then? The situation of the average home? Home life and financial problems? The relationship between culture and family? The influence of home life on the individual? The comforts and sorrows that home life bestows upon a person? Whether everyone does or should have a family? Whether home is something to be cherished or abhorred? These questions all get intertwined with each other in my mind, driving me to distraction. As the old novels would put it, this topic is haunting me like a nightmare.

I came out tonight with my mind all entangled in these thoughts. See how clear the sky is at this time, as clear as if it had been washed! The moon is like a discus thrown up to the sky by a Greek youth in antiquity, or a breastplate left there by an ancient warrior, radiating a cold and dazzling glow as the stars around it shine their brilliant light onto it. At this moment, I am on the lake, and the boat is moving along the shadows of the hill. Under the dark blue sky, clusters of trees adorn the islands that are scattered over the vast white water. I imagine what it must have been like before these places were "civilized": inside the huts in the quiet moonlight, boatmen lay down in front of the oil lamp on the stove. The women sat behind it, and the boatmen could not help noticing how their wives' faces glowed, illuminated by the fire. They must have felt much more secure than what we can hope for nowadays with all our freedom. I remember not too long ago seeing the fishermen at Cai Shi Ji living in their boats. All of their daily activities—eating, resting and working—are done in the small cabin. Floating from place to place the whole day long, do they find it enjoyable or trying? I think of your topic again. It was so easy and simple for you to come up with the topic, but if you go ahead and ask a fisherman the above question— a small question, really—he will look at you, his eyes wide, and not know what to say.

There are quite a few "genteel souls" out here tonight, and more than just the bookworm types have come out to admire the moon. Dignitaries and bankers are here to look at the moon during the Mid-Autumn Festival, their cars lined up by the bridge. To do that, one has to come with offerings of flowers and fruit, together with a reverent state of mind. If we could fly to the sky at this moment, we would see red candlelight flickering and incense smoke rising all over the city. We would even hear the crackling of firecrackers coming from the distance. This is indeed a solemn night, a night that belongs to the deities. All the sightseers have shed their flippant façades tonight, and although there are so many people on the lake, it is not as chaotic as during ordinary times. One by one, the boats glide by gently and slowly. Sitting in the boats are people of all descriptions: Some are murmuring to themselves, some are whispering to each other, some are tilting their heads back to soak in the moonlight, exposing their pallid faces. Young people, imagining the scenery of the south, strum their guitars and sing "Aloha Oe," the tropical love song.

At this moment, a boat that I have not seen before comes by with a dimly lit glass lamp hanging on its deck. Under the lamp, three or four people are sitting around playing guessing and drinking games. There is another person sitting all by himself on the bow. His face is a patch of darkness and it is impossible to make out what he looks like. I hear the sound of chanted poetry coming from this dark shadow. He chants with a drawn-out sound, the pitch relatively low in the beginning, but rising gradually. After it reaches the peak, it slowly dies down again, until it disappears half in moaning and half in sighing. Listening to the dying cadence, you can imagine a small hill in an ancient painting, half-shrouded in mist. There is a winding stream, too, splashing drops of water as it flows along. The sound of his chanting lingers, trembling all the while, like the shadow of a lone wild goose in the sky gliding in a flash across the water. That, I think, is an appropriate comparison, because the sound itself is half real, half imaginary. While half of it is still coming from the person's mouth, half of it has already burrowed its way into our dreams.

Amidst the chanting, I hear two lines clearly: "Meeting by chance on horseback, we lack paper and a writing brush/ Please tell my people at home that I am safe."[1] You will see, therefore, that on this happy festival, somewhere on this vast lake are a few broken souls trying to drown their sorrows in wine under a dim light in the back cabin of their boats. They have left their families and their hometowns—only heaven knows what kind of a life they are leading. On this night, for these two ancient doleful poetic lines to come bursting from their hearts, their minds must be filled with longing. Perhaps at this moment, somewhere in a corner concealed in reeds or withering lotus leaves, someone else may also be thinking of home. When he hears the chanting, will he be able to hold back his tears and stop himself from sobbing? Will it take many soothing words from his friend to calm his quivering heart? How can I not think of "home," the topic you gave me, and suddenly come to realize its meaning? Now I know that, however heavy a burden it may be, however profound the pain it inflicts, we will carry them home with us, like a snail crawling sluggishly with its heavy shell on its back. All of a sudden, I seem to get a glimpse of a clear vision of something. As Xin Qiji said in his poem, "I looked for her everywhere. Unthinkingly, I turned my head and was startled to find her among the lanterns growing dim."[2]

---

[1] Cen Shen (715–770), "Feng rujing shi" (On Meeting the Envoy on Its Return to the Capital).

[2] Xin Qiji (1140–1207), "Qing yu an" (In the Tune of *Qing Yu An*).

Liang Shiqiu

For many readers, Liang Shiqiu (1903–1987) is forever linked with *xiaopin wen*, in large part due to the popularity of his *Yashe xiaopin*. His essays are characterized by the kind of wit that one associates with the English familiar essay. Most of the titles of his essays concern human situations and daily objects, which he explores from a variety of angles, citing relevant anecdotes and literary references to illustrate his points. The three essays anthologized here are works of this kind.

Liang received his education at Tsinghua College, before going to Colorado College and Harvard University in the US to further his studies. When he was at Columbia University, he studied under Irving Babbitt, whose philosophy on New Humanism he brought back to China. As a professor of English, Liang advocates a belief in the transcendence of literature over social classes. Such a view of literature puts him at odds with leftist writers, with whom, chief among them Lu Xun, he carried a bitter long-standing debate.

Of Liang's many literary accomplishments, he is the first scholar to have translated single-handedly the complete plays of Shakespeare—a monumental endeavor that took him some thirty-seven years to complete.

Middle Age (1949)

The hands of a clock or watch move slowly—so slowly that one hardly notices. Age is like that, too. It advances imperceptibly, year after year, until one day you are startled to find that you have reached middle age. By then, there are probably two things you cannot help observing. First, obituaries arrive with no letting up: Some of your more impatient friends have decided to move on ahead first, which can spoil your fun quite a bit. At the same time, you suddenly notice hordes of young people cavorting before your eyes, and you wonder where they have been hiding all this time. Now they swagger in front of you, flaunting their strong, steady gait and youthful, merry faces, looking as if they were on their way to a wedding. Meanwhile, most of your own peers have long since gone into hibernation, handing the whole world over to the young. As the saying goes, "All one hears is news of old friends' deaths, all one sees are young people." This is the true portrayal of middle age.

It used to be that the back covers of magazines often carried an advertisement for "William's Red Tonic Pills," with a picture showing a wan and sallow man, who stooped, his hand on the small of his back. Next to the picture were the words, "Pay attention to the implication of this picture." That "implication" was probably rather obscure for young people. But this picture often sprang up in the minds of middle-aged people, and though they did not necessarily want to partake of the "red tonic pills," that implication they fully understood. If a pillar made from the trunk of a yellow pine might on occasion bend and even collapse, how much more likely would this be for the human spine, made as it is of twenty-six little bones?

There is not a single young person alive who does not enjoy looking in the mirror. Even a quick glance at his reflection in a shop window is an opportunity not to be passed up; he always feels he is on the whole not at all bad-looking. This habit of looking at one's reflection and admiring oneself slowly fades with time. Then, one day, when you inadvertently pick up a mirror, you find that several lines have been engraved on your forehead, clear and forceful like the brush strokes of the famous artist Wu Daozi.[1] You will still think they only show when

---

[1]   Wu Daozi of the early eighth century was an important Tang dynasty painter. He is famous for the murals he painted on palace walls.

you raise your eyebrows, but there they are even when you look down. Careful examination reveals that the hair on the top of your head has begun to move to the area beside your cheeks and under your chin. The most shocking sight of all is of the few white hairs around your temples. They should not be taken lightly! Even if you are the proverbial scrooge who "would not pull a single hair even if it would benefit the whole world," the time has come to steel your resolve and get rid of those white hairs. And thus will your hair be pulled out, roots and all, perhaps with even a little glob of shiny skin attached to the end. But it's all in vain—time won't let you go easily by!

The average woman is even more anxious than a man when she gets to middle age. Who among young women is not as full and lustrous as a milky white grape, likely to burst at the slightest touch? Who among them is not as agile and delicate as a swallow that hops and skips about so nimbly? At the arrival of middle age, however, things begin to change. The curves are still there, but nothing is quite right. What should curve in now bulges out, and what should protrude outward now caves in. The white grape has turned into a honeyed date, and the sparrow has become a quail. The part of a woman's body that receives the most exposure is her face, where "fish-tails" spread out like a fishnet, the lines crisscrossing and overlapping with each other. There may not be too many of them, but they leave nothing uncovered, until her whole face gradually assumes the appearance of a very well-developed railway map.

It is quite enough that wrinkles appear that could never be ironed out, but on top of that, every now and then one also finds on one's face moles that look like fly droppings. Unless one's face is already as dirty as an earthen wall, age can always find something to make it worse. The easiest solution, perhaps, is to paint with make-up another face on top of one's own. Yet, before applying and removing cosmetics, one cannot help being reminded of the story, "The Painted Skin,"[2] in the *Strange Tales Recorded in the Studio of Idleness*.

The muscles of a woman's body are no match for gravity, either. As soon as she reaches middle age, they hang down loosely in clumps from her face and around her ankles. I've heard that many Western women

---

[2]   A story from *Liaozhai zhiyi* (*Strange Tales Recorded in the Studio of Idleness*), a seventeenth-century collection of supernatural tales, in which the ghost of a woman, lacking skin, has to have it painted on her face.

use a rolling pin on themselves from morning till night, hoping to firm up their puffed-up muscles. Others simply stay away from fatty and starchy food and tighten up their belts, trying to starve themselves back to youth. How effective these measures are, I have no idea.

Don't think that when you reach middle age, you've come to the end of your life. No, as with mountain climbing, at middle age you've only reached the peak. Turn around and you will see crowds of young folks struggling on their way up—"their heads set firmly forward, their perspiration flowing, unwiped." Take a closer look and you'll see many rocks that once tripped you up, and many traps that once ensnared you and turned you into a "frog at the bottom of the well."[3] When I think back on my younger days, I remember the times I behaved like a moth flying toward a lamp, almost perishing in the fire, or like a fly banging its head continuously against the window, hoping to go out into light but only ending up stuck on the flypaper. One can only see these things clearly when one is on the peak. As one looks ahead, one sees the downward slope that by comparison, is far easier to traverse.

Shi Nai'an wrote in his preface to *Outlaws of the Marsh*, "If one is still unmarried at thirty, one should foreswear marriage; if one has not assumed any office by forty, one should stay away from the world of officialdom." In fact, both "marriage" and "officialdom" are trivial matters, and there is not much to lose if one is not married or not an official. The only problem is that this sort of advice somehow rings of defeatism. As a Western proverb has it, "Life begins at forty," which seems to suggest that, before forty, one merely sees previews of the real show to come. I think the whole matter hinges upon one's health. Those who have grown up on the coarsest kind of corn bread and rice cakes find it no easy feat to live to middle age. Their energy for life has been almost entirely sapped. How can they think of marrying, and what is the point of their becoming officials? It is too late even to take vitamin pills. I have also seen men and women who are blessed with good health in youth, complete with an ungainly energy, thick brows, big eyes, and straight backs. They are just like those bitter green young peaches, down to the fuzzy hair on their faces. But when they get to middle age, they glow radiantly and their step grows so sprightly that one might think

---

3   See "Qiushui" (Autumn Flood) in *Zhuangzi*, where a frog living at the bottom of a well is described as being so limited by his environment that he cannot possibly know anything about the vastness of the sea.

they have installed springs under their heels. You can tell at a glance that they have substance. Their lives are like fine wine stored in the cellar for years, unadulterated and fragrant. To them, there is no sadness in middle age.

It is not too late to begin living at forty. The question is how to understand the term "living." If it is only at the age of no perplexity[4] that one begins to learn to ice-skate, kick a shuttlecock, fly a kite, or in other ways "find the time to learn from the young folks," well, that would be forcing it a bit, like celebrating spring in the fall. It is also depressing for a matronly woman to let down her bangs and practice walking in high heels in the privacy of the bathroom, as if walking on stilts. The wonderful thing about middle age is the knowledge one has found in life and in oneself, from which one then proceeds to do what one can do, and enjoy what one can enjoy. Junior actors fresh from acting school can handle the acrobatic roles in a standard full performance, but only middle-aged players are qualified for roles in the finale—only they can truly understand the heart of the opera.

---

[4]   The "age of no perplexity" is forty.

The Send-off (1949)

"Sending people off is the one thing that overwhelms one with sorrow."[5] To my mind, the ancients must have gone about this business of sending people off with elegance and profound feelings. In the past, when getting about was by no means an easy thing, it was never known how long a person, once departed, would be gone, and whether one would ever come to meet him again. This is why people of those times went to such great lengths with parting rituals, such as singing songs of farewell at Nanpu,[6] and breaking off willow branches as souvenirs on Ba Qiao.[7] A cup of wine drunk as far out as the Yang Gate[8] under such circumstances carried a special significance. Even now, one can still almost see what it must have been like for Wang Lun to walk on the shore with big strides, singing all the while, when Li Bo's boat was about to pull away.[9] What is so wonderful about such a parting scene is the purity and genuineness of Wang Lun's emotions, and the spontaneity and lack of inhibition of his actions. To see someone off who has always shared one's thoughts is of course difficult. But if I have always disliked the way you look, and you have always taken exception to the way I talk, then there is nothing better than to see the other person go. One's only fear is that the world might be too small a place and we might run into each other again. In that case, what would be the point of taking all that trouble to see each other off?

In our lives as modern people, send-offs have become a social ritual, like attending birthday parties and funerals. You get up so early in the morning that you could even "catch the tail of the crowing rooster" and, still half-asleep, you hurry to the train station or the pier, squeezing your way through the chaotic crowd to look for your target. Finding it, you cast around for some inept thing to say until the time when the whistle finally blows. Everyone gathered there then disperses like birds and beasts. Letting out a sigh of relief, they go home, their mouths pursed. That is considered to be thoughtful. For his part, the person being sent

---

[5] See Jiang Yan (445–505), "Bie fu" (Rhymeprose on Parting).

[6] Nanpu, south of Pucheng County in Fujian.

[7] Ba Qiao is to the east of Chang'an in Shaanxi, a traditional place for sending people off.

[8] Yang Gate is located to the south of Dunhuang in Gansu. See Wang Wei (699?–761), "Wei Cheng qu" (Song of Wei Cheng).

[9] See Li Bo (701–762), "Zeng Wang Lun" (To Wang Lun).

off appreciates the bustle around him, which goes to prove that he is well liked and has not muddled through his days in vain. It is also very gratifying to have so many people come to show their unwillingness to see him go. Comparing himself with other passengers who may not have a single person to see them off, his sense of superiority grows and his spirit soars. He only wishes that he could shake every hand eight times, and thank everybody ten times. If we attach so much importance to the number of friends and relatives who come to take part in the funeral procession to express their lingering remembrances for the dead, how much more should we try to do for the living? It simply won't do unless there is an impressive send-off!

It seems disconcerting to leave quietly without having someone there to see you off. If other passengers around you are making a display of their send-off party, it will make your trip even lonelier. Things are no different outside of China. In his essay on seeing people off, Max Beerbohm relates an incident at a train station where he runs into an old actor friend of his who is there to send off a woman passenger. At first, the two whisper endearments to each other. Before long, tears flow down their cheeks. When finally the whistle blows, they can hardly manage to hold back their tears. His friend then waves to the woman again and again, and gazes at her for a long time as the train pulls away. It turns out, however, that the actor is just playing a role—he does not actually know the woman at all, but is employed by a "send-off service." Anyone who has to go on a trip and wishes to have someone come to the train station to see them off can avail himself or herself of this service. With his acting background, his friend is of course a virtuoso of the trade. He can project his feelings and put up a convincing performance, and for a modest fee, the customer is entitled to a handsome spiritual reward. American tourists in particular have money to buy everything they want when they are abroad. If "send-off services" become a widespread business, there will never be a shortage of sender-offers.

Send-offs being an unavoidable fact of life, one can ill afford to ignore the proper techniques. If sending off were limited to merely showing up at the station or the pier and shaking hands to say goodbye, then the whole thing would be simple. However, food is an important item in any ritual in China, and when a friend is about to take a long trip, we make sure he doesn't leave with an empty stomach. There is no avoiding a farewell banquet, where our only wish is to stockpile in his stomach over the course of one meal the nutrients he will need for several days. I believe that all of us have had similar experiences. If the news—often advertised by the traveler himself—is abroad that a trip is impending, the traveler has every reason to expect that invitations to farewell banquets will pour in and that for a short time, there will be no need for his family to cook. Other more considerate souls even bring food to the train or boat, as if hunger on the road were a real danger.

I shall never forget a most miserable send-off I once witnessed. It was a bitter cold winter night, and there was not much sign of life at the train station. Most of the passengers, as well as the people who had come to see them off, were trying to keep themselves warm in the train cars, but on the long platform, which seemed to extend interminably, there was a dark pack of sender-offers. Some had capes around their shoulders, some had felt hats on their heads, and some were tapping their feet as if playing drums on the cement floor. I came up to the crowd and found that they were all friends of mine gathered there to send off a lady friend. The train was about to depart, but she was nowhere in sight. It turned out that she was still obliged to go to several farewell banquets that night.

At the last minute, she showed up and all of us who had gathered there felt that we were there to receive rather than to send her off. When we saw her arrive at the train station, we were simply too happy, and didn't have time to express our sorrow at her departure. In one arm, she was holding a small child, who was startled by the crowd and started to cry. With her other hand, she was dragging another child along. Half walking, half running, her hair all disheveled, she was breathing steam from her mouth like a donkey carrying a heavy load in winter. She could not afford to socialize with us, and with a few steps, hopped onto the train, which had already begun to move. Most of the people gathered around had things in their hands and did not have a chance to present them to her. I happened to be standing closest to the train door, so they all handed their presents to me, saying, "May we trouble you to take these to her?" I was like Santa Claus, holding a pile of presents. I dashed onto the train. There was no time for words, so I dumped everything on her, turned around, and fled. When I hopped off the train, I had to spin around a few times before regaining my footing.

Later, I received a letter from her, in which she said:

"Who were those people who came to see me off? And who gave me those things that you dumped on me? It took me quite a while to sort everything out on the train and finally gather them up into a bundle! Thanks to the good intentions of my friends, I ended up having another piece of luggage.

I would like to know who gave me what. Since you came up to the car as their representative, you must know, and I hope you will tell me as soon as possible who these things are from, namely:

> Three baskets of fruit, four cans of Taikang food, two bottles of fruit syrup, four boxes of sweetmeats, four tins of crackers, four cans of fermented tofu, four boxes of cake, eight boxes of pastry, eight tins of cigarettes, a box of letter paper and envelopes, two pairs of silk stockings, one bottle of perfume, a set of ashtrays, a small clock, two pieces of fabric, four baskets of pickled vegetables, a pair of embroidered slippers, four large loaves of bread, a tin of coffee, two toy swords...."

I couldn't come up with an answer to her query, and to this day, it remains a mystery waiting to be solved.

I do not like to see people off, nor do I like other people to see me off. Going through the moment of parting from people whom one cannot bear to let go is like undergoing surgery, and as a rule, all surgery requires anesthesia beforehand so that, half-conscious, the patient can survive the pain. That is why it is best to avoid the pain of parting. A friend once said to me, "When you leave, I won't come to see you off, but when you return, I will come to meet you, even in the heaviest rainstorm."

I admire this sentiment most of all.

Travel (1949)

Of all the races in the world, the Chinese are the most disinclined to travel. Even in times of famine, they do not lightly set out on the road to escape from hunger, preferring to stay in the same spot to eat grass, gnaw on tree bark, and swallow Guanyin Tu.[10] They are afraid that once they leave their homes, they may die on the road and thus lose their final right—to die in their own beds. The better-heeled are even less willing to travel: Instead, they hang a picture on the wall and claim to have engaged in "armchair travel" simply by looking at it. This is what is meant by the saying, "Being active is not as good as being idle." What this really means is that "there is nothing new under the sun." After all, what are the famous sights of great mountains and rivers, anyway, if not merely a few piles of stones and a puddle of water?

I remember that when I was a primary school student, going for a picnic in the wild could set my heart beating with excitement. We would get all prepared well in advance, getting up early in the morning, falling in line, and holding up our school flag, the band marching in front of us. A week after the picnic, we would even be required to hand in a composition with the title "Our Outing." Only then was the whole matter considered to have come to a satisfactory conclusion. Such was the solemn undertaking of a picnic!

My maternal grandmother lived in the city center of Hangzhou, and in the eighty-some years of her life, she had never been to West Lake. At long last, she went, but by then she could no longer walk and had to be carried there. She never returned—she was buried in the hills by the lake.

The ancients asked, "How many pairs of shoes can one wear in one's lifetime?" The idea was to urge people to pursue happiness while they could and not be deterred by thoughts of the number of shoes they might need to wear. But is traveling really an enjoyable thing, or is there something somehow aggravating about it?

One cannot do without luggage when one is on the road. A bundle of bedding weighing twenty or thirty *jin*[11] is the first obstacle that a traveler has to overcome. It should be tied up tightly and handsomely in the shape of a square with sharp, tidy corners, easily distinguishable

---

[10]   A kind of white clay eaten by famine victims.

[11]   *Jin*, a measurement of weight equal to about 1 1/3 pounds.

from bundles that are loosely wrapped in cloth with the inside showing. This task alone is not for those of us who lack the strength to tie up a chicken. It sometimes happens that curious souls at domestic customs stations like to open up your bedding to take a look, and once the inspection is over, it is not that easy to restore it to its original shape. The ancients spoke of travel in this way, "Go when the mood strikes you, and return when the mood passes." For many people, once they have endured the process of rolling up their bedding, the mood to travel has almost run its course. In some countries, it is not necessary to carry one's bedding when one travels for wherever there is a bed, there is a mattress; and wherever there is a mattress, there are bedsheets which can be washed and changed at any time. Travelers can come and go unburdened, and do not have to carry their bedding like snails carrying their shells on their backs.

When all is said and done, carrying one's bedding is still not such an impossible task, but I have never heard of people carrying beds on the road. There are very few beds in the world that do not come with bedbugs, and I seriously doubt how much energy is left for touring after a whole night spent giving one's blood to the vermin. I have a friend who designed for himself a set of seamless sleeping clothes that snugly covered his head and limbs. When he crawled inside, only his eyes were visible through the two holes in the front, and he was completely insulated from the world outside. The problem was, with these sleeping clothes on, he looked like a member of the Ku Klux Klan. I heard it said that when he came out in his sleeping clothes one night, a person who caught sight of him nearly fell dead from fright.

A primitive means of transportation is not necessarily a source of trouble for travelers, and I find that a *huagan* or *jiazi che*[12] are much more interesting than airplanes. "The wonderful feeling of riding on the wind"[13] is only possible for immortals. To travel in this mortal world, the criterion should be that one can touch the ground with one's feet. We like the sight of white clouds, but that does not mean we'd like to weave our way in and out of them. We like to see those hills that, as one poetic line has it, look "like a range from the front but a peak from the side, tall from afar and short when one is near

---

12   *Huagan*, a kind of sedan chair found in Sichuan, usually with no cover; *jiazi che*, a kind of push cart.
13   See *Zhuangzi*, "Xiaoyao you" (Free and Easy Wandering).

them,"[14] but that does not mean we have to shrink the whole world into a miniature rock for us to toy with. I regret never having rode on the "wagons with sails" that, according to Milton, could be found in China.[15] No, there is nothing wrong with the primitiveness of one's means of transportation. The problem lies in the difficulty of securing service, and in dealing with drivers and boatmen. It goes without saying that one should watch over one's belongings, but one must be careful of bandits on the way, as well. When Liu Ling exhorted others to "bury me where I fall dead," he did not mean that he was ready to face an unnatural death.

Although travel is beset with worries, there is nevertheless a lot of joy in it. Traveling is a kind of escape from the ugliness of human company. It is said that, "the greatest recluse hides himself in the sea of humanity." Since we are by no means great recluses, we could hardly survive in that sea. Not only that: We also find it less than easy even to hide in our own homes. Confined to a courtyard house the whole year round, one hardly needs to look up to the roof to sigh;[16] forced to look at the same face at home for twelve months of the year, one does not need to put on a grass cloak intended for cattle in order to shed tears.[17] What you can see of the sky at home is but a small corner of it, and the cool wind and bright moon described as "inexhaustible" by the Song poet Su Shi are not to be had there.[18] To fly a kite, you have to climb up to the roof and hold it up with a bamboo pole. To watch the sun rise or the moon set, you have to find a place not blocked by your neighbors. When you walk on the street, the people you see amid the hustle and bustle around you are either beasts in disguise or pathetic vermin. Given all of this, even if we lack the courage to let loose our hair and retire to the mountains, why shouldn't we at least pack up our toothbrushes and roll up our bedding for a few days of travel? Once on the road, there will be no escaping the pelting wind and rain, which then will so tire us out that

14 Famous lines from Su Dongpo's "Ti Xilin bi" (Inscribed on the Wall of the Xilin Temple).

15 *Paradise Lost*, IV, p. 439.

16 Han Lang, as recorded in the *Hanshu* (*The History of Han*), remained quiet about his troubles, but often raised his head to the roof and sighed.

17 In his impoverished days, Wang Zhang of the Han dynasty was once reduced to wrapping himself in a grass cloak meant to protect cattle from the rain. Thinking that he was about to die in this sorry state, he said good-bye to his wife in tears. See *Hanshu*, "Wang Zhang zhuan" (Biography of Wang Zhang).

18 See Su Shi, "Chi Bi fu" (The Red Cliff).

we will return, having realized the truth of the saying, "one can stay at home in comfort for a thousand days, but leaving home for a short while is difficult." In this way, we will be able to tolerate temporarily that intolerable home, and once it becomes intolerable again, we can then take another trip. After enduring this cycle a few times, we will find our lives almost over.

There is no escaping the feeling of loneliness on a trip, but loneliness also has a certain charm. William Hazlitt suggests in "On Going a Journey" that one should not travel with a companion: "If you remark the scent of a bean-field crossing the road, perhaps your fellow-traveller has no smell. If you point to a distant object, perhaps he is short-sighted, and has to take out his glass to look at it." An incompatible traveling companion is, of course, a nuisance, but human beings are indeed strange animals. When there are too many of them, we frown at all of their bustling about, but when there is no one around, we feel bored. One tends to shrink from senseless jabbering, but one also wonders whether clamping one's mouth shut the whole time will not give one bad breath. On the road or in moments of silence, then, one somehow wishes to have someone for company. Only the spirits and animals can endure solitude, yet in our society, most of the people we meet are detestable in appearance and insipid in speech, and we do our best to avoid them. Out in the world of nature, on the other hand, one somehow feels that relationships between humans should be intimate. Some people who have traveled to the Rockies in the United States once told me that when they ran into other travelers in the mountains, everyone, regardless of age or sex, took off their hats as a rule to greet one other and exchange a few words. This is an interesting custom. It seems we only discover we are of the same species in the wilderness, for during ordinary times, we pay too much attention to the differences between us.

An ideal traveling companion is hard to find, and a good friend in the living room is not necessarily a good partner on the road. An ideal traveling companion should possess many qualities. For one thing, he should not be too dirty, like Ji Shuye, who often "left his hair and face unwashed fifteen days in a month," and "would not take a bath unless he could no longer stand the itch." Nor should he be so obsessed with cleanliness as to clean everything with alcohol. He should not be as wooden as a statue, or as unresponsive as a dead fish that cannot open its mouth. He should not jabber all day long, or snore throughout the night; but neither should he appear unctuous or clumsy. He should be able to engage in conversation or laughter, and be alternately active and quiet. When he is quiet, he should sit by you wordlessly to watch the clouds and listen to the evening rain. But when he is active, he should flop like a fish on the grass! Now, tell me, where is one to find such a traveling companion?

Zhu Xiang

Like Liang Yuchun and a few other essayists featured in this anthology, Zhu Xiang (1904–1933) led a short but remarkable life. Also like Liang, he comes under the heavy influence of English literature, having studied it first in China and then in the US. He is better known as a poet, having made his fame as a writer when he was still a student at Tsinghua University.

After he returned to China from the US, Zhu taught English literature at a number of universities. He was soon ostracized by people who found him aloof and conceited. In the end, driven by poverty, he jumped overboard from a ferry and drowned himself.

Zhu's poetic talent is evident in "Books." While the format is prose, the care with which the images are developed, especially in the beginning few paragraphs, reminds one of poetry.

Books (1934)

Pick up a book. Don't be in such a hurry to study its contents: Its appearance alone will offer much to admire.

The part of a book most soothing to the eyes is the yellow paper made from bamboo pulp. The color can lead us on flights of fancy as we contemplate how this book must have escaped the depredations of time. The fact that it has survived these trials and come to meet with us is a history that could fill a volume in itself. A book thus deserves our reflection and awe, quite apart from the truth and beauty one might find in its pages.

There are, moreover, those beautiful characters. The construction of each is a poem, and its evolution a book of history. The word "strong wind" is made up of three dogs and wind: Amidst the withered grass in the open autumn wilderness, when the sky above is blue and the ground below reddish-brown, hunting dogs dash by like the wind, sniffing and following the scent of blood left behind by the injured animal. They listen to the rustling of the grass, and run like a gust of autumn wind.

The word "evening" is the ancient character for "marriage." When the sun has set and it is no longer possible to see a person standing right in front of you, a throng of people comes riding on horseback. Grasping burning torches, they approach a house stealthily. They arrive at the bamboo fence and wooden gate; before the people inside have a chance to close the door, they barge in amidst the barking of dogs. On the threshing ground, the groom snatches up the bride, who lets out a scream of surprise. He turns back, while his companions ward off the bride's father and brothers. In marriage as much as in trade, there's no conclusion without contention.

There are many fonts in printing. The Song font is as upright as the calligraphy of Liu Gongquan, the Masha script is as nimble as that of Ouyang Xun, the calligraphy script is as elegant as Chu Suiliang's, and the standard script is as stately as that of Yan Zhenqing.[1] The standard script, which is the most common, can be further divided into several types: The most popular type is square in shape; another type is long, narrow, and angular; yet another short and flat, appearing so full as to invoke antiquity in one's mind. Of course, books can be handwritten

---

[1]   Liu Gongquan (778–865), Ouyang Xun (557–641), Chu Suiliang (596–659), Yan Zhenqing (709–785). The Masha script was traditionally used in books printed in Jianyang county in Fujian province.

too, and some of these use the standard font exclusively, while others use it only in part. They not only give the reader a sense of intimacy, ancient handwritten editions can sometimes even correct mistakes in our present-day printed copies and help us trace the evolution of a Chinese character.

If you have an ancient edition lying in front of you, you will see many red-colored seals at the front of the book. Some of these seals indicate a polite sobriquet, while others give you the formal name of the owner. From these names, you may discover that the previous owner of the book was a celebrity whose name was known far and wide. You can then allow your imagination to run free in this vermillion world, constructing castles in the air. You can also see the red circles used to punctuate the text. Some were dashed off with a flourish, while others were written with care and solemnity. You can deduce from their appearance and position in the book whether the previous reader was young or old, whether he was a genius with irrepressible flair or a scholar of decorum and composure. You can even speculate on his fate, and on how his book came to circulate in the world. Did his unworthy descendants dispose of the book? Did his disloyal servants raid his collection during wartime? Did a twist of fate cause a decline in the family's fortunes, such that he had to sell the book himself in order to pay off loans and support his family? If this is what befell him, then what about me—the present owner of the book? When he sat down facing his carved inkstone, a faint scent of incense in the air, and picked up his new brush to punctuate his favorite book, thoughts about the future of this book or his own fate could not have crossed his mind. In just the same way, as I read this book now, I cannot tell what my own fate will be.

Let us take this even further and try to imagine the fate of the writer. His sadness and disappointment merge naturally from the lines on the page, and as we read, we are prompted to cry and sigh with him. If, disaster of all disasters, his book should fall into the hands of a Qin Shi Huang or Dong Zhuo,[2] then this product of his blood and sweat would be burned to ashes. Or, like *Jin Ping Mei*, *Hong Lou Meng*, or *Shuihu Zhuan*,[3] it might court the displeasure of prudish people with shallow

---

[2]   Qin Shi Huang (259–210 BC) and Dong Zhuo (?–192 AD) were both capricious rulers who wielded dictatorial power.

[3]   All have been considered licentious books and were proscribed at various times throughout Chinese history.

views and be banned. What a pity that would be!

Life is full of disappointments. For the moment, let us put aside other things and focus on books. Nothing in the world can be as harmless as a book, but even then, there are times when it has to submit to the fate of its own destruction. It is self-evident that beautiful women, as fragile as glass, or fine scholars, as outstanding as white cranes, should arouse jealousy in others. Think of scholars whose ambitions are yet to be realized. When they are not appreciated, some work as woodcutters and some as cowherds. Not only are they regarded no differently from the most mediocre people, they also have to suffer contempt and insults from their kin or masters. Nonetheless, they are born with an indomitable character, and the more the world treats them with disdain, the more self-respecting they become. Some, as woodcutters, carry firewood on their backs so their hands will be free to hold a book. Some, as cowherds, ride on the back of a water buffalo, and prop up their books on its horns. Some read in the summer night when mosquitoes hum like thunder, and some read under the light of fireflies captured in a muslin bag. On winter nights so cold that fingers freeze in the wind, some read in the light reflected by the snow. Time, however, will not wait, and by the time they have become learned, their eyesight has gone dim and their hair has become white. Their knowledge has only added another long, deep wrinkle to their foreheads.

Well! While our eyes are still bright and our hair has not yet turned to frost, let us read more of this book of "life"!

Ba Jin

Ba Jin (1904–2005) is one of the most influential Chinese writers of the twentieth century. During his long life, Ba Jin was tireless in promoting the course of modern Chinese literature. Many of his works remain classics, including *Family*, probably the most well known of his novels. *Family* represents the strongest indictment of the traditional Chinese family structure and inspired many acts of family rebellion among its readers. At the late age of seventy-four, Ba Jin began a series of essays known *Random Thoughts* with pointed references to the social and political reality of China at the time, an act of courage for which he was highly respected.

Ba Jin was born to a gentry family in Sichuan, and was educated in Chengdu and Shanghai. Between 1927 and 1929, he studied in France, where he was exposed to various schools of Western thinking popular at the time, most notably anarchism. After his return to China, he maintained a close relationship with the Communist Party, even though he considered himself to be politically independent.

"Outside the Garden Ruins" bespeaks Ba Jin's anger toward the Japanese aggression against China. Yet, the language is far from incendiary. Rather, one detects a note of irony in his description of the lonely maiden whose life was terminated by the bombing while the flowers in the garden remain fresh and lush. Such is the cruelty of war, which crushes even the humblest wish of an ordinary woman.

Outside the Garden Ruins (1941)

After dinner, I went out for a walk and, without meaning to, once again arrived at that spot.

I looked into the garden through the gap in the wall. Inside, the garden was still alive and lush. In one corner, a cluster of red flowers was in bloom, and next to them was the bare frame of the destroyed building. The tiles of the roof had been blown away, but the green banister from the front of the building was still there, hanging on precariously.

I looked at the flowers blooming magnificently with their full petals and long green leaves. They must have been planted in front of a window that was no longer there. A week ago, I thought, someone inside this handsome house might have opened the little window to look at the garden, his eyes falling in admiration on this cluster of flowers. Just as likely, someone else might have spent the whole day leaning against the window to look at the plants and trees, his youthful yearnings projected onto the red flowers and green leaves.

But now, the window was no more, and the whole building was threatening to collapse. The garden had remained green throughout, however, and the flowers were blooming furiously. If they could have talked, they would have told me about the young and the middle-aged faces they had seen through the window inside the house. Oh yes, the young faces, but now they had disappeared forever, because... the flowers would then have told me something more. They would certainly have told me about the tragedy on the fourteenth of August, the day when this fine building was destroyed. On that day, in less than fifteen minutes, the whole garden had been reduced to rubble.

I looked at the garden; its green color was soothing to my eyes. Rubble, did I say? No, the garden had come back to life after the enemy bombing, and there were no signs of destruction among the robust plants. Just then, a woman's voice came to my ear. "That is the third daughter of the Chen family, just now dug out." I turned around, but no one was there. What I had heard had been spoken a few days before—in fact, on the day after the bombing.

I had walked by the garden that afternoon, too—not on this side, however, but behind the building, right by the air-raid shelter that was hit. There were three bodies covered with grass mats, but I forget whether they were laid on the ground here or up on the knoll. A small thin leg stuck out from under the mat in the middle. There was mud all over it, and if one did not look carefully, it would be impossible to say whether it was a human leg. People were still digging among the rubble. Standing on a mound of earth newly piled up, I looked from a distance through the gap in the wall and saw seven or eight people looking at the dead bodies. Stunned, their faces were filled with grief, for they must have known the victims. A middle-aged woman pointed at the body whose leg was exposed, and said, "That is the third daughter of the Chen family, just now dug out." Later, I found out from another person about the tragedy that had befallen the air-raid shelter.

A mud-covered leg. The life of a young woman. I did not know her, had never even set eyes on her face. Looking at the plants in the garden, however, I thought of the loneliness of youth captured in this garden, and my heart ached at the thought, almost as if I had been stabbed. In a quiet place like this, the air-warriors with their sun-emblazoned flags would not even permit a humble life to live. Two or three bombs had taken away the yearnings of this young woman. They had destroyed everything, even the nebulous hopes of her lonely life. Though now freed from her captivity, she would never see the wide world outside the garden.

The flowers shook their heads in the wind, as if sighing. They would never again see the familiar face in the window, and must have felt lonely and sad. The building separated them from the air-raid shelter, and thus they were spared the sight of the girl being suffocated to death, and that of her mud-covered leg. I, however, saw everything. How am I to tell the world about it?

Evening had fallen, and the garden gradually became invisible in the dusk. Darkness began to surround me, but I could still see the flowers shaking their heads. There was nobody around, and I was suddenly assailed by feelings of desolation. Why was it so quiet? Why did no one come to tell me angrily the tale of the young woman? Was I in a dream?

Something cold and wet fell on my cheek. I looked up and saw that it was raining. So, this was not a dream after all. I could not stay here in the rain forever. I had to go home, to the house which, damaged by the shock of the shelling, was now leaking all over.

Ye Lingfeng

Ye Lingfeng (1905–1975) was educated at Shanghai Arts Institute. He was an active member of the Creation Society, and is well known for creating characters with great psychological depth.

He moved to Hong Kong in 1938. He developed such an interest in his adopted home that he spent the latter half of his life researching and writing about the history of the city.

"The Weary Sound of the Fiddle" describes a vignette of the city from the point of view of the homesick writer, who is led to ponder the irrevocable passage of time by the plaintive music coming from an aging musician on the street.

The Weary Sound of the Fiddle (1932)

Day after day, she passed by below the building where I lived.

Day after day, I watched her from above as she passed by below the building where I lived.

The silent evening. The pallid streetlamps. The coolness of the new autumn air circulating around the dark shadows of the trees.

In the coolness of the new autumn evening, awakening thoughts of home, the plaintive sound of her three-stringed fiddle drifted aimlessly in the quiet, lonely air like a bird without a nest to fly back to at the end of the day.

There were no other instruments or singing to accompany the fiddle. It wasn't, at any rate, a sustained grand performance, but only fragmented chords casually strummed on a string. But from these fragmented phrases, there seemed to emerge all on its own a boundless sorrow.

A grayish white coat and a pair of dark colored pants. Her hair and face formed an indistinguishable, blurry patch. With the streetlamps behind her, she cast a heavy shadow through the gaps in the trees. She disappeared around the corner, seemingly not on her feet, but slowly gliding away like a spirit.

Her silhouette disappeared around the corner in darkness, but the fragmented sound of the fiddle remained in the quiet, lonely evening air.

Twenty or thirty years ago, the same woman now roaming the street today was perhaps a woman at the height of her beauty, enchanting one and all. But ruthless time, heeding the turning of the wheel of life, had whittled away unsparingly at this masterpiece of creation. Time flies inexorably, just as water flows to the east.[1] The sound of the fiddle might be the same as before, but the hand that strummed the string was definitely not the slender youthful hand of the past.

Leaning against the quiet balcony in the evening, I stared at her shadow slowly moving amidst the chaotic sound of the fiddle. A wave of pity for the swift passage of time swept over me.

Day after day, she passed by like this below the building where I lived.

---

[1] All major rivers in China have their sources in the northwest part of the country and empty into the sea on the east coast. The eastward flow of rivers has thus traditionally been used as a metaphor for the irrevocable course of events.

Day after day, I watched her like this as she passed by below the building where I lived.

After several days up on this balcony in the autumn rain, my longing for home increased. I got up from my short nap, and looked out to the street in the evening rain. The lamps were lit as before, but in the humid air, the sound of her fiddle was absent.

The first night after the rain cleared, a few fallen leaves, blown down by the autumn wind but wet with rain, were still stuck to the steps and had not flown off yet. After the streetlamps came on one by one, I leaned against the window forlornly. I knew that tonight, under the shadows of the trees, I would be united again with the sound of the fiddle that I had missed for a few days.

The darkness under the trees deepened, and the water puddles on the street reflected the autumn stars in the sky. But after the sound of traffic had died down under the pallid light of the streetlamps, I still did not see that heavy shadow pass by.

The second night after the rain cleared, the sound of the fiddle was still absent.

There were more and more fallen leaves in the autumn wind. I leaned against the balcony in the evening and faced the new chill in the air. Besides thoughts of home, there was now another nameless yearning inside me.

The autumn wind was growing all the more violent. Outside the window, the two trees had exposed their bare trunks in several places. Beneath the evening streetlamps, there was only the rustling sound of leaves fluttering down. The sound of her fiddle was heard no more.

Autumn was growing old. The weary sound of the fiddle had most likely passed away with the weary autumn, I sighed.

Day after day, I still leaned against my balcony.

And day after day, I never saw her pass by the building where I lived.

Li Guangtian

Li Guangtian (1906–1968) began his writing career as a poet, publishing *Hanyuan ji* with He Qifang and Bian Zhilin, but later came to be known mostly as a highly original prose writer. He was educated in the foreign language department of Peking University, where he also studied French on his own and Japanese with Zhou Zuoren. During the war years, he taught in various secondary schools and universities, while continuing to write prolifically. After 1949, he assumed leadership positions in different official writer associations, but his literary output gradually declined in quantity until he died under persecution during the Cultural Revolution.

Li's early works, two of which are presented in the following pages, demonstrate what He Qifang (also featured in this anthology) describes as the characteristics of Li's essays, namely, they embody the "perfect seamlessness of poetry and the plotted meticulousness of novels." Both "Mountains and Water" and "Two Thoughts" have a plot-like quality reminiscent of novels but the language that is used in the unfolding of the plot is so fluid that one is reminded of poetry. The two essays are filled with nostalgia for his childhood in his rural hometown when life was presumably simpler if not better. The latter, moreover, is ridden with anxiety with life in the city, underscoring yet another characteristic of Li's work.

Mountains and Water (1936)

Sir, I have read all of your essays on mountains and water and think they are superb. However, I haven't been able to suppress a rather peculiar thought, namely that I don't think I will read any more of your writing. I suspect that your writing is all something of an exaggeration, and that kind of exaggeration can bring sorrow to children growing up on the plains. Why, I wonder, do you always come up with such beautiful descriptions of mountains and water? Has it never occurred to you that those lovely mountains and water may have a not-so-lovely side to them? Let me, a son of the plains, tell you something from my heart about them.

Unlike the expansive, unobstructed plains, mountainous areas, with all their rough and craggy terrain, make traveling difficult. It is not easy for people living there to see the sky, or the sun rising from its edge, or meteors vanishing beneath its horizon because their view is blocked by the mountains. To behold in a glance the sights of a thousand miles is a privilege with which only people living on the plains are blessed. People like you like to write about sailboats and bridges, waves and the surging sound they make, but as a man of the plains, I think they are less appealing by far than fields of rice and wheat in the autumn wind or horses sauntering on an abandoned road. And the rumblings of wagon wheels are perhaps something that you people of the mountains can never hear. Besides... there are many other reasons besides, but since I am inept with my pen, I don't think I can put them into words. Oh, how stupid I have been! I started out with the thought of playing a joke on you, but the joke is on me. At first, I thought I would tell you about the sorrows of the people of the plains, but reading your pieces about mountains and water has led me to think of my hometown, where I spent a dozen years of my life. I cannot forget the sadness of those plains.

Naturally, on that plain of ours, there are neither mountains nor water. Yet, how we descendants of that place cherish even a puddle of water or a rock the size of a fist! Of course, there are springs that serve as wells, but people have to go down twenty or thirty yards before, with the help of a well-sweep, they can obtain the clear water they need. We treasure water in the same way we treasure money. Children long for rain, and a few drops of rain from an overcast sky are enough nourishment for their souls. On days when it pours in torrents, they are mad with joy, just as one might expect. They swim in pools of water that are only knee-deep, and float their grass toy-boats in ditches. They imagine rivers from tracks of water left behind by cart wheels, and oceans from rivulets not much wider. Wherever water collects becomes a place to play all kinds of games. Even if their parents scold them, they still feel drawn to water. They ask fish vendors from distant lakes and rivers about scenes of water, and fruit vendors from the mountains about what is produced there. If someone from the mountains brings them a small smooth pebble, it becomes virtually the most prized thing among them. They pay a high price for it, when the pebble moves from the pocket of one child to that of the next. They speculate on the origin of the pebble, saying that it was acquired from such and such a lofty mountain, and nurtured in such and such a valley, where it was washed by mountain springs for thousands and thousands of years. This is why it is so smooth, so round, and so lovely.

People who have been to far-away places come back to report, in wonder, "I have seen the mountains! Indeed, I have! They are full of rocks, nothing but rocks." Whereupon their listeners, based on what they have heard, conjure up mountain ranges in their dreams. Looking up at the fabulous clouds in the sky, they point them out to the children and say, "Look! Look! Now, *that's* what the mountains look like!" And the children look at the changing clouds, quite lost in amazement. Indeed, children of the plains are full of fantastic thoughts about distant mountains and waters, and their solitude is as boundless as the plains. Sir, when will you come to this plain of ours and take a look for yourself at the trees, villages, and endless stretch of wilderness—and, what is more, the great number of graves, the eternal resting places of our ancestors? The wind on the plains blows from horizon to horizon, and one can only sigh in awe.

Our ancestors who arrived at this plain and built the first village here already understood this solitude all too well. They planted trees and grew vegetables and various kinds of flowers and grain on this land. Generation after generation, they tried every way they could to enhance the beauty of this place. The plain was then covered with trees and flowers and grass, vegetables and grains, houses and graves, but the solitude that they felt remained. People here often thought about the climate in faraway places and events of the distant past. That might have just been dreaming, but it was also a kind of remembrance, for they seemed to have seen beautiful places in their former lives. They thought to themselves: Why is this place so flat? Why isn't there some variation? And thus they thought of bringing about changes to their land with their mortal hands.

You may think that this plain of ours must be vast. Not so, there is a small river three hundred *li*[1] to the south, and a big one three hundred *li* to the north. The sea on the east and the mountains on the west are likewise about three or four hundred *li* from the village. That is the entire area of our plain. It is really not that big, but to our ancestors who lived in the center of it, it was so vast as to seem limitless. For them, life here was akin to that of a child abandoned on a desolate island. The thought of transforming their land with their own hands prompted them to embark on a noble project. They worked when they were not busy with farming, every man on the plain becoming an engineer. With the help of chisels, spades, knives, shovels, and anything else that could be used to remove earth from the ground, they dug up a large watercourse around the very first village they built. They connected one end of it with the small river to the south and the other end with the big river to the north. Our ancestors did not leave behind any records, and hence we are unable to estimate how long this project took. But in the minds of the people of the plain, there are specific numbers: Some say it took thirty years to finish, some say forty, some even say fifty. From that time on, our ancestors were able to fish, swim, and walk on wooden bridges. From their boats, they could look at the clouds and see smoke rising from the city gate.

There is another thing you should know: In those days, our ancestors were all very hardworking, with men tending the fields and women rearing silkworms and weaving. This is how they managed to live their days in warmth, plentitude, and safety. They even had leisure for other things, especially the leisure to contemplate what was lacking in their emotional lives. They had brought the water closer now—although it was not as beautiful as the rivers you describe in your writings, it was flowing water nevertheless—but they still found their achievement far from complete, and wanted to create a lofty mountain on the plain.

Now that there was a river flowing by the east side of the village, our ancestors decided to begin their second project on the west side. With carts of various sizes, shoulder poles, baskets, burlap sacks, shirts, and anything else that could be used to carry dirt, they moved earth

---

[1]   *Li*, a measurement of length, about one-third of a mile.

from north and south of the village to the west. They applied themselves to the work with the same diligence with which they had opened the river before, digging deep and wide and transporting all the earth to the west of the village. Then they directed water from the river into the two ponds newly formed to the south and north of the village. These they called the South Sea and the North Sea. And thus, as if by itself, a hill of twenty or thirty yards high rose up to the west of the village. However, it was made entirely of earth, so they went farther to the west to take rocks from the mountains there, and to the south to bring back trees from the southern mountains as well. Thus was the mound of earth that they had constructed adorned with elegant ranges and luxuriant forests. As the days went by, the trees became so abundant that they provided an inexhaustible supply of timber and firewood. Rare birds and other animals also stopped at the hill for rest and shelter. When they had a free moment from their work in the fields, our ancestors would climb up the hill with their old and young, bringing with them food and drink. In the South Sea and the North Sea, fish and turtles proliferated and various kinds of water plants multiplied. At night, one could see the lights of fishing boats, and during the day, one could hear the songs of the lotus-gatherers. My dear sir, you see what a good life our ancestors led!

Ah, it brings me sorrow just to talk about it. Although I did not mean to exaggerate things as you have done in your writings—indeed, any descendant of the plain would regard what I have told you as truth and would be happy to have the glories of those days related—I have ended up lying to you nonetheless. For this is a page from our history—or perhaps it is just a legend, but this legend is forever engraved in the memory of those of us who are the sons of the plains.

I left that plain long ago, but have skirted it in my travels on many occasions. Time has made an old man of this traveler, but I still believe that the plain has remained the way it was in the past, expansive and unobstructed, still so simple and ordinary. There are, as in the past, villages, trees, fields of grain and vegetables, travelers on abandoned roads, galloping saddled horses. You may ask: Isn't there anything left of your ancestors' projects? Aren't there any traces of the hills and the rivers from long ago? Of course there are; otherwise, how could those stories about the hills and the rivers have been passed on to us, and how else would anyone believe in them? I am reminded of the time when, as a small child, I followed my grandfather to the west side of the village, the first settlement that ever came into existence on the plain. As if in a dream, my grandfather pointed at the tip of a black rock buried deep in the earth and said, "This is the hilltop of our ancestors." We then went to the south and north of the village and found two long and narrow places that were slightly lower than the surrounding earth. He pointed them out to me and said, "They are our ancestors' seas." As you might expect, on the east side of the village, there was also a place that was relatively lower. That naturally was our ancestors' river. I grew up on that plain, and spent my childhood there. On the basis of a rock and several depressions in the ground, I dreamed about the tall mountains, long rivers, and large seas in distant lands.

Two Thoughts (1941)

Last night, it rained the whole night through. Although the rain was not heavy, the pitter-pattering kept me awake. In the past, or I should say in the distant past, I liked to listen to the rain at night while sleeping by myself in the school dormitory. The sound used to refresh me, transporting me to thoughts of many beautiful things. Everything is different now. These days, I find the sound of the rain at night noisy and annoying, especially when Zhao leaves the wooden and enamel basins lined up under the eaves before going to bed. This way, she says, we can collect enough water in one night for the laundry and cooking the following day, and we can save money on water. (The price of rice has gone up recently, and so has that of water.) Great, so now on top of drip-dropping, we have dibble-dibble-dop the whole night! How is a person to fall sleep?

As I listened to the rain last night, scattered thoughts arose in my mind. At times I would fall asleep and then have strange dreams. When I awoke—who knows whether I was truly awake or not?—my imagination would begin to wander. No, it was not just my imagination; rather, illusions began to appear before my eyes. I dreamed that I was walking on a very slippery road covered with stone slabs, which seemed to lead up to a high mountain. The road was very steep and narrow— so narrow that there was only enough room to put one foot down. On both sides of the road was a deep pool. The water was very clear, but the bottom was not visible. One could only see waves crashing upon each other. Was this a dream? No, I was revisiting a familiar place. I had often been here in my dreams, and had often climbed up this steep road, just like the difficult and dangerous road we have to travel in our waking life.

Then I dreamed that I was walking in the open field in my home village. I saw my father working among the thick rice seedlings. Oh yes, he was always working in the fields. But I did not call out to him. When I woke up, I could not help wondering why I had not called out to him. Don't I always want to call out for him? Thousands of miles away from home, in cities, in villages, on wide streets or country roads, whenever I see an old farmer with a dark face and kind eyes, wearing clothes of faded blue.... I am startled: Isn't that man Father? Has he fled from some calamity at home? Has he come to look for his son? Let me catch up with him, call out to him, hug him! But by then, he has already gone away. Why, then, hadn't I called out to him in my dream? Perhaps I was afraid he would ask, "Didn't you say you would send me some money to fix up the run-down house back home?" "Yes," I would say, "I did promise you that, and it is wrong of me not to have lived up to my word. But you can't really blame me. Then again, I know you would never reproach me like that, because you are too kind. As for the house, I know how broken down it is. I have seen it in my dreams—holes in the walls, wood chips falling from the eaves, and wild grass growing on the rooftop.... I know that there have been too many storms in the past few years."

Stranger still, I saw—not dreamed—a baby. This baby had not smiled for a long time. Perhaps he was dying.... But then, all of a sudden, the glimmer of a smile appeared on his face. There clearly was a brilliant world in that smile, and it lit up everyone's heart. Unfortunately, very soon after that, his smile fell under a shadow, and I said to myself, this is our country, this is China. Half-asleep and half-awake, I murmured a few lines, all incomprehensible and bewildering. They lingered on my lips—no, in my heart—over and over, as if they would drone on forever. They seemed to go like this:

> There is warmth in the coldest place,
> There is cold in the warmest place.
> In ice and snow, one can find growth
> And the place near the sun is most desolate.

What does this all mean? Even I cannot say.

What else did I see in my dreams? What else did I think about? Let me see.... Oh, yes, I remember.... There seemed to be a lot of things that I missed in my dreams, things that passed by me, or came so close that they touched my fingertips, but then slipped away, like a fish that escaped the grip of a fisherman by swimming through his fingers. We tell ourselves to "hold on to" things, but hold on to what? A fistful of sand? A handful of water?

When I awoke in the morning, it was still drizzling and I felt melancholy. I always long for a sunny world after a night of rain. It doesn't matter how dark, cold, or wet it is at night or how strong the wind is, as long as you can see the sun and the blue sky when you open your eyes in the morning, how wonderful it is! But what appeared in front of my eyes now was still the same dreary rain. Then my wife, Zhao, also my supervisor, was here again to remind me of my duties.

She whispered into my ear, "Go and buy three *jiao* worth of bean paste, three turnips, one *jiao* worth of garlic sprouts...." She was keeping her voice down for fear of waking Xiao Xiu, but I wanted to scream and wake up the whole world.

Of course, I had to go get food for the day. As I stepped out of the house, a gust of chilling wind sprinkled water all over me. Sure enough, the basins were full of water. The Yong Ning River must be like an ocean now, I thought to myself. I walked into the kitchen. Oh, no! The roof was really leaking badly, and the rice and flour were all a mess. It's so true what they say about having to be prepared for rainy days as long as you live. Zhao has always been a very meticulous person, but this time, even she had been careless. I felt as if even my heart was soaked through and through. What can you do?

When I came back from the market, I found Zhao cleaning up the wet rice and flour. What else could one do? Nothing, as far as I could see, but she is always so patient, and knows exactly what to do in situations like this. She even smiled and said, "When I was in college, it rained one day when I was out. The wind blew open the window, and the whole place was covered with rain. My books were all damaged, so you know what I did? When the sun came out, I aired them, page by page, page by page...." But rice and flour are not the same as books. With rice, you can still separate it grain by grain, but surely you cannot dry it that way. Flour is even more aggravating. If the weather does not improve, it will get moldy and rot away. Oh well, let's just pretend that we ate it.... But look at you, Zhao, you're really something—you even filled up the big wooden basin with laundry.

After this, I had time to myself, and needed to begin my day's work. I sat down by the window and refused to pay any more attention to that morose sky. I quickly opened a finely printed book. A stream of light, like a streak of sunlight, flashed across the page. On it was printed the following passage:

> There are two contradictory thoughts that have for a long time come into conflict in the human mind—to be better or to live better. In our present muddled and chaotic world, it is impossible to reconcile the two.

Liang Yuchun

Liang Yuchun (1906–1932) is a precocious and prolific writer. He began to introduce foreign literature to Chinese readers when he was still a student in Peking University. He later turned to writing essays, which show clear signs of influences from the English familiar essay. In his short life of twenty-six years, he established himself as an original stylist, leaving behind two volumes of essays and over twenty volumes of translation.

Liang has been described as holding a "cynical" view of life, but clear-eyed may be a more appropriate phrase—he is able to detect contradictions even in the most mundane situations. The way that he questions the meaning of tears and laughter is but one example. His essays do not contain overwrought emotions. Instead, he apprehends what life has to offer in a leisurely and a somewhat ironic manner. In this light, "On the Road" may well be an apt metaphor for his literary endeavors. Life is a journey, full of sights and happenings waiting for a detached writer to observe with his keen eyes.

Tears and Laughter (1929)

More than twenty years have gone by in a flash. Like other people, I naturally often laugh and cry, and I have seen other people laugh and cry numerous times. I have always managed well at the sight of tears, be they emotional tears of my own, or the choking tears of others, but there are several kinds of laughter that strike fear in my heart, to the point that I do not even dare breathe too loudly when I witness them. Some of these peculiar kinds of laughter have actually come from my own mouth. When a most intimate friend utters heartless words as cold as ice, and what is worse, does not seem to realize that his words have sent a chill to his listener's heart, one can only burst out into some meaningless ha... ha... ha. Under the circumstances, what else can one do but laugh? This kind of forced laughter may come from realizing the contradiction between his true character, as revealed in his unfeeling words, and what we used to think his character to be. Or, we laugh in order to show that we are not shocked by what he says, and that we have a life that transcends everything and his words cannot hurt us in the least. Or....

The fact is, though, that at that moment, we laugh only because we feel that it would not do *not* to laugh, and do not have the time to carefully analyze ourselves. When our hearts are in the grips of inexpressible pain and we are looking for someone to talk to, a person whom we respect at other times may dismiss our heart-piercing sadness with the most frivolous (or even the most despicable) explanation. Confronted with such a deep gulf between them and us, what else can we do but lamely turn from tears to laughter?

There are times when, as luck would have it, there is not a single thing from morning to night that we do not botch up. By evening, we are tired and full of exasperation at ourselves, and neither regret nor weeping brings any relief. We can only swallow our tears and laugh a vacant laugh.

We keep ourselves busy our whole lives, frittering away our irretrievable time in traveling and pointless socializing. We scheme the whole day long, but do not know what for. We do everything possible to prolong our lives, but do not see what is so good about living, and have never actually enjoyed our lives. In short, it is like living in darkness. When we reflect upon this in the quiet of the night, how can we not chuckle at ourselves and as we do, come to feel the boundless sorrow of our lives? Even assuming that we are indifferent to life and death, our exasperation at this world and our loathing of human affairs still wriggle their way in like a poisonous snake, wrapping themselves around us, and we can truly say that we are tired of everything. It is a pity that we are not in love with the god of the dead, and thus do not find it worth expending any great effort to seek death. In this limbo of not living and not dying, we see waves of sorrow assailing us.

Occasionally, we might put up a fight and let out a sigh, and after sighing, there's nothing to do but break into laughter. But what bitter laughter! It comes from our own mouths, but when it reaches our ears, it gives rise to an inexpressible fear in our hearts, perhaps even bringing forth a ghost-like sneer. The bitter laughter may come from other people, and as soon as we find out its source, our hearts empathize as sorrow sweeps over us. At the same time, however, we may tremble all over in fear. The idiotic laugh of the disappointed, the fawning laugh to the master of servants who have been scolded, the icy laugh of arrogant officials to their old but now destitute friends, the hollow laugh of old maids at other people's wedding feasts, the bitter laugh of people facing separation in life as well as in death—all come to us when "nature" is being difficult with us. Left with no other choice, we admit defeat by laughing. It is the white flag of surrender, painful to our eyes, that flies at the foot of the castle of our soul. Shakespeare's admirable line, "smiling at grief," articulates to the fullest the tribulations therein, as do the two lines from Byron's masterpiece *Don Juan*:

> Of all tales 'tis the saddest—and more sad,
> Because it makes us smile.

I like to recite these two lines again and again when I am down and listless, because they can in truth convey the tragic sense of "laughter."

Tears, on the other hand, are an expression of our faith in life. Because life is to be cherished, and because the past is like a spring gone by, we shed the clear tears of mourning. If life itself is not worthy of a glance, then whence would come our feelings of regret? When a middle-aged woman loses her husband, she howls in grief at the thought that her son should lose his father so early in life, and that no one will guide him in the years to come. She cannot help but cry her eyes out, but her heart harbors vaguely boundless love and hope for her son. But if her son dies, too, this time she may go through the funeral arrangements without a word, or burst into uncontrollable laughter because she has grown weary of life and her feeble heart has gone numb.

Whenever I see people cry, whether from the pain of falling out of love or the sadness of losing loved ones, I always feel that this world is worth living in. Tears are the ambrosia of life. When I was a small child, I often felt an inexpressible sadness, and would fabricate unhappy events in my mind. When I was totally overtaken by these thoughts, tears would sometimes come before I knew it, and I would feel indescribably happy. These rootless tears don't come to me anymore, even if I look for them.

Is there anyone among those of us with hearts who does not like watching tragedies? Aristotle was certainly right about catharsis. The spiritual pain that sits entangled in our hearts is given a chance to untie itself as we follow a tragic plot unfolding on stage. After we cry, we feel relieved beyond words, as if our spirits had taken a breath of fresh air, and our souls suddenly display signs of extraordinary health.

People say that there are tears amid the laughter in Gogol's works; in fact, it is precisely because there are invisible tears that his novels can be so hilarious and exhibit a joy encompassing all aspects of life that lingers even after we put the book down. Chinese poetry is never very moving when it comes to descriptions of delight and pleasure, but it is particularly poignant on the subjects of sorrow and regret, because those rueful lines are crystals formed of tears, which at times can provoke us to shed tears of sympathy. This is why the dethroned Li Yu and the sentimental Li Yishan remain our favorite writers.

There is no one who loves crying more than passionate maidens and young men struggling in the sea of love, but their lives are energetic and colorful, and they do not live in vain. By the time a person gets old, his zest for life has gradually come to naught, and the well of his tears has run dry. All that is left of him is a state of mind approaching death that does not care one way or the other, and the seemingly compassionate smile that comes in truth from a feeling of utter fatigue with life—the kind of smile I fear. The Romantic poet Thomas Gray of the eighteenth century wrote in "Ode on a Distant Prospect of Eton College":

> The tear forgot as soon as shed,
> The sunshine of the breast.

Only young people can shed tears of passion such as these, for they disappear with the dreams of youth. When our tears dry, we become indifferent. As Su Dongpo once wrote, "Used to the sights of life and death, I have no tears at all." The shadow of the grave has come to taint our declining years.

On the Road (1929)

Today was an exhilarating autumn day, with a slight drizzle. I was sitting in a tram, and noticed along the way that almost all of the clerks in the shops on both sides of the road were listlessly chatting, reading newspapers, or drinking tea—above all, drinking tea, because it was indeed growing rather chilly outside. Others were leaning on the counter, watching the sky. All in all, a leisurely air had suddenly come to permeate this bustling center of commerce, and the shops in those tall buildings each seemed to have been transformed into a recluse's retreat. Even the shop clerks, who at ordinary times would be busy putting on smiles for the customers and making money for their employers, had been given a chance to savor a few leisurely moments in their lives. They were all going about their business at their own unhurried pace, as if they were cultured hermits of the past. On the street, there were also only a few pedestrians. Even the foreigners on their way to work were smoking pipes on the trams, aimlessly looking at the advertisements in the newspapers. They had none of their usual haughtiness, thanks probably to the raincoats they were wearing. I arrived at the north station, where I changed to the bus to the western suburbs.

There is something unique about fields in the autumn rain. The drizzle made it impossible to see anything outside, and all one could see were the raindrops falling continuously on the window and the tiny dimples they left scattered on the surface of the river. Water droplets as fine as powder also seeped in through the broken glass and clung to my face. Although I was shivering slightly, this baptism by rain had made me all the more clearheaded. Having stepped into the net of world affairs and lived a life of mindless tedium, it was unusual for me to feel so alert and refreshed. I looked at the scenery outside again. There was nothing quite like the splendor of spring to impress one with its transience, or the desolation of winter to suggest the world's impending end. Today, though, there was only quiet layer upon layer of mist and rain, which concealed as much as they revealed, making the whole world all the more beautiful. I could not help murmuring the lines of Jiang Baishi, an earlier poet of my hometown, "How rarely is one blessed with the sight of rain before autumn!"[1]

---

[1]   Jiang Baishi, 1155–1221 AD.

Suddenly, I thought of what she[2] had said this morning with a frown: "Such dismal wind and bitter rain and you still have to travel such a distance! How dreadful!" I smiled secretly. How could she have known that at this very instant, I would be leaning against the window, admiring the view along the way? Perhaps she was thinking I must be all frowns, like a prisoner on his way to the execution ground. She would never have thought that I would be lingering over this autumn scene, with its leaves not yet wilted but its grass already brown. Sympathy is hard to come by, and, misplaced though it may be, I don't turn it down. That is why I allowed her to feel sorry for the time I spent on the road. Besides, whenever things go against me and I cannot keep misery from showing on my face, I can then hide behind my supposed hardship on the road and stop her from enquiring any further. This way, I don't have to tell her the truth, and cause her unnecessary worry.

As a matter of fact, I like people who roam about in this world of red dust most of all. These days, I have to spend over two hours or so a day on the road and, though this has already gone on for a few months, I am not a bit bored by it. I get on the tram every day, and it feels like the beginning of a honeymoon trip. For the most part, people traveling on trams and on the road do not know each other, which is why they don't need to put on any sort of veneer toward each other, unlike people who have to keep up appearances in a lecture hall, at a party, or in an office. At a park, cinema, amusement park, or restaurant, customers tend to be all smiles, or at least they have to put up such a front; in a graveyard, court, hospital, or pharmacy, they are all frowns, their faces engulfed in wrinkles. In both cases, things are simply too monotonous, and one feels the mediocrity and blandness of our world.

People on the tram or on the road, however, come in all hues and types. All you need to do is keep your eyes open and observe continuously for thirty minutes on the tram, and you will see every shade of happiness and sorrow and every other sentiment in life on people's faces. There you are, sitting quietly in your own seat, and your fellow passengers allow you without reservation to speculate from their appearance and behavior about their life stories and present state of mind. Pedestrians outside the tram will come into your view one by one, and you can scrutinize them to your heart's content and compare them without their ever knowing as they go by you like water in a stream.

---

[2]   Mostly likely the author's wife.

Such a procession of ordinary people is certainly much more interesting than any parade; indeed, it is virtually a parade designed by God, and as such is of course superior to those colorful playthings we come up with for our festivals.

One's mind is most receptive to silent viewing when one is on the road and it is most able to pick up stimuli from the world outside. Ordinarily, we tend to have things to do, be they good or wicked, and our attention naturally is focused on one particular thing. When we are traveling, however, especially over a long route with which we are familiar, we can be in a leisurely state of mind before we arrive at our destination. We are not focused on any particular thing, yet there is not a single thing that we miss. Amidst the haste of our daily lives, it is only in such a situation that we can take a good look at the real face of life. That is why, from whatever angle, the best place to understand this life of ours is on the road, and traveling in a car, on a boat, and on a sidewalk can be considered three tickets to the exhibition of life. It's a pity that so many people take them as merely three pieces of wastepaper, and travel down the road of life in vain.

We have an ancient saying, "Read ten thousand books; travel ten thousand *li*." To "travel ten thousand *li*" naturally refers to visiting all the famous mountains and rivers and major cities, but I think we can interpret it in a different way: You can travel back and forth on the same route thousands of times until you have covered ten thousand *li*. As long as you really use your eyes, then you qualify as someone who has gained an understanding of life. A common saying has it that "A true scholar needn't leave his front door, yet knows everything there is to know in the world." Since we are not fortunate enough to qualify as true scholars, the only way for us is to put our feet to the road and see more of the world.

As soon as we can reflect lucidly on life, our inner tranquility will not be disturbed by worldly honor or disgrace, misfortunes or blessings, and our souls will thus gain eternal freedom. It can be seen, therefore, that all roads, and not only the few decreed by Mr. Russell, lead to freedom. Worst of all are people who, like devout Buddhists, choose to meditate on life with their faces turned to the wall, ignoring the possibilities awaiting them on the road. They willingly opt for their own wrongheaded ways, and refuse to set out. There is really nothing to be done about them. Study is but an indirect way of understanding life; traveling is the direct way. As soon as language gets in the way, the truth disappears. That is why I think that one can set aside the ten thousand volumes one is supposed to read, but there is no doing without the ten thousand *li* one has to traverse.

If one wishes to understand nature, there is simply no avoiding a trip on the road. But I find that those who travel with an objective are not as close to nature as those who find themselves routinely on the road. People who are on a trip think only of their destination; their spirits are tense, and they lack the relaxed state needed to accept nature's beauty. The scenery of the world is fluid and alive, not confined to one particular valley, river, cave, or rock. Yet people on trips for the most part go to see the same famous but artificially designated scenes and, without knowing the reason, follow the custom of singing the praises of these well-known sites. With few exceptions, most travelers become slaves to an unchanging tradition.

Why subject oneself to this? It is only by facing beautiful scenes one has discovered by oneself that one can experience a heartfelt intimacy and find one's whole soul moved. One runs into such scenes mostly by chance, and there is no way to will them by force. It is for this reason that the images of farming cottages one happens to glimpse while traveling by train on business can leave a deep impression on one's mind, whereas the famous sites we come to admire by spending money and taking sick leave only float in the sea of memory like mist and fog.

I went to Hangzhou twice this year, once in spring and once in fall. When I was not sitting in a boat heeding the commands of the boatman, I was on my way up the hills respectfully following orders from the rickshaw puller. My thin travel guidebook also seemed to possess indisputable authority. By the time I had checked out each and every one of the so-called famous sites and returned to my train, I felt as if a burden had been lifted from my back. When I later resumed my normal mechanical life—freely looking here and there every day and never having to endure the reproaches of boatmen, rickshaw pullers, or traveling companions, or rush to see sights that should not be missed—I was almost crazy with happiness. The scenery of Xi Ling in Hangzhou of course gradually faded from memory until nothing was left. The pity is that it faded away too slowly, and for a while, provided the setting for quite a few nightmares. In my dreams, I saw those selfless rickshaw men pulling me up Baoshi Hill over the rough and uneven terrain, or to Dragon Well over roads made of rocks so slippery that one could hardly get a footing. No matter how much I begged to be excused, they would still force me to go look at the mist in the Misty Cave and the dragon antlers at the Dragon Well. Thank goodness, West Lake no longer appears in my dreams!

The most enjoyable sights on which I have set eyes in my whole life are to be found beyond the window on the bus to the western suburbs. Sitting in the bus, I let it jostle me about as it jumps up and down and turns left and right, while I try to finish one of those eighteenth-century novels that never seems to end. At times, I shut the book and allow my eyes to wander to the weather outside. All of a sudden, I am greeted by a stretch of green, with fragrant flowers covering the ground. The sky is blue beyond description. All at once, I have a feeling that spring has returned to the world, and my soul has taken flight to the distant sky above. I take a closer look, but the beautiful scenery is now gone. All that is left are the filthy streets of Zhabei. Tomorrow I will come to this spot again, and, although everything will be the same, somehow something will seem to be missing and thus it will be different from today. And so the scenery of this day will remain forever in my mind.

Even the most wondrous sight becomes tiresome if we look at it for too long. The truly wonderful scenery should be just like that—here for a blink of an eye and then gone forever. (The major shortcoming of marriage lies precisely in that it forces a couple to be together day and night. All of each person's good points are thus turned into bad points because they become so familiar.) In both scorching summer and snowy winter, moreover, I also often run unexpectedly into indescribably wonderful scenes that nurture my soul. Opportunities like that are always just around the bend. Just as Lu Fangweng said, "Where can one find a balcony not graced by the presence of the moon?"[3] As long as you cultivate a sensitive mind, traveling really can provide a shortcut to understanding nature.

Traveling not only gives us a lucid understanding of life and nature, it is a poetic undertaking in itself, and nothing could be more romantic. The fluttering of snow and rain and languid waving of willow branches—these are scenes only travelers can enjoy. Many adventures have come to pass solely because of the wanderings of a few individuals. *The Journey to the West*, *The Flowers in the Mirror*, Cervantes's *Don Quixote*, Swift's *Gulliver's Travels*, Bunyan's *Pilgrim's Progress*, William Cowper's *John Gilpin*, Dickens's *Pickwick Papers*, Byron's *Childe Harold's Pilgrimage*,

---

3   Lu You (1125–1210), "Pai men" (To Dispel Boredom).

Fielding's *Joseph Andrews*, Gogol's *Dead Souls*, and other incomparable masterpieces all have travel as the skeleton of their stories about life on the road. I think that next to love, "travel" is the most romantic theme in literature. Lu Fangweng is a poet with a free spirit, whose most distinguished works are his seven-character poems about traveling. I have chosen two of his poems at random as illustrations of the romance of traveling.

"Running into Light Rain on the Road to Sword Gate Pass"

On my clothes the dust of travel mingled with wine stains.
On a distant journey—no place that doesn't jar the soul!
And I—I am really meant to be a poet?
In fine rain straddling a donkey I enter Sword Gate Pass.[4]

"Meeting Pelting Rain at Nanding Tower"

In my travels, I covered all of Liangzhou and am now moving on to
    Yizhou,
Once again, I am crossing the Lu River this year.
Rivers and mountains clamor to present themselves to my eyes,
Wind and rain, pelting this way and that, find their way into the tower.
Running into people of the Dong and Liao tribes—their language strange
    to me,
The song of the boatman lingers on as I head toward Wuzhou.
I have long been used to a life on the road—home I seldom think of,
But here up on the tower, I look around, lost, as a wave of sorrow assaults
    me.

Since traveling can thus awaken in us poetic impulses, we can obtain the highest spiritual satisfaction from it. This is why traveling is the best way to dispel our boredom. People who have fallen out of love and are on the verge of suicide as a result can be consoled by wandering. At times, when one's mind is tainted by melancholy, a walk can take away a considerable amount of one's sorrow. Hawthorne and Edgar Allan Poe are fond of describing people who wander endlessly back and forth in the streets of a city with the hope of forgetting for a short while the hunger of their souls and the sorrow of emptiness in their hearts. Raskolnikov, in Dostoyevsky's *Crime and Punishment*, also wanders aimlessly after committing murder, as if taking a walk could lighten

---

[4]   Translation by Burton Watson, *The Old Man Who Does As He Pleases*, New York
    & London: Columbia University Press, 1973, p. 9.

his burden. Some people are even so interested in traveling that other interests are pushed to the side. There is such a character in Stevenson's "The Vagabond":

> Wealth I seek not, hope nor love,
> Nor a friend to know me;
> All I seek, the heaven above,
> And the road below me.

Walt Whitman is another poet who sings the praises of roaming about. His "Song of the Open Road" is indeed a superb eulogy to travel. Let me quote the sublime lines at the beginning of this poem as a conclusion to this section:

> Afoot and light-hearted I take to the open road,
> Healthy, free, the world before me,
> The long brown path before me leading wherever I choose.

What lies between our cradle and our grave is but a road. It can be said that we grow old traveling on this road before coming to our eternal rest. Naturally, we can expect hardship along the way, but the scenery surrounding our fellow travelers and us is all extremely interesting, and it's worth all that wandering in order to appreciate it. Apart from what this long road leads us to, we do not have any other destination. And by the time we finish this journey, we will also have left this world and returned to the beginning. Scientists say that we will cease to be, and will never travel on the same road. People who uphold the eternity of the soul, on the other hand, believe that there is still a long future ahead of us, and we can get back on the road again millions of times. All of this is in the future, so who cares? Maybe this road too will one day cease to be. For now, let us walk on the road before us. The most important thing is not to go through life with our eyes closed, oblivious, and in the end fail to see the world around us.

Wu Boxiao

Wu Boxiao (1906–1982) was born in Shangdong and entered Beijing Normal University in 1925. He made his fame as an essayist, but also pursued a tireless career in language education.

Under the influence of the New Culture Movement, Wu had strong communist inclinations, which led him to Yan'an in 1938. He joined the Chinese Communist Party in 1941 and participated in propaganda work with the army during the war. The experience of those years is partly reflected in "Conversations at Night."

As a writer with leftist leanings, Wu explores the experiences of the common people in his work. He is adept in deriving significant meaning from ordinary events. His plain narration is imbued with profound sentiments. "Conversations at Night" describes several kinds of such conversations, some restful, some romantic, some secretive, some with one's family and friends, some with strangers, and yet some with comrades-in-arms, in the process giving a cross-sectional view of Chinese society.

Conversations at Night (1934)

I might well be a melancholy character. Otherwise, why would I have come to prefer the dark hours of the night?

I like the overlapping shadows of people on the street at night, and a lone flickering lamp in a quiet house. I like the passing wild geese, screeching across the cool autumn sky. I like the knelling of bells deep in the night to which the traveler distressed at sleeping on a riverboat far from home listens so intently. I like the crashing of waves on the shore, and the nighttime echoes from the hills far and near. I like the crowing of roosters coming in waves, which must have roused Zu Di from his bed to practice his sword.[1] I like the continuous barking of dogs in the dark, on back streets and in bleak alleys. I like the sound of a gunshot at midnight, the down-and-outers who stagger down the alleyways, the jazz that comes blaring from dance halls until daybreak. I like the brightly lit painted candles in the nuptial chamber, and seeing the abashed bride under their light. I like it when, deep into the night, there are still people in the hotel calling out to attendants to bring tea. I like to stretch languorously, drowsily open my mouth wide, and sneeze. Because I like the night, I like all the things that come with it.

That's right, I like the night. That's why I also like talking deep into the night.

The scorching part of the day is when people are busy tripping over themselves ordering others around or being ordered around themselves. While peasants toil in sweat and dirt with ploughs and hoes, businessmen flick the beads of the abacus, spittle bubbling at the corners of their mouths as they calculate each fraction of a cent and try to second-guess and trick each other. The hands and hearts of the workers have become machines. In the schoolroom, the teachers pontificate, not caring whether they make sense or not. Students fool around, looking forward to a respite when the teachers go for a short nap. Amidst all of this bustling about, how could anyone really talk, even if they wanted to? If you want to talk, better to wait until evening. It's the best time by far.

On summer nights in the villages, no sooner have you put down your chopsticks from supper than you can see stars scattered all over the

---

[1] Zu Di (266–321 AD), a general of the Eastern Jin, who subjected himself to a regimen of rising when the rooster crowed to hone his skills with the sword.

sky. There are many mosquitoes in the yard and it is a bit muggy, so you pick up the dogskin cushion and the water pipe for Grandpa and walk to the edge of the village to the threshing ground surrounded by willow trees. A crowd of people is already sitting on the ground there chatting. Some have wrapped their reed capes around them. Some sit on stools, others take off their shoes and sit on them like cushions, and still others spread grass mats on the ground and lie down on them, legs folded beneath them. They have all come out to cool off. The old grandfathers, the middle-aged uncles, and the young brothers all warmly greet each other:

"Have you eaten yet?"

"Come, sit over here."

As they speak, some bow slightly, while others get to their feet. How peaceful and comforting it all is! At first, those who smoke do so for a while. Those who don't go about catching fireflies and counting the stars. Gradually they begin to talk to each other, and gradually they begin to tell stories... the Rebellion of the Long Hairs[2]... the love story of Liang Shanbo and Zhu Yingtai... the year "when the draught lasted for forty-nine days and there was not a single bit of grain to harvest in the fields." They talk of ghosts and fox spirits, their homes and neighbors. How interesting it is! When they come to the scary parts of their stories, each tries to huddle closer together with the crowd. When they come to the happy parts, everyone bursts into laughter together. They look out at the boundless open fields where darkness reaches all the way to the edge of the sky. They look at the stars, the fireflies, and the faint light of pipes flickering in the dark. Each feels quiet and peaceful inside as the crowd melds together with the night. A meteor shoots across the sky, and everybody calls out, "Look at that bandit star!"[3]

A lantern passes by on the road, and the dog starts barking.

"Go away, dog!" someone bellows.

---

[2]   A reference to the Taiping Rebellion, a revolt that took place in the mid-nineteenth century led by Hong Xiuquan, a frustrated scholar who suffered under the illusion that he was the son of God. The rebels were called "long hairs" because they let their hair grow long in defiance of the Manchu rule requiring men to shave the tops of their heads.

[3]   A meteor is called a "bandit star" because it has strayed from its normal orbit. There is also the belief that a bandit, like those found in *Outlaws of the Marsh*, has a star to his name in the sky.

"Where are you going?"

"To the inn," or "To the town," the one with the lantern replies.

Such a moment of uneasiness is often followed by a feeling of peace. They watch as the lantern goes farther and farther away, and the stories begin anew. Every now and then, someone sings a few Shanxi folk tunes. Listen: "The golden plague...," sung with the tremor of a falsetto.

This is conversation at night, the kind that you find in the villages. Conversations like this often last until the third watch or until the dew gets to be too much. Very often, someone will fall asleep and begin to snore while the conversation continues. Others, too, may begin to yawn and doze off. A mother will call to her child, "Come back here and get to bed!" The child will rub his sleepy eyes, unwilling to go, but leave at last. And a wife will come to call her husband, "I say, are you coming?" The compliant good husband is also unwilling to go, but he too stands up to leave. And thus, one by one, the crowd gets thinner, and the words grow fewer. By the time everybody has dispersed, the dog growls and stretches its back, and only the screeching bats and buzzing mosquitoes are left, as if suspended in animated conversation.

Away from home, exposed to wind and rain, you may find yourself roaming across hills and rivers. Thinking of home, you drag your tired steps forward to find an inn before the sun sets. You walk in, stomping your feet to shake off the dirt, wash your face and blow your nose. Once inside the room, you drink some tea. You are rather thirsty, and drink quite a few cups. You have no appetite, but still order a few random things. But just when it is time to wrap up the day and go to bed, you find you cannot sleep. Looking at the lamp, feeling lonely, tired, bored and sad, you just want to cry. Suddenly, the doorway for carts opens, and in comes another customer. Is he a vendor? Is he a cart pusher? Or is he a wine seller with a mule? It doesn't matter what he is, as long as he is here to spend the night at the inn. Look at him: He comes in and, as is the custom, stomps his feet to shake off the dirt, washes his face, blows his nose, and comes into the room to take food and tea. At first, you are not in the mood to greet him; you are so sad you just want to cry. But later, you begin to talk to him:

"Where did you come from?"

"Where are you going?"

You ask his name, and he yours. Is it any surprise that you gradually begin to feel comfortable with each other, and begin to talk? You are both travelers on the road, both afflicted with the same homesickness; it is only natural that you should share the same feelings. As you talk, you seem to feel a certain intimacy, a certain consolation. In this way, you forget your loneliness and are not as sad as before. Thus, quietly, you slip into your dreams, even if you still find traces of tears on your pillow when you awaken. At least this is better than listening to the wood-claps of the watchman, tossing in bed like an eel the whole night while sleep eludes you.

What if you were to run into an old friend in a distant land? That would give you even more reason to drink a few cups to celebrate. There would not be enough time in one night to say all you wanted to say, but couldn't you stay up till dawn? If you were happy, you could hold on to each other's hand tightly. If you were sad, you could allow your tears to fall, or pat each other on the back with an understanding smile on your face. Who knows what you would talk about? Nighttime is lonely, but you would have forgotten that. The night is long, but you would have forgotten that, as well. You would feel the excitement, the inexplicable flow of happiness and waves of sadness that come to your heart.

Here is another kind of night conversation.

In another place, as rumors grow ever more rampant by the minute and encirclement by spies everywhere becomes so impenetrable that even water could not flow through, a group of revolutionaries still gathers in a small attic or a stuffy basement, deep in discussion or argument. A small candle is burning, its light so dim that a breath could easily blow it out. The droning of their words can only be understood with the full attention of their eyes. But they do not panic; on the contrary, calm hovers over their fiery hearts. They look at each other happily with light in their eyes, and seem to be waiting for someone or for an important command. A long time passes, and they wonder:

"Why isn't he here yet?"

"Nothing has gone wrong, has it?"

Suddenly, they cannot believe their ears when they hear three gentle raps on the door. They look at the door, and see a young man in a tattered blue gown slip in through the narrow gap of the open door. That's him! They see a slender build, piercing eyes, and tightly closed lips, as if clenched between them were a will as strong as iron. Unconsciously, they stand up solemnly to welcome him, and then unconsciously sit down again to listen.

At first, he smiles like a girl with frankness and composure, giving a dose of sedative to every edgy soul. His low but clear and flowing voice rings like the tinkling of spring water emerging fresh from the hills. When he speaks of traps and snares, it is as if he were speaking about the fickle love of taxi dancers. When he speaks of prison, it is as if he were talking about an ancient book. When he speaks of life, he says it should be like thunder and lightning on a rainy day. There should be sound and light, and even if they are short as a flash, that is as it should be. He speaks of death as the beginning of another dream, where there is nothing either to hope for nor to fear, because it does not have anything to do with living. He speaks of the stupidity of the spies, the grandeur of uprising, and also the joyful days ahead for the masses. You see? Before you notice it, a happy smile emerges unimpeded from the hearts of all the people gathered there. Their faces glow, as though in bashfulness, and they are both exhilarated and inspired. Like bullets, each is filled with an irrepressible force.

This is yet another kind of night conversation. Certainly, no one could doze off in a conversation like this!

Night conversations are fascinating. On lunar New Year's Eve, the entire family—old and young alike—drink yellow rice wine while awaiting the arrival of the new year. With a fire blazing in the fire pit, they talk about forgotten anecdotes of their ancestors. Amid the riotous sound of firecrackers, their conversation is pervaded with the warmth that only family members can share. Somewhere else, two old watchmen walk among the crops in the fields equipped with a hunting rifle, a dog walking beside them. In the bleakness of the night, they smoke, talk and listen to the rasping sound of seedlings growing. This kind of night conversation has a rustic feel to it. In another place, several young people gather around an amiable old scholar with questions, talking about the Zheng airs of the *Book of Poetry* and Greek mythology. Such an eloquent, knowledgeable and urbane conversation is filled with the flavor of learning. In times when an unintended word straying beyond what is sanctioned by the authorities might bring one the fate of public execution,[4] a meaningful look can say more than what the mouth can utter. When the country is under the threat of foreign invasion, one's tears bespeak the repressed anger inside.[5] Or, in better times, one might

---

[4]   Under the strict control imposed during the reign of Qin Shi Huang (259–210 BC), the First Emperor of China, people found discussing state affairs in public places could be executed.

[5]   A reference to court officials of the Eastern Jin (317–420 AD), who were known

"sit at a banquet set among the flowers and play drinking games while watching the moon."[6] But who cares whether it is an elegant pastime or not? Night conversation is always enjoyable.

You don't believe me? Come, let me prepare for you a big pot of boiled water, a small urn of good wine, a can of cigarettes, several tabloids from Shanghai, roasted sweet potatoes, turnips as sweet as pears, and a few volumes of proscribed books, and let's invite a few close friends in. It doesn't matter what the occasion is: A spring evening when the fragrance of flowers fills the air, a stormy summer night when the sky is charged with thunder and lightning, a night in autumn when the wind whistles and insects chirp, a deep winter evening when everything is covered with snow.... It makes no difference if it's a time when the moonlight is as clear as water, when a single night brings several alarms, or when you meet up with friends whom you have not seen for a long time—it is all up to you. We invite you to a whole night of conversation, and when we line up our beds next to each other by the candles under the west window, shouldn't that be a night when sleep will elude you?

Hey, friends, would you like to come over tonight to have a conversation with us?

---

to cry over their lost territories north of the Yangtze River at a celebration in spring.

6   Li Bo (701–762 AD), "Chunye yan congdi taohuayuan bing xu" (Feasting My Cousins at the Peach Blossom Garden at a Spring Night).

Lu Li

Lu Li (1908–1942) received an education in mechanical engineering and made a living as a science teacher, while his interest in literature led him to pursue a creative life of writing and translation, in addition to managing a publishing house in Shanghai during the years of Japanese occupation. His editorial policies, however, brought him the displeasure of the puppet government, which ordered his execution in 1942.

In his essays, Lu Li fixes his gaze on the minute details of daily life, especially those surrounding the dispossessed and the underprivileged. With descriptions that can best be described as earthy, Lu Li is unflinching in his castigation of social inequality. "The Water Pestle" employs nature imagery to highlight the unnatural act of human beings preying on one another.

On the other hand, the world of nature is pitted against human selfishness in "Greenery Imprisoned." It is difficult to comprehend what perversity of mind would lead the character to deny the sunlight for which the ivy plant naturally yearns, but the mention of the Marco Polo Bridge Incident in the essay suggests a possible political reading. At any rate, the symbolism is quite clear. The green plant stands for "life, hope, consolation and happiness," which is finally set free at the end of the essay.

The Water Pestle (1933)

How many of us have heard the monotonous sound of a pestle on the bank of a rushing river at midnight?

You can often hear it on a bank far away from any human habitation by the side of murmuring, splashing, flowing water; on the edge of a pine forest where a lone owl is meditating like a philosopher; next to a cluster of short young willows where an egret is spending the night, its long legs curled up and its neck and stomach tucked in. Every now and then, an armadillo scurries out to the river to have a drink of water, or a beaver looks around in fear, twitching its ridiculous eyebrows and whiskers. Wolves out hunting howl intermittently from mountain ridges far away, and schools of fish swim against the swift currents in the dark night. The sound of their fins moving against the water reminds one of the rapid but steady splattering a startled wild duck makes as its wing tips flap on the surface of the water.

You can often hear the sound of a pestle in the winter when rain intermingles with snow. Heaven and earth are frozen together, and the water mill appears all the more solitary. The wind rises suddenly in the deep of the night, making this exposed water mill as cold as the pit of hell.[1] Underneath the thatched eaves are hidden some sparrows, who remain there even when human beings and lamplight approach. They rely completely on human compassion for their safety, although they must be trembling with fear inside. It is colder than ice all around, but there is, after all, still a scant trace of warmth by the water mill.

You can often hear the pestle at the end of the year when every household is preparing cakes and buns to please and tempt the impartial Old Man of Time so he will bestow upon them a lucky year ahead. They do not begrudge the precious lamp oil, making use of the water pressure that wields the cumbersome pestle to grind flour and other ingredients. And thus, this water mill, which at ordinary times serves only as a place for shepherds to take naps and urchins out collecting firewood to play their game of "tiger feeding its cubs," is now whirring away day and night.

What a sorry water mill it is! Having endured the cold and heat, drought and humidity, the straw mat that drapes over the door has now

---

[1]   Unlike hell in the Western tradition, which is marked by its scorching fire, the Chinese hell can be bitterly cold at times.

faded into a light gray and hangs down in shreds. Every now and then, the northerly wind comes wailing inside, cutting a wide opening through the mat. It also rises through the cracks in the floor, carrying with it the dampness of the water. The cold is unbearable for the watchman, who feels as if his fingers are about to break off and his skin about to crack open. In one corner of the roof, specks of flour cling to the spiderwebs, reminding one of dewdrops hanging like so many strings of pearls from spiderwebs on an early summer morning. The flour, however, is denser and lacks the dew's luminous transparency. On the floor in the corner, an oil lamp stands on a tin box. Because the room is drafty, its frail yellow-greenish light flickers off, then on, off then on. A pair of enormous pestles thunders steadily.

The watchman of the mill sits on his curled knees and can feel them going numb. Hypnotized by the rhythmic pounding of a pair of pestles, he has forgotten the deserted bank that he now finds himself on, the year that has almost come to an end, the cold that is hardly distinguishable from numbness, and the stern orders from his master. Instead, he dreams of his shabby, warm bedding by the corner of the wall, the roaring fire in the stove, and the long winter nights when he never seems to get enough sleep. His eyes grow bleary.

When I hear the heavy midnight thuds of the pestle, I cannot help but think of the child-bride who used to live on a street nearby. She came from a poor family, which lacked the means to bring her up and sold her off as a child-bride to a family that owned a cake shop. She was fifteen years old then, her husband, only eleven. As their family's own flesh and blood, the children around her were all considered precious, but the girl was cursed as "a mere weed that happened to grow in the field for no apparent reason." She endured the torture and abuse that all child-brides are expected to bear: hunger, whipping, having her fingers tied together with a string soaked in oil which was then set on fire. Her clothes in winter were made of thin foreign cloth, and those in summer were of coarse fabric. All manner of tasks fell to her to do— drawing water, pushing the grindstone, and making cakes. In fact, she did everything a fifteen-year-old should not be expected to do, from the most strenuous to the most painstaking. Even more heartlessly, she was often asked to guard the water mill by herself on winter nights. The pestle, like a giant spirit, thus assailed her frail soul. The terror of the night surrounded her, and the fatigue from endless restless nights slowly wore her down. I heard that one winter night toward the end of the year she was dragged by the pestle into the mortar, where, mixed with the flour there, she was reduced to pulp. It was even said that the flour was then made into cakes, and sold with extra red sugar mixed in.

On hearing this, I cursed the reverberating sound of the mill at midnight, and those who have partaken of the cakes made of human flesh and blood. I hope that one day a thread from the spiderweb may fall on that flickering lamp, spreading fire to the straw canopy and destroying this death-dealing mortar and pestle. Or a summer torrent from the mountains may come, sand and earth and all, and wash away the mill so that no one will ever hear of this bloody story again, and the owl that is now eating its own mother in the forest will not ridicule us for preying on our own kind. But for now, I can only close the window that opens out to the river and cover my head with the comforter to stop the sound of the water mill on the other bank from reaching my ears.

Greenery Imprisoned (1940)

Here is something that happened last summer.

I was then living in an apartment building in Beiping, occupying a room no higher or wider than one *zhang*.[2] The dank floor was made of bricks, and the walls and ceiling were papered. There was a wooden window frame with a pair of glass panes, and hanging in front of the window was a set of delicately designed paper blinds. One seldom finds rooms like this in the south.

The window faced east. In the north, it gets light early in the summer. The sun would come into my little room at about five o'clock in the morning, filling it with a frightful glare and driving up the heat until eleven o'clock, when the sun finally withdrew. There were a few other vacant rooms in the building, one of which I could have taken. But I ended up picking this eastward-facing room, and came to occupy it to my delight and satisfaction.

I had a little reason for my decision. On the south wall of the room was a small round window about one foot in diameter. Despite its round shape, the window was covered with a hexagonal pane of glass, the lower left corner of which was broken, leaving a hole big enough for a hand to go through easily. Outside the round window was an ivy plant. When the sun shone into my room through the dense tendrils and leaves, it cast a green shadow. It was because I liked its green shadow that I had picked this room. When the caretaker of the building, with my little suitcase in hand, showed me the room, I caught sight of the green shadow and a sense of delight overtook me. Without further thought, I decided right then to take the room. The caretaker was astounded by the promptness of my decision.

How precious the color green is! It is life, hope, consolation, and happiness. My yearning for green had my heart burning with impatience. I like the whiteness of water and the greenness of grass, and was weary of the grayness of the city sky, the aloof yellow of the plains. I yearned for green as a fish, trapped in a wheel track where once had been a puddle, longed for rain. My need had become so urgent that I became indiscriminate, and came to value a green branch as the most precious treasure in the world. As I settled down in the small room, I moved the little table under the round window so I could face the wall

---

[2]   *Zhang*, a measurement of length, slightly longer than ten feet.

and the little window when I sat down. The door was open all the time, but no one came to disturb me because I was a lone stranger in this ancient city. I did not feel lonely, however. I forgot the fatigue of the journey and the many unpleasant memories of the past. I looked at the little round hole, and the green leaves conversed with me. I understood the wordless language of nature, just as it understood mine.

Contentedly, I sat in front of the window. A month passed, and then two months. I was mesmerized by this patch of green, and began to understand the joy of those who lay eyes on an oasis after crossing the desert. I also understood the delight of seaward explorers when ocean waves carry stalks of flowers and blades of grass to their boats. Human beings grow in nature, and green is nature's color.

Every day, I watched the ivy grow on the window. I saw how it stretched its supple tendrils and gripped a dead branch or a string placed there to guide its growth. I saw its folded young leaves slowly unfurl, then gradually turn dark green and old. I observed closely its delicate veins and fresh sprouts. Like the farmer who impatiently yanked up the young seedlings to help them grow,[3] I wanted so much for the ivy to grow fast and flourish. When it rained, I enjoyed listening to the rustling sound of the ivy and watching its tendrils dance.

Suddenly, a selfish thought occurred to me. I reached out through the broken glass and pulled in two soft, plump tendrils. Stretching them out on my desk, I became all the closer and more intimate with the greenness of the plant. I would use its color to decorate my shabby room and my frustrated mind, and take it as a metaphor of thriving love, happiness, and luxuriant youth. I imprisoned it in the same way one would imprison a songbird. I would have it sing its wordless songs for me.

The green tendrils hung down over my desk, and stretched out as before, climbing and unfurling their leaves. They grew even faster indoors than they would have outside. I seemed to discover a sort of "joy of living," which surpassed any other kind of joy.

I once lived in a thatched hut in a village. The floor was covered with fresh earth, and grass roots that had not been removed sprouted new shoots under my bed, while mushrooms started to grow in the corner of the room. I could not bring myself to get rid of them. One day, a friend pulled them out nonchalantly as we were chatting. I found

---

[3]   See *Mengzi*, "Gong sun chou I," book III.

it a pity that my friend removed them, and blamed him for not minding his own business.

Every morning when I came to visit my captured "green friend," its tips were always pointing toward the window. Even the smallest leaf and the tiniest curling tendril were turned in that direction. How stubborn plants can be! The ivy plant understood neither my love for it nor my good intentions. My feelings were injured and I became displeased with this plant that kept its face to the sun. Nevertheless, I continued to keep it imprisoned, insisting on having its branches hang over my desk.

Gradually, the plant lost its luscious color, and began to turn light green, and then light yellow. The branches got thinner and became frail like a sick child. More and more, I came to regret my mistake of locking up in a dark room a plant that should have been growing under the sun. My pity for its ailing branches and leaves grew, though I was still angry at its stubbornness and lack of feeling. Still, I would not let it go. An evil obsession had taken hold of my mind.

I had originally planned to return to the south at the end of July. I made a note of the date of my departure, the day when I would release this "green prisoner." When I left this city, its freedom would be restored.

Later, the Lugou Bridge Incident[4] broke out, and friends who were worried about me telegraphed to urge me to hurry up and return to the south. I had no choice but to change my plans. By mid-July, I could no longer linger around the ancient city, which was now threatened on all sides by warfare. The trains had stopped running for several days, and every day I had to pay attention to when they might start again. One morning, the moment had finally come. Before I left my room, I reverently set free the prisoner that would not bend to darkness. I placed the frail yellow branches back in their original place and gave them my sincerest blessing. I hoped that they would grow and flourish.

I have been gone from Beiping for a year now. I miss my round window and my green friend. If one day I were to see them again, would they recognize me?

---

[4]   Better known as the Marco Polo Bridge Incident in the West. On July 7, 1937, Japanese soldiers opened fire at the site when requests to enter the city of Wanping were denied. The incident signaled the beginning of all-out aggression against China by Japan during World War II.

Qian Zhongshu

Qian Zhongshu (1910–1998) is one of the intellectual giants in twentieth-century China. His fame as a writer is built upon a volume of essays, a book of short stories, and a full-length novel. Yet, his scant literary output does not in any way reduce his stature, as his writings are generally held up to be the work of a genius, which one can only admire but cannot emulate. After 1949, he concentrated his energy on classical literary research, for which he is equally famous.

Qian is the son of the scholar Qian Jibo, who gave him an excellent education in classical studies. In 1929, he entered Tsinghua University to study foreign literature; there, his talent for languages was widely recognized. Later, he went to Oxford University and the University of Paris.

In both his creative and critical writing, Qian is known for his erudition and ready wit. He is decidedly apolitical in his writing but shows keen perceptiveness in human affairs, which he often depicts with irony and humor. In "Windows," Qian summons a large array of literary references, both Chinese and non-Chinese, to shed light on his topic. For the most part, however, the topic is but a starting point. His main business, in this and other essays, is to comment on the different facets of human life.

Windows (1941)

It is spring again, and the windows can often be left open now. Spring comes in through them, while the people inside, finding it hard to sit still, go out through the door. But outdoors, spring comes way too cheaply. Sunlight is everywhere, but nowhere is it as bright as the light that shatters the darkness inside the house. The wind, too, is everywhere, lazy and warm under the sun, and not as energizing as the breeze that stirs up the still air indoors. Even the chirping of the birds seems broken and frail out in the open, needing the contrast of the stillness indoors to set it off. We thus come to understand that, as with a painting in a frame, spring should be set within a window to be viewed.

We also come to realize at the same time that doors and windows serve quite different functions. A door, of course, is designed for people to enter and leave a house, but a window is sometimes made to serve the same purpose. Thieves and secret lovers in novels, for example, like to go through windows. The basic difference between a window and a door does not lie therefore in whether they allow people to come in and out. When it comes to admiring the beauty of spring, we might put it this way: A door makes it possible for us to go out, while a window makes it unnecessary for us to do so. A window helps to bridge the gap between nature and the human world: It entices the wind and sun to come in so that the house can capture a part of spring, and allows us to enjoy the season indoors without needing to go out looking for it.

Tao Yuanming, the ancient poet, had an intimate understanding of this function of windows. There are two lines in his "Homeward We Shall Go":

> Leaning against the south window I look upon the world with disdain.
> I'm easily satisfied with a room barely big enough to rest my knees.

Is this not the same as saying that, as long as there is a window for him to look out, even a cramped little house is habitable? He also said, "In the leisurely summer months, I lie down beneath the north window where the cooling wind blows in. My joy is so great that I compare myself to the legendary sages before Fu Xi."[1] This means that, as long as the wind can come through the window, even a small house can become the Western Paradise. Although he lived in Chaisang, with

---

[1]   Fu Xi, a legendary hero whose many contributions to the progress of human civilization were said to include domesticating wild animals.

Mount Lu right nearby, Tao Yuanming felt no need to go there to escape the heat. Hence, a door makes it possible for us to pursue, symbolizing desire, whereas a window allows us to possess, symbolizing enjoyment.

Such a distinction between windows and doors applies not only to those who already live in a house, but at times also to others who come in from the outside. A visitor who knocks on the door for admission comes with a request or a question; at most, he will be a guest who must submit himself to the wishes of his host. On the other hand, someone who pokes in through the window, be he a thief of wealth or of the heart, has all along made up his mind to take over temporarily the place of the host, and could not care less whether he is welcome or not. Musset, in his poetic drama *What Do Young Maidens Dream of?* (*À quoi rêvent les jeunes filles?*), put it wonderfully when he said that the father may open the door to invite in the *matériel époux*, but the *idéal* lover always climbs in through the window. In other words, he who comes through the front door is the son-in-law in form only, one who might have already gained the father's approval but still must win the daughter's heart. Only the person who comes in through the back window is one to whom the daughter entrusts her full body and soul.

When one walks through the front door, one must go through the doorman, wait for one's host to appear, and mumble words of greeting before coming to the purpose of one's visit. This all takes a lot of thought and time. How, then, could a visit like this be as simple and direct as coming through the back window? The same is true of scholarship: The shortcut lies in going directly to the index at the back of a book, while starting with the main text in the front is simply too pedantic. Needless to say, all of these distinctions only apply under normal social circumstances: In times of war or other abnormal periods, even the house itself may not remain standing, let alone doors and windows.

All houses have doors, but we can still find some in this world that are not equipped with windows, showing that windows represent a higher stage of human evolution. A door is a necessity for people living in a house, but a window is a kind of luxury. The whole purpose of a house is like that of a nest for birds or a cave for animals: It is there for one to return to at night, and by closing the door, one can enjoy a certain degree of protection. Now, by creating a window in the wall, one lets in light and air, and eliminates the need to go out even during the day. One can even live with the door closed if one chooses to. A house thus assumes a new meaning in a person's life. No longer is the house only a place to hide from wind and rain or to spend the night; it also begins to acquire furnishings and decorations, and pieces of calligraphy and painting begin to appear on the walls. From morning to night, it is now a place for us to think, work, entertain—a theater where all our human comedies and tragedies will be staged.

Thus it can be said that a door is a passageway for us mortals, and a window is a passageway for the sky. The original function of a house is to enable human beings to escape from the threat of nature and face four walls and a roof, while a window entraps a corner of the sky, taming it and putting it to human use, just as we used to capture wild horses and tame them into domestic animals. From that point on, we can communicate with nature even inside our houses, and instead of our having to go out looking for sunlight and fresh air, they will come to us. That is why we should count the invention of the window as one of mankind's victories over nature. It should be pointed out that this victory is like women's victory over men. On the surface, it may appear that we are making concessions to nature, since with the window open, the wind and sunlight can come in to conquer our space. But little do they suspect that by staking out such a conquest, they are actually being conquered by the very space they invade.

We said a while ago that a door is a necessity, and a necessity is something that is not for us to deny: When I am hungry, I have to eat, and when I am thirsty, I have to find something to drink. Similarly, when someone knocks on the door, you are obliged to open it. On the other side of the door may be, as Ibsen calls them, the young people of the next generation. Or, it may well be what De Quincey (in "On the Knocking at the Gate in *Macbeth*"), in discussing the banging of doors after a murder, describes as the bright and shining world making an attack on the dark and sinful one. It may be a prodigal son returning home, or someone requesting a loan—or more likely demanding repayment of one. The more uncertain you are, and the more fearful you are about opening the door, the more you will want to find out who is knocking, and the more you will want to open the door. Even the postman's daily knocking arouses in you an uncertain hope, because you do not know—but would like to know—what news he is bringing. Hence, it is not for you to decide whether to open the door or not.

But what about the window? When you wake up in the morning, all you have to do is open the window and you can tell what is awaiting you outside. Is it snow, fog, rain, or bright sun? You can then decide whether to open the window or not. I said earlier that windows are a luxury, and as such they are something you can take or leave, depending on the situation.

I have always thought that windows are the eyes of a house. Liu Xi said in his phonological study, *Shi Ming*, "The word window means to see through. Looking through a window is thus akin to seeing light with one's eyes." Likewise, Gottfried Keller's *Abendlied* begins with the lines, "The Eyes are like windows/ Letting in picture after picture."[2] Both of them, however, describe only half of the equation. Eyes are the windows of our souls, through which we can see the world outside. At the same time, other people can get a glimpse of our inner selves, too. The look in our eyes often changes with our hearts. That is why Mencius believed that there was no better way to read a person's character than to look in his eyes. Lovers in a Maeterlinck's play do not close their eyes when they kiss because they want to see how many of the other's kisses rise from the heart to the lips. That eyes can reveal the heart also explains why, when we speak to someone wearing dark glasses, we find it difficult to divine his intentions, as if he were wearing a mask. According to Eckermann's record of April 4, 1830, Goethe loathed anybody with glasses, saying that, while these people could clearly see the wrinkles on his face, he himself was distracted by the reflection of their glasses and therefore could not fathom their hearts.

A window enables people to look out from inside and in from outside. Curtains are therefore needed in busy places to provide some protection of one's privacy. When one goes to visit at night, a look at the window to see if the light is on gives one a general idea whether one's host is in or not, and one need not wait for the door to open to find out. In the same way, by looking at people's eyes, we can read their thoughts without waiting for them to open their mouths. Closing the window is thus the same as closing one's eyes. There are many images in this world that one can only see with one's eyes closed—dreams, for example. When it is too noisy outside, closing the window gives our souls the freedom to explore and meditate in peace. Sometimes closing the window is related to closing one's eyes. When you find that the world outside the window is too mundane and fails to bring you any

---

[2]   Qian Zhongshu gives only a truncated translation of the four lines in Keller's *Abendlied*. My translation is based on Qian and not Keller.

satisfaction, you like to go back to your hometown to see friends and relatives from whom you have been separated. This you can only do by closing your eyes to go to sleep and seeking them in your dreams, so you get up to close the window. As it is only spring and there is lingering cold in the air, you cannot really leave the window open all day and all night long.

He Qifang

He Qifang (1912–1977) was born to a wealthy land-owning family in Wanxian, Sichuan. To escape from his authoritarian conservative family, he moved to Shanghai for his education. He eventually entered Peking University where he befriended Li Guangtian and Bian Zhilin. The three collaborated in the publication of *Hanyuan ji* in 1936. In 1938, he moved to the Communist base in Yan'an where he served as the secretary to a number of top Communist party leaders. After the war, he took up key positions in leading literary associations until his death in 1977.

He Qifang is often mentioned together with Li Guangtian in large part because of their early collaboration. Yet, their aesthetic inclinations are quite distinct from each other. Despite his political involvement, He follows a romantic and apolitical orientation in most of his writings. The title of his essay anthology *Record of Painted Dreams* is telling in this regard, containing works with a dream-like quality. This is not to say, however, that his essays are devoid of social messages. The two essays featured in this anthology depict pedestrian life. "Hunger" affords a view of life on the brink where food is scarce, while "Old Men" offers a group portrait of three ordinary old men who live with dignity, ending with a reminder to himself to make good use of his time before old age sets in.

Old Men (1937)

I think of a few old men.

*   *   *   *   *   *   *

The first who comes to mind is an old servant in the home of my maternal grandmother, where I often spent my days as a child. Her home was an enormous ancient mansion located at the foot of a bluish mountain crag. Behind the mansion was a forest of bamboo whose knotty, whip-like roots draped over the cracks of a low wall. There was an abandoned well beneath the wall. Covered completely by duckweed, the well had become an ideal place for frogs. I was frightened by— yet felt drawn to—the quiet stillness of this part of the estate, because on those overgrown trails that seemed so far from any human presence were butterflies with colorful wings fluttering about, and red and green dragonflies that were difficult to find elsewhere. Like the grass and trees that had escaped everyone's attention, I, too, grew up behind the mansion undisturbed.

The family living in this huge old mansion was made up of only four people: My grandmother, who was already very old; my grandfather, who was sick most of the time; my first uncle, who was studying in a middle school in the county seat; and my second uncle, who, only two years my senior, liked to go out and play with the local urchins. How was I to pass the time? I seldom wandered into the locked-up courtyards, the lofts used for storage, or the area behind the mansion. As for the rooms with patterns carved on their windows, they were full of shadows. One day, when my grandmother opened a vanity case that she had long since stopped using, she found a small snake coiled up inside. I never again had the nerve to rummage through the things in those rooms.

I often played alone in front of the terrace outside the main hall. The terrace was long, complete with stone railings and black-lacquered stools. If you stood there and looked up, you could see three big plaques hanging high along the eaves. Beside the dragons carved around the eaves, sparrows found an ideal home. Every now and then, a wisp of grass or a feather would come drifting down.

All of this, however, has become merely the backdrop against which the old servant appears in my memory. I can see him now, holding a bunch of burning incense sticks, walking in from the left end of the terrace, stepping over the two-foot high threshold (that seemed to be intent on playing tricks on children's legs) to go inside the main hall. He would put sticks of incense in the burner of each of the altars, and then devoutly strike the bowl-shaped copper chime. A clear and distant silvery sound would vibrate in the air, spreading far outward until it vanished in the solitude of the old mansion. This was one of his tasks in the early morning and evening.

The old servant was deaf, and people tended to shout at the top of their lungs when they talked to him. When, every now and then, his hearing allowed him to catch a few simple words, he would smile and nod, satisfied with his own comprehension and guesswork. He almost never spoke, except when he had something to report to the master of the house. On those occasions, he too would shout loudly and make gestures, a smile on his face. As for how old he was, or when he first started working in the old mansion, no one ever mentioned it and I never asked. His white hair indicated his advanced age, and his numerous but skillfully executed daily chores revealed his long history of service in this household.

I don't know how best to describe his daily duties. Should I provide a long list of his chores, or should I mention a few at random? Besides attending to the incense in the morning and evening, I found every day when I got up that, thanks to his labors with the broom, the stone courtyard shone with cleanliness like the early morning. He also had his share of miscellaneous duties in the kitchen, and was alone responsible for caring for the stove used for cooking fodder for the hogs. Every morning, he led a flock of cackling ducks to the river, and brought the little team back in the evening. One could often see him stooping over to work in the vegetable field, whose harvest appeared on our dinner table. When we went for a walk, moreover, we could see the golden blossoms of sunflowers atop high stalks outside the gate, and light purple and white flowers that looked like little crosses in the turnip field.

The sunflowers were dignified and cheerful; the turnip flowers, humble. How fond I was of that patch of grass outside the gate! The ancient spruce towered high like a giant, and the castor oil plant spread out its large, starfish-shaped leaves. Then there was the Chinese evergreen, with its long tendrils like human hair. They seemed to have come together to sing a eulogy to that hard-working old man.

I cannot say exactly how long he worked as a servant in my grandmother's home or when he left the old mansion, but when, at some later date, life found me squandering my time in another setting, I heard that one day he had fainted by the kitchen stove. When he came to, he went home by himself. Only then did people begin to notice his age. Some time later, I heard that he had returned to the old mansion, carrying out the same numerous duties as before. Later, was it another fainting bout or was it some other thing? Whatever it was, he went back home once again and left the old mansion forever.

*   *   *   *   *   *   *

I lived in a fortified village, growing up among cold, hard rocks.

Adults demanded of a ten-year-old the circumspection of someone three times his age, but an honest and compliant child can sometimes exhibit a tendency toward mischief, just as grown-ups sometimes engage in meaningless or even harmful actions against others out of loneliness. Under similar circumstances, I sometimes played tricks on the gatekeeper.

He was an irascible old man. A graying goatee hung down from his chin and a pigtail from the back of his head. He had served as gatekeeper for a number of years. He kept a room by the gate and would go to a different family by turns for his meals. In more peaceful times, when most of the families moved back to their regular residences outside the fortified village, he would go around to these families each month to collect several *sheng*[1] of rice, which he cooked for himself. One will never know whether it was his own impatient nature or the poverty in the world that gave him his fiery temper, but most of the time when he appears in my memory, he is sitting on a short wooden stool in front of the blockhouse gate with an angry look on his face. Muttering and grumbling, he knocks the stone slabs of the street with the metal bottom of his long bamboo pipe.

That bamboo water pipe, which had turned yellow with age, was also his walking staff. On its top was a copper mouthpiece, and on the bottom an iron bowl for holding tobacco. This was the source of enmity between us. When he was not paying attention, I often hid it so that he would have to look all over for it.

One time, I made myself a toy, which I called a water gun. It was made of a segment of bamboo with a hole drilled through the node and a chopstick with one end heavily wrapped in a piece of cloth. It

---

[1]   *Sheng*, a measurement of grain, equivalent to about 31.6 cubic inches.

could draw in a large glass of water, and the water, when forced out, would shoot a long way. I cannot recall for sure whether this weapon had offended the old gatekeeper. In any event, he told my grandfather about it, who, as a punishment, rapped my head twice with his knuckles and gave me a round of scolding. My weapon was then confiscated and thrown over the village wall, landing at the foot of the cliff.

Later on, the old man got himself another job on the side. Sitting on a specially designed wooden structure, he spent his time weaving sandals out of straw and hemp. In the rugged mountain villages, one sees these simple, practical sandals on the feet of every laborer. At first, the old man's skill was rather crude, but it slowly improved and he began to sell his shoes at three copper coins (each worth 100 cash) a pair to sedan-chair carriers, artisans, and servants who came in and out through the fortified village.

I seem to see him now, sitting on that wooden structure. Work has made him more mellow and kindly. Another old man in turn appears in my imagination. He lives in a thatched hut by a major road, and spends the whole day weaving straw sandals and selling them to people of all walks of life who happen to pass by. He himself has never gone beyond a distance of ten li,[2] but the straw sandals made by his hands have traveled to many places and encountered many strange experiences.

When will I begin to write "The Adventures of the Straw Sandals?"

*   *   *   *   *   *   *

Evening. Dusk closed in as softly as a flower. We were sitting on the steps in front of the village gate. The distant hills were slowly vanishing from our sight. Bats were flying above us. We were just back from an excursion around the foot of the village wall. We had walked through a forest with pine needles and pinecones scattered on its floor, gone by the thatched huts of several peasant families, passed by wheat fields and blooming patches of garden peas, and made a full circle around the small hill on which the village wall was built. Finally, exhausted, we had climbed up several sets of meandering steps and sat down to rest in front of the gate.

There were three of us: My grandfather, an old man who used to come every now and then to spend a few days with us, and me.

In his booming voice and gesturing with his hands, the old man was describing a horse to us. It seemed as if a tall brown horse were standing

---

[2]   *Li*, a measurement of length, about one-third of a mile.

right in front of us, neighing and stretching its neck, which was draped in a long mane. He was very knowledgeable about horses, and was good at riding and appraising them and curing them of sickness.

He was a county military officer. I heard from him the way to pass the martial arts examination: how to wield a halberd, push weights, and mount a horse, then set it galloping, and turn around suddenly to shoot three arrows at a target. Whenever he came to the part about shooting the arrows, he would flex his arms powerfully and strike a pose as if holding a bow in one hand and pulling the string with the other.

I also heard legends from him about martial artists. In an ancient temple somewhere, he said, there lived an old monk who was well known for his skill with the staff. He had many students. One day, he carried a clay pot on his back, stood against a wall, and asked his students to attack him. If any of them could tap the clay pot with his staff, he would admit defeat. And the result? Well, it goes without saying that the old monk was never defeated.

He was very old himself, but he had the kind of resounding voice one does not expect from an old man. He enjoyed talking about anything that had to do with martial arts. I was a small child then, and knew nothing of the many misfortunes and instances of injustice in the world. I took as mere idle stories the many things he told me, and never envisioned becoming a wandering knight myself to roam the world. On the contrary, I was more interested in hearing about the world beyond the hills. The old man had traveled to faraway places to sell horses. Beyond the hills where the white clouds meet and swallow up the setting sun, what kind of a place is it? What kind of people and adventures can one find there? Whenever I sat outside the blockhouse gate and gazed into the distance, I would be occupied with solitary thoughts such as these. The old man's stories could not satisfy my curiosity or give me a clear idea of what the answers might be. Gradually, his visits became less frequent, and after a few years, I heard that he had entered another world. Life is brief.

*   *   *   *   *   *   *

Finally, I see that I myself have become an old man, alone and calm, like a tree quietly tucked in the countryside in the winter. I study plants. I live among humble vegetables, tall-standing fruit trees, blooming shrubs. Like them, I follow the cycle of nature's seasons. A hoe is always in my hand, and through it, I get close to the earth. Perhaps I will raise bees under the eaves where there is some sun. Life is too bitter: Let us put a little sugar in our tea. On long nights when sleep is ever shorter, I will sit by the flickering oil lamp and slowly, meticulously, recall and write down the stories of my life.

But suddenly I awake from deep thought. What a preposterous dream this is! Between my mature years and my old age, there is still a long way to go. What should I fill it with? It should not be dreams but serious work.

Hunger (1941)

I

I once went with a friend to the Shao Cheng Park to practice riding a bicycle. It was one of those summer mornings when the sun had not yet come out and the street was quiet. The stores on both sides of the street still had their boards up, as if they were taking a morning nap. When we entered the park and came to the big playground, there were already some people there circling the field on their bicycles. However, the person who rented bicycles to us every morning, with the guarantee that we would learn how to ride them, was nowhere to be found. We were still a bit early.

We went to a teahouse nearby and ordered two cups of plain boiled water. Chengdu is a strange place—at such an early hour, there were already people sitting in the teahouse. There was an archery ground nearby, and usually when I walked by that part of the park, I would see men in traditional Chinese clothes and women dressed like concubines standing around, pulling their bows, and sending long arrows to the red wooden targets. I always instinctively loathed that kind of place and that kind of people. But it was better this morning: The archery ground was quiet. We sat on opposite sides of the tiny low tea table. We opened the lids, which were ordinarily used to hold back the tea leaves, and drank the water.

A vendor selling sweet steamed cakes walked by our table, and I called out to him, remembering that it was time for breakfast. His was a kind of steamed cake made of rice flour. White and round, the top of the cake had cracked a little while steaming. The vendors in the county city called them "white sugar cupcakes." When I was a child, what a temptation it was for me when I heard the vendors call out its name in a sweet, clear voice as they walked from street to street! But now I watched the vendor as he picked up the cakes with a pair of chopsticks from the tin pail and put them one by one on the overturned cup-lids on our table and felt none of the excitement I used to feel.

As he was doing this, a crumb fell from a cupcake and rolled down to the ground. A little girl walked by just at that instant, and, to my surprise, she bent down, picked up the crumb from the ground, and put it in her mouth. Then she walked quickly away.

She was thin, no more than ten or so years old. She had on a light blue cloth jacket, faded from washing but otherwise quite clean. Her left hand held an old, empty bamboo basket, which had turned black from use. She walked away quickly, and did not once turn back to look at us, as if embarrassed by what she had done. That crumb of cupcake was very, very small, not much bigger than a grain of rice.

I seemed to be seeing hunger for the first time. That it should appear to me in the form of such a lovely girl made it all the more shocking to me. But at the same time, it seemed as if I had just witnessed a solemn spectacle. I remained silent—I was not thinking about anything in particular, nor did I say anything to my friend, although ordinarily we enjoyed debating every sort of issue, be it large or small.

Oh, peaceful city, with your peaceful residents! While you were sleeping soundly in the quiet white light of the morning, you would never have guessed that I had glimpsed a terrible secret of yours.

II

Again, it was in the vicinity of Shao Cheng Park. I was sitting in the public dining hall on the ground floor of a restaurant. In Chengdu during the summer, if you eat in a small restaurant such as this one, there are always little homeless children in tattered clothes around who suddenly walk into the restaurant, stand behind you, and fan you with their torn rush-leaf fans. I was very embarrassed the first time this happened to me. I turned down the children's offer, but was very uncomfortable throughout the meal. I could feel their eyes staring at my back, as if, by eating my meal, I had done something unforgivable. However, I soon got used to it, and would habitually turn them down with a word or two, or give them some money and ask them to go away. My feeling of embarrassment also passed away, and I was able to appreciate the taste of food and have a satisfying meal. Human beings are like that sometimes.

This time, we again started our meal by sending those homeless children away. When, at the end of the meal, we stood up from the table and were preparing to pay, three little children suddenly came over, hurling themselves onto our table. I thought they were about to fight over the food, but when they got what they had come for without any interference from us, they immediately became quiet. An older child among them scooped out rice from the metal container and put it on the leftover food on the plates. After briefly stirring the food with chopsticks, he divided it into three equal portions, and the children started to eat.

"Are you brothers?" I asked.

"No," answered the child who I had thought was the older brother.

I did not go away, but stood there with them. I wanted to know more about them. I asked again, "What does your family do?"

"My father is a rickshaw puller."

"Doesn't he feed you?"

"He cannot find enough to feed himself."

I instantly recalled one time when I was riding a rickshaw. When the rickshaw passed by a certain store, the puller stopped and disappeared inside. After a while, he came out and picked up the rickshaw again. I asked him what he had bought from the store, and he told me that his addiction to opium was acting up again, and he had gone in to swallow a few opium pellets. I saw the face of that honest middle-aged man again, and imagined him to be the child's father.

I looked on gently as they finished that pathetic lunch so they would not be harassed by the waiters. When I walked out of the restaurant, I felt as if something heavy was resting on my heart. I did not know what to say, though. If what I felt inside was a kind of weeping that had yet to turn into tears, then I cried not only out of grief that the human world was like hell, but, more importantly, out of a certain consolation that I had derived from that insignificant tragedy—for now I saw how hunger could unite people together like brothers.

III

We were chatting in the faculty dormitory at a university. Someone who had been to England was talking about the theaters in London and the man-made storm on stage in the scene when King Lear appears in Shakespeare's play. Another person, wearing clothes made of some kind of shiny material, had just arrived in Chengdu, and suddenly asked us whether we had been to a certain street. I said I had not, and didn't know what was so special about that street. He seemed very surprised that I had lived in Chengdu for half a year and still did not even know about that street. He then told me that prostitutes of the lowest class inhabited that street. He had been there, and said, as if offering advice, "You should go and take a look." He then added, "I am the kind of person who looks at life in heaven as well as in hell."

I suddenly recalled the two incidents that I just wrote about. I seemed to be thinking, isn't it easy enough, as things are now, to indict the injustices of human society? Need we look around for further evidence? Besides, I was dissatisfied with his way of merely looking at things, whatever they might be.

I did not put these thoughts into words, except that, from then on, I didn't like the kind of person who wears silk that gleams and rustles. I also didn't like professors who, with complete ease of mind, lectured on Croce or taught Greek. I was dissatisfied with some of my friends who insisted on the value of style and wit in literature, and picked at their food when they ate out at restaurants, complaining about this dish or that. I know they should not be blamed, but I was too radical then, like someone who had discovered his own weakness and become hypercritical of other people. I wrote: "I would rather be a laundry man than someone like them, for a laundry man can wash dirty clothes until they are clean, while these people only know how to sully what was once clean."

IV

Another time, another place, and another group of people.

Before crossing the Beiping-Hankou line that had been blocked by the enemy, I stopped at a small village where a detachment of troops was camped. I was staying with someone who was a friend in literature and a comrade in revolution. That afternoon, we were returning from a small town nearby, and instead of going by the main road for carts, he insisted that we take a detour through the aspen forest next to the road. He said he wanted very much to take a walk in the forest.

But as we were walking slowly on the hard frozen ground, bare of either grass or paths, weaving our way through the aspen trees whose smooth naked bodies stretched toward the clear winter sky, he said sarcastically (and I do not know whether it was directed to me or to himself), "Don't you enjoy wonderful scenes like this? But I would exchange such a wonderful scene for two baked buns any day."

At times, I was a little displeased with this comrade. Whenever he showed any reluctance to eat food made from old millet (which might at times even be blended with sand) and bitter, sour, dried vegetables cooked in water, preferring to go without food, I made it a rule for myself to finish my food right in front of him without saying a word.

At that time, I was fonder of another young comrade, who in 1935 had endured whipping by policemen dispatched to his school to arrest students during the December 9 Movement in Beiping,[3] and who, together with other demonstrators, had forced open the city gate. He once said to me with a sigh, "The livelihood of the average Chinese person is really just too low! What we are getting is only our fair share of food."

I am someone who has never experienced hunger that tortures the body and soul in the most fundamental way. That is why I sometimes regard the hardship of poverty with the aloof arrogance of a non-proletarian, unlike my comrade, who exposed his own weakness in such an undisguised manner. In fact, his wish at the time, the wish to substitute a meal of millet with baked buns, wasn't it one worthy of sympathy and by no means extravagant?

Although life was somewhat harder on the front line, I'm afraid I cannot say that I fully appreciated the meaning of hunger. Sometimes when we tried to cross the blockade, we went without food for a day and a night. But on such occasions, fatigue always overwhelmed hunger. Besides, when we awoke from our sleep, cooked millet from the troops would be delivered to our *kang*.[4] I remember that the worst food I ever tasted was soup made solely from green onions, and the worst staple was purple bread made of sorghum, which had a nice color but tasted like mud. What cause do I have to complain?

V

I am a man of many dreams. Romain Rolland once said, "There is such a thirst for happiness in the human spirit that, denied happiness in reality, it will think of some way to create it." When it is impossible to create happiness, human beings will substitute dreams for it. I am not speaking metaphorically, by the way; I am speaking of the kind of real dreams that appear in our sleep at night.

Dreams are in fact a kind of reflection of our lives and thoughts. If I were to categorize all the dreams I have ever had, it would be clear that there are two kinds of new dreams that I never had before. One is

---

[3]   December 9 Movement is a student movement organized in 1935 to protest Japanese aggression toward China.

[4]   A bed, usually made of bricks, that is warmed from below.

political, and the other has to do with hunger. My arm was dislocated once when I fell from a horse at the front. After a doctor put it back in place and bandaged my arm, I was told to rest. I dreamed of milk on that occasion. In my dream, I saw a tall, white Swedish porcelain jar, complete with handle and spout, filled with milk. When I picked it up by the handle and poured the milk into a cup, it was thick and steaming. There was even a thin layer of cream floating on top. But before I could drink the milk, I awoke from my dream. I have that kind of dream every now and then. More recently, I dreamed that I passed by a room filled with cakes and pastries, and could not stop myself from stuffing my pockets with goodies. Then I dreamed that I was sitting at a feast, eating many dishes of delicious food. Would someone laugh at me for having such dreams of food and gluttony? I suppose that when dreams like this become no longer the sole property of a special minority of Chinese people, but are that of the majority, or close to the majority—those now poor and hungry—then there will be nothing to be ashamed of.

Among our ranks, there are perhaps some who may have come with the white wings of the angels, but I feel much more intimate with the humble ones, with their less-than-beautiful stigma of suffering, who have come along this uneven road step by step on their coarse, even bleeding, feet. They are much more like brothers born from the same mother. I shared only for a short time the fate of these people who, while entertaining golden dreams of the future, had to endure the most ordinary hunger and poverty in the present. But I realize that the hunger that I felt for a long time in the past was of a different kind altogether, insignificant by comparison, and could only be used as a metaphor—my hunger for love in the human world.

Su Qing

Su Qing (1917–1982) made her literary fame on the Lone Island, as occupied Shanghai was known during the War of Resistance against Japan. Like Zhang Ailing, another Lone Island writer to whom she is often compared, Su's reputation is attributable to her literary achievements as much as her well-publicized personal life. As a divorcee, she was the subject of many rumors, which she fanned with the frank depiction of her unsatisfying marriage in her writing.

Understandably, gender issues are one of the recurrent subjects to which she turns. Su is extremely critical of the social hypocrisy that keeps women under men's thumbs. The system of marriage often comes under attack, as is evident in "My Hand." Even "Sweet Bean Cakes," an otherwise nostalgic essay about Su's grandmother, is wrought with gender tension: The father is depicted as an intrusive force that disrupts the close relationship between grandmother and granddaughter. In writing if not as much in life, Su shows that it is possible for women to be independent of men, even if it can only be realized at a high emotional cost.

Sweet Bean Cakes (1943)

For a while, I had four packets of sweet bean cakes on my desk. I thought I would never eat them, but I still could not bear to throw them out.

A week ago, Cousin He Guan brought me these sweet bean cakes specially from Elgin Road. When he saw me, he didn't waste any time on pleasantries, but immediately put the sweet bean cakes into my hand with great care, saying, "Your grandmother asked me to bring these to you. I went to Ningbo last month and only got back yesterday." When he was finished, he wanted to leave and go home because the rickshaw that had brought him here was still waiting at the door.

I held onto him tightly and wouldn't let him go, at the same time asking the servant to send the rickshaw away. So, he sat down and told me all about things in my hometown. "These sweet bean cakes," he said, finally returning to the topic, "are Shanbei products. Someone gave them to your grandmother, but she thought they were too precious for her to eat, and insisted that I bring them to you. 'Ah Qing loves to eat sweet bean cakes most,' she said. 'She used to sleep with me in the same bed when she was little. When she woke up in the middle of the night, she'd fuss around and want to get out of bed. Then I'd pick up some sweet bean cake crumbs and put them in her mouth, and she would swallow them and quiet down.'"

I was abashed to hear that, and to hide my embarrassment, I interrupted him with, "Cousin He Guan, how is my grandmother these days?"

Cousin He Guan cocked his head and thought for a while. Then he replied, "Her health is good, but she's getting on in years, and her memory has failed somewhat."

Then he told me a story. It happened that when she had asked him to bring me the sweet bean cakes, she had also insisted that he stay to have a snack with her. She had groped around under her pillow for a long time, and then pulled out a black woven bag used to hold loose change. She opened the bag carefully, pulled out a few small paper notes, and looked them over again and again. Finally, she picked out an old green one, and put it in my younger brother's hand. She said, "Ah Xiang, take this ten-cent note... this is ten cents, right? and buy ten stuffed steamed buns. Be quick about it!... Make sure they're hot.... Cousin He Guan is going to take these sweet bean cakes to your sister, and we have nothing good to treat him with.... These are just ordinary things, just ten steamed stuffed buns.... Here you go, ten cents, hold on tight, now...." When he heard this, my younger brother could not suppress his laughter, and he winked at Cousin He Guan and went out. After a while, he came skipping back with a bowl of steamed stuffed buns. My grandmother picked out two for Cousin He Guan, and two for my younger brother, mumbling all the while, "Ten whole cents for just ten steamed stuffed buns, and they're so small... ten cents for ten stuffed buns, that's one whole cent for each bun.... One cent is three copper coins, and when you add them up...." Hearing this, my younger brother's mouth opened all the more widely with laughter and he choked on his last small bite of bun. Cousin He Guan thought it was funny, too. Later, he said, my brother told him that the cheapest steamed stuffed buns you can find in Ningbo these days are fifty cents each. Besides, the paper note my grandmother had given him was an old note issued by the Central Bank, now worth only five cents, which the people selling the buns took only reluctantly.

When I heard this, I also felt like laughing, but when I looked down at the four packets of sweet bean cakes in my hand, my smile disappeared. Soon afterward, Cousin He Guan took his leave, and I carefully put the four packets of sweet bean cakes on my desk.

After sitting for a while on my desk—a place ill-suited to storing such things—the sweet bean cakes had already become rather damp. Even the paper wrapping was moist with melted sugar. I thought to myself, "Since my grandmother entrusted someone to bring these to me from a long way away, I really should eat and enjoy them." But then I thought, "It's not good to eat things that are already damp. I'll just keep them around as a souvenir."

That's why the four packets of sweet bean cakes had remained on my desk all that time.

A common saying puts it well: "Look at the object, and you'll think of the person." Whenever I caught sight of the sweet bean cakes, I very naturally thought of my grandmother. My grandmother is of slender build, and she has a light complexion with well-formed features. Her only shortcoming is that her teeth are very bad. At six years old, when I came home from my maternal grandmother's home, I began to share a bed with her. At the time, she had only three front teeth left, but she liked sweet things and used to eat them in bed whenever she awoke in the middle of the night.

We used to sleep in a big bamboo Ningbo bed. There was a net made of blue linen hanging over it that hadn't been washed for years. Even the white top of the net had turned gray. On the inner side of the bed was a propped-up board, which she used for storing her snacks. I slept on the inside, and had to burrow my way right under the board. If I were careless when I sat up in the morning, my head would bump against it, and the snacks placed on top would jiggle up and down like a boat being tossed about on rocky seas. Sometimes they would even fall down from the board. When that happened, they had no chance of survival: Either I would devour them all by myself, or my grandmother and I would share them.

By nature, my grandmother liked to move around, and the thing she liked to move the most was her mouth. After she got up in the morning, her mouth would start mumbling until nighttime when everybody went to bed. Only then would she stop. As soon as her mouth stopped moving, she would fall sleep, snoring very loudly. Sometimes she made so much noise that I was unable to sleep. Whenever this happened, I would grope around in the dark and reach up to steal food from the board. Most of what was up there were sweet bean cakes. I would grab a packet, quietly lie down again, open the wrapping, and start eating. The crumbs would fall all over the pillow and the bedding, and sometimes even into my eyes, but I didn't care. I would break up the bean cakes into small bits and eat them in the dark, sometimes even tearing the wrapping into pieces and eating it as well.

In the middle of the night, if my grandmother stopped snoring, she too would reach up for something to eat. She had a remarkable ability to find things in the dark, never bumping into anything or needing to rummage around for what she was looking for. Whatever it might be, she always managed to find it. Sometimes she would count the sweet bean cake packets in the dark and discover that one was missing. Then she would nudge me awake and ask me about it. I would stretch my back, rub my eyes and mumble, "Ah Qing has no idea. Uncle Mouse must have eaten it." But her hand knew better. She would feel around the pillow and find crumbs scattered on the bedding. Laughing, she would then pinch me and say, "No, it must be *this* little mouse who stole it!"

Feeling her pinch, I would wake up completely, and the two of us would eat the sweet bean cakes in the dark. She never lit the lamp in the middle of the night because she didn't want to waste any lamp oil and she was afraid that we might accidentally set the net on fire. She would put a pinch of crumbs in my mouth, telling me to wait till they melted before swallowing them. Then, with a gulp, I would swallow them, and she would pick up another pinch and put it in my mouth again. Thus, slowly and quietly, the two of us would eat sweet bean cakes in the small hours of the morning. When we finished one packet, I would clamor for more. She would not let me have it, though, and would try to put me to sleep again by gently patting me. Before long, I would drift off to sleep, and her snoring would resume again.

We never made our bed, so all over the pillows and underneath the quilts there were bean cake crumbs and bits and scraps of other things. As we climbed into bed, we would hear a rustling sound, but we were used to it and never felt any discomfort. When we woke up in the morning, we would simply straighten the quilt a little, but never dusted the bedding. The crumbs were thus allowed to remain where they had dropped.

Sometimes, crumbs from the bean cakes would stick to my ears and face, and when my grandmother saw this the next day, she would carefully pick them off my face and put them in her mouth, saying it would be a crime not to eat them. I would pester her when I saw this, asking why, if they were stuck to *my* face, she didn't give them to *me*. When all efforts to appease me had failed, she would go into our room, open another packet and give me a small pinch. She would then carefully wrap up the remainder, and save it for later that night.

To my grandmother, sweet bean cakes were a special delicacy, and the old bamboo bed, her treasure house. Later, I too was drawn to the treasure house. When I did not get enough sweet bean cakes by asking, I would resort to stealing. After that, she started storing them in another place, and would not put them in the treasure house until nighttime. My craving for them got stronger and stronger, however, and I could barely wait for nighttime to come. When night had fallen, I would hurry my grandmother to bed, hoping that she would wake up a bit earlier to eat the sweet bean cakes.

One day, my father came back from Shanghai. Everybody talked and talked until late into the night.

I woke up in the middle of the night and could not find my grandmother. I groped around for some sweet bean cakes and could not find any. I wanted to call out, but was afraid of the stranger who was my father. I was extremely distressed. After waiting for a long time, I could not bear it any longer. I began to feel around my pillow and under the blanket, picked up the crumbs that were lying around, and started eating them. Just when I was about to swallow, I suddenly heard people coming into the room. I dared not make a sound, and quickly hid my head under the blanket. I lay there motionless, pretending to be asleep.

"Where is Ah Qing?" my father asked, putting down the lamp.

"She must be under the quilt," my grandmother answered.

"It's unhealthy for her to sleep with her head covered," my father said. He got closer, and was about to pull the quilt off my head.

My heart jumped. Fortunately, my grandmother stopped him, and said, "She's sleeping. Don't disturb her."

My father did not say anything. I heard the rustling sound of my grandmother taking off her clothes to get ready for bed.

Some sweet bean cakes were in my mouth; the melted sugar mixed with my own saliva and flowed down my throat, making it itch. It was hard to bear, but I tried with all the strength I could summon not to make any sound. After a while, though, a gurgling sound finally escaped from my throat. My father pulled away the quilt at once, and asked, "What are you eating, Ah Qing?"

I was very frightened. Looking at the flickering lamp, I answered, my voice trembling, "I'm not eating anything—Uncle Mouse is eating the sweet bean cake crumbs."

"Sweet bean cake crumbs? Where did the sweet bean cake crumbs come from?" my father asked. He pulled back the quilt, and with the oil lamp in his hand, inspected the bed. With my hands, I quickly covered the spot where the largest collection of crumbs was so that he would not take them from me, but my father took my hand and shone the lamp onto the crumbs. "Where did all this dirt come from?" he asked. "How can you sleep in such an untidy bed?" As he spoke, he reached out to flick the crumbs and other things off the bed.

My grandmother had taken off her day clothes, and she climbed into bed with a huff. "What is so dirty about this perfectly good food?" she grumbled to my father. "Sweet bean cakes from Shanbei, quite famous. Now, take the lamp out of here—I'm going to sleep. Blow out the lamp and try to save some oil. Look at you, so reckless! If you set the net ablaze, it would be no laughing matter! That's the thing a family has to watch out particularly for—fire."

The more she grumbled, the more my father frowned.

The next night, my father set up a small bed for me, and wouldn't let me sleep with my grandmother anymore. This made her very angry, and she wouldn't speak to my father for ten full days.

My father has been dead for a long time, and I have not seen my grandmother for six or seven years, but I haven't forgotten her for a single moment. I wonder if her three remaining front teeth are gone by now? She should have kept the sweet cakes for herself. Why did she go to all the trouble of asking someone to bring them to Shanghai from such a distance?

I could not bear to eat them—in truth, I was actually afraid to. When I thought about how I would gather up crumbs from the pillow and the quilt when I was a child, it turned my stomach and I didn't have the courage to open the wrapping. Was I repelled by how dirty they were? If my grandmother should find out what was going on in my head, she would probably be all puffed up in anger, and wouldn't speak to me for ten days or more, or even the rest of her life. I couldn't just let them sit there and not eat them. But how could I bear to eat them?

I wavered for more than a week, and finally ate all the sweet bean cakes. Although they were damp, they were the real thing—the true Shanbei kind—and very sweet. I tasted the sweetness in my mouth, and in my heart. I wish you good health, my dear grandmother!

My Hand (1944)

After dinner, I took out a clean glass and made myself some strong green tea. As I sipped it, I mulled over the writing I still had to do. Suddenly, I caught sight of my hand holding the glass. My white tapered fingers, set against the green tea, looked like five small, slender pieces of ivory.

—Is this my hand?

—Yes, my hand.

I slowly set down the glass and put my hand on my knee, studying it carefully: long fingers, a thin palm, skin so pale it seemed to lack any sign of life. It was almost a bit frightening to look at it.

This is my left hand, I thought, perhaps my right hand is better. I put my right hand on my knee, comparing the two—this way and that—but they looked more or less the same, and I could not see any difference between them. The only thing was that on the tip of my right index finger, there was an ink stain, left there inadvertently when I was writing. All it would take was some scrubbing with soap, and my hand would be clean.

These pale, skinny hands—I did not want to look at them again. I picked up the glass silently, lightly sipping the tea. I thought to myself, they should take a rest. Otherwise, with hands as bloodless as these, how could I ever hope to come up with writing endowed with flesh and blood?

I have heard it reported that many great writers in the West never have to pick up a pen with their hands when they work. All they need do is recline comfortably on a sofa, cigar between their lips, smoking as they dictate. A stenographer sitting by their side then types out or takes down what they say. What a comfortable way to write! My status, however, is nowhere near theirs, and these kinds of descriptions seem like fairy tales to me. After indulging in such fantasies for a while, I still had to trouble my own hands to do the work. To earn my keep, I had no choice but to put down the tea, reach for the draft paper, and start writing.

I wrote and wrote, until my hand had gone numb and my fingertips had stiffened. I took a look at them, and forgot all the phrasings about happiness that I had prepared in my mind. All that was left was limitless sorrow that no words or sentences could express. Dazed, I stared at the blank piece of paper.

After a while, I suddenly got an idea. I put my left hand on the paper and, holding a pencil in my right, I traced around it. Soon afterward, the outline of a slender hand was clearly visible on the paper.

—Is this my hand?

—Yes, my hand.

My hands were surely not like this in the past. I once had ten strong, thick fingers, nails cut short. My palms were thick and plump, their color, red and lustrous.

When I was a child, my hands kneaded mud balls, caught grasshoppers, and picked field thistles for my mother.... In school, they were busy taking notes in class, playing tennis, and they could even play melodious tunes on the piano.... Later, he came along, and put a diamond ring on my ring finger. He kissed it, and said, "So competent, this hand!"

With my hands, I did many things for him....

With my hands, I did many things for my children....

Together, grease and dirt made their way into the creases in my palms. Washing and scrubbing could not remove them. In the end, my hands became dirty and rough.

But I was not ashamed of my hands, because as long as they worked, they could bring joy and happiness to others.

In winter, the back of my hand cracked like the pattern on the shell of a turtle. But I endured the pain, and sewed satin-covered cotton-padded robes for my children. My rough hand touched the patterned satin, and made a scratchy sound, which my children found curious. They asked, "Mother, why do your hands make that sound?"

I laughed. But when I looked at him, I saw he was not laughing. After a while, he frowned, and said in a disgusted tone, "Look at your hands! Isn't my precious diamond ring wasted on you?"

I was speechless. The next day, I gave the precious diamond ring back to him.

But neither the law nor my financial situation allowed me to keep my children. I have nothing. I can only rely on my cracked hands to make a living, all alone.

—Is this my hand?

—Yes, my hand.

My hand will no longer change my children's diapers, or wipe their noses. All day long, my left hand can only hold the tea cup, while my right hand writes, writes, writes....

The strong tea tasted bitter. I sipped my tea as I silently thought about what I was writing. But what word or line could convey what I meant to express? Moreover, even if I managed to express it, who could I hope would understand?

After a while, I got an idea: I will send my children the piece of paper with my handprint on it, so that they will know that my hand... has grown thin.

Zhang Ailing

Just as Lu Xun is the icon of twentieth-century China in crisis, Zhang Ailing (1920–1995) is the icon of Shanghai under siege in the late 1930s and early 1940s. She captures the reader's imagination with her distinctive writing style and legendary personal life, which she consciously depicted with a fair amount of embellishment in her works.

Born to a privileged family, Zhang nevertheless had a torturous childhood after her parents divorced. She was educated in Shanghai and Hong Kong, both of which appear prominently in her writing. She established her fame as a writer during World War II in Shanghai, but her career stalled after the war, partly due to her short but widely publicized marriage to Hu Lancheng, a collaborator under the Japanese puppet regime in Shanghai. She later moved to Hong Kong and then emigrated to the United States, where she became increasingly reclusive until her death in 1995.

Despite their autobiographical nature, Zhang's writings can be read as serious explorations of such issues as urban life, gender relations, and the moral implications of everyday life, especially as they relate to wartime Shanghai. She seldom spoke out directly against patriarchal oppression, but her own writing quietly asserted the right of a woman to speak on any issue, making her perhaps more radical a feminist that any woman writer of her age.

The two essays here reveal two recurrent themes in Zhang's works. "My Little Brother" captures a scene of her unhappy childhood, while "Love" conveys the fortuitousness of human encounters, where isolated and seemingly insignificant events may turn out to possess deep meaning.

Love (1944)

This is a true story.

There once lived a beautiful girl from a well-to-do family in a village. Many people came with matchmaking proposals but nothing came of them. She was no more than fifteen or sixteen that year.

One spring evening, she was standing by the back door, her hand resting on a peach tree next to her. She remembered that she had on a moon-white blouse. There was a young man who lived across the road. They had seen each other before, but had never greeted each other. He came over and stopped at a place not too far from her. He said softly, "Oh, you're here too?" She did not say anything in particular. Neither did he. They stood there for a while, and then went about their own business.

That is it.

Later, the girl was abducted by a relative and sold elsewhere as a concubine, after which she was sold three or four more times. She still remembered in her old age the incident that had taken place so long before, though she had lived through a life of numerous terrible upheavals. She often talked about that spring evening... the peach tree by the back door... the young man.

When, among the tens of thousands of people you might have met, you meet the very person you were meant to meet, and when, among the tens of thousands of years in the boundless wilderness of time, you arrive at just the right spot at just the right moment, not a step too soon, not a step too late, there is nothing else you can say, but to ask softly, "Oh, you're here, too?"

My Little Brother (1944)

My little brother was born a handsome boy, but I was not attractive at all, not even a bit. Ever since we were little, our family had found this regrettable. What a waste that his small mouth, big eyes, and long lashes had been bestowed on a boy! The elders loved to tease him, "May I borrow your eyelashes? I'll return them tomorrow." But he always flatly turned them down. One time, we were saying how beautiful the wife of a certain person was, and he asked, "Is she as beautiful as I?" We often made fun of him for being so vain.

He envied the pictures I drew, and when no one was around, he would tear them up or put two bold black lines across them. I can imagine the kind of psychological pressure he was under. I was a year older than he; I could speak better; I was healthier. I could eat things that he could not, and do things that he could not.

When we played together, I was always the one who came up with the ideas. We were the two seasoned and valiant generals of the Jin Family Village; my name was Yuehong, and his was Xinhong. My weapon was a double-edged sword, and he wielded a pair of bronze maces. We also had many imaginary companions. The setting of our little drama was always evening, when we started to play. Nanny Jin would be chopping up the vegetables in the shared kitchen, so we would enjoy a feast before the battle. Then we would ride over the hill under the moonlight to attack the barbarians. On the way, we might kill a tiger or two and steal their eggs, which were like fur-balls as big as crotons. When we opened them, they looked like poached chicken eggs, but the yolks remained round. My little brother often refused to listen to my orders, and we often ended up arguing. He was the kind of person who "could not lead but would not be led," but he was indeed such a lovely boy. Sometimes, I would let him weave his own tale: A traveler was being pursued by a tiger, running as fast as the wind, and right behind him the tiger was chasing, howling—but before he could finish, I would be rolling on the ground laughing. I would give him a peck on the cheek, treating him like a little toy.

After we had a stepmother, I lived at school most of the time and seldom came home. I had no idea how my little brother spent his days. One time I came home for vacation and was shocked to see him. He had become tall and slender, and was wearing a blue cloth dustcoat that was far from tidy. He was reading a pile of comic books he had rented from somewhere. At the time, I was reading Mu Shiying's *The North and South Poles* and Ba Jin's *Destruction,* and felt that his tastes needed some improvement. But he made only a brief appearance and was gone. Everyone told me about his horrid behavior: truancy from school, defiance of my father, and a lack of ambition in his character. I was more furious than anybody and agreed with what was said about him. I got so excessive in berating him that, in the end, everybody turned around to mollify me.

Later at dinner, my father slapped his face over some trivial matter. I was shocked, and held up my bowl before my face, tears streaming down. My stepmother laughed and said, "Hey, what are *you* crying about? No one is saying anything about you. Look, *he's* all right, and there you are, crying!" I put down my bowl and ran into the bathroom, latching the door behind me. Choking, I wept silently. I stood in front of the mirror, and looked at my twitching face and the many tears flowing down it, like a montage in a movie. I clenched my teeth and said, "I'll get back at you, some day! I *will* get back at you!"

The glass window of the bathroom opened up to the sun terrace. *Boing,* a rubber ball hit the glass and bounced off. My little brother was kicking the ball on the terrace. He had forgotten about what had happened, having grown used to incidents such as this. I did not cry anymore, but felt a chilly sadness come over me.

Works Cited

Some entries below bear two dates. The one that appears immediately after the name of the author indicates the date on which the item was first published. The one that appears at the end of the citation refers to the date of the modern reprint which this study uses. References in the Introduction are made to the first date.

Bo Han. 1935. "You zaren xiaopin dao suren xiaopin" (From *Xiaopin* for the Genteel to That for the Vulgar). In *Xiaopin wen yishu tan*, edited by Ning Li, 120–125. Beijing: Zhongguo guangbo dianshi chubanshe, 1990.

Cao, Shujuan. *Wan Ming xinling xiaopin yanjiu* (*A Study of Late Ming Xinling Xiaopin*). Taipei: Wenjin, 1988.

Chen, Shaotang. *Wan Ming xiaopin lunxi* (*An Analysis of Late Ming Xiaopin*). Hong Kong: Bowen shuju, 1981.

Chen, Shuhua. 1935. "Meiyu ti xiaopin wen shili" (Explication of the *Meiyu* Style of Essays with Examples). In *Xiandai zuojia tan sanwen*, edited by Shusen She, 129–148. Tianjin: Baihua xenyi chubanshe, 1986.

Chen, Suyu. 1989. "Yashe xiaopin xianxiang: wo guan Liang Shiqiu de sanwen" (The *Yashe Xiaopin* Phenomenon: My View of Liang Shiqiu's Essays). In *Xiaopin wen yishu tan*, edited by Ning Li, 349–350. Beijing: Zhongguo guangbo dianshi chubanse, 1990.

Chen, Wangdao, ed. *Xiaopin wen he manhua* (*Xiaopinwen and Cartoons*). Shanghai: Shenghuo, 1935.

Chen, Zizhan. 1935. "Gongan Jingling yu xiaopin wen" (The Gongan and Jingling Schools and *Xiaopin Wen*). In *Xiaopin wen yishu tan*, edited by Ning Li, 206–216. Beijing: Zhongguo guangbo dianshi chubanse, 1990.

Epstein, Joseph. *The Norton Book of Personal Essays*. New York: Norton, 1997.

Fan, Songpei. *Zhongguo xiandai sanwen shi* (*A History of Modern Chinese Prose*). Suzhou: Jiangsu jiaoyu chubanshe, 1993.

Feng, Sanmei. *Xiaopin wen san jiang* (*Xiaopin wen: Three Lectures*). Shanghai: Daguang shuju, 1936.

Ferguson, Suzanne. "Defining the Short Story: Impressionism and Form." *Modern Fiction Studies* 28, 1 (1982): 13–24.

Gerlach, John. "The Margins of Narrative: The Very Short Story, the Prose Poem, and the Lyric." In *Short Story Theory at a Crossroad*, edited by Susan Lohafer and Jo Ellyn Clarey, 74–84. Baton Rouge and London: Louisiana State University Press, 1989.

Gong, Pengcheng. "Wei zai sheng fan zhi jian di qingyan xiaopin" (*Qingyan Xiaopin*: Situated between the Sacred and the Secular). In *Wan Ming sichao*, 243–291. Taipei: Liren, 1994.

Hanan, Patrick. "The Making of *The Pearl-Sewn Shirt* and *The Courtesan's Jewel Box*." *Harvard Journal of Asiatic Studies* 33 (1973): 124–153.

He, Yubo. *Xiaopin wen zuofa* (*How to Write Xiaopin Wen*). Shanghai: Guangyi shuju, 1934.

Hesse, Douglas. "A Boundary Zone: First-Person Short Stories and Narrative Essays." In *Short Story Theory at a Crossroad*, edited by Susan Lohafer and Jo Ellyn Clarey, 85–105. Baton Rouge and London: Louisiana State University Press, 1989.

Hu, Menghua and Shuzhen Wu. 1928. "Xuyu sanwen" (The Familiar Essay). In *Xiandai zuojia tan sanwen*, edited by Shusen She, 14–16. Tianjin: Baihua, 1986.

Hu, Shi. 1922. "Wushi nian lai zhi Zhongguo wenxue" (Chinese Literature of the Last Fifty Years). In *Hushi zuopin ji*, Vol. 8, 65–150. Taipei: Yuanliu, 1986.

———. 1928. *Baihua wenxue shi* (*A History of Vernacular Literature*). Taipei: Hushi jianlan guan, 1967.

Huters, Theodore. "From Writing to Literature: The Development of Late Qing Theories of Prose." *Harvard Journal of Asiatic Studies* 47, 1 (1987): 51–96.

———. "A New Way of Writing." *Modern China* 14, 3 (1988): 243–276.

Kao, Yu-kung. "Chinese Lyric Aesthetics." In *Words and Images: Chinese Poetry, Calligraphy and Painting*, edited by Alfreda Murck and Wen C. Fang, 47–90. New York: Metropolitan Museum of Art; Princeton: Princeton University Press, 1991.

Laughlin, Charles. *The Literature of Leisure and Chinese Modernity*. Honolulu:

University of Hawaii Press, 2008.

Leung, Gaylord Kai Loh. "The Eye of a Storm: The Familiar Essays by Liang Shih-ch'iu during the Anti-Japanese War Period (1937–1945)." In *La Littérature Chinoise au Temps de la Guerre de Résistance Contre le Japon*, 67–82. Paris: Éditions de la Foundation Singer-Polignac, 1990.

Li, Jingbin. *Luxun Zhou Zuoren bijiao lun* (*On Comparing Lu Xun and Zhou Zuoren*). Tianjin: Nankai daxue chubanshe, 1987.

Li, Ning. "Zhongguo xiandai xiaopin wen gaiguan" (An Overview of Modern Chinese *Xiaopin Wen*). In *Xiaopin wen yishu tan*, 401–424. Beijing: Zhongguo guangbo dianshi chubanshe, 1990.

Li, Subo. 1932. "Shenme shi xiaopin wen" (What Is *Xiaopin Wen?*). In *Xiaopin wen yishu tan*, edited by Ning Li, 46–55. Beijing: Zhongguo guangbo dianshi chubanshe, 1990.

Liang, Yuchun. 1930. "Xiaopin wen xuan xu" (Preface to *Xiaopin Wen Xuan*). In *Xiaopin wen yishu tan*, edited by Ning Li, 41–45. Beijing: Zhongguo guangbo dianshi chubanshe, 1990.

Lin, Yutang. 1934a. "Xiaopin wen zhi yixu" (The Heritage of *Xiaopin Wen*). In *Xiaopin wen yishu tan*, edited by Ning Li, 101–107. Beijing: Zhongguo guangbo dianshi chubanshe, 1990.

———. 1934b. "*Renjianshi* fakan ci" ("Inaugural Preface" to *Renjianshi*). In *Xiaopin wen yishu tan*, edited by Ning Li, 88–89. Beijing: Zhongguo guangbo dianshi chubanshe, 1990.

———. 1934c. "Lun xiaopin wen bidiao" (On the Style of *Xiaopin Wen*). In *Xiaopin wen yishu tan*, edited by Ning Li, 97–100. Beijing: Zhongguo guangbo dianshi chubanshe, 1990.

Lopate, Philip. *The Art of the Personal Essay*. New York: Doubleday, 1994.

Lu Xun. 1933. "Xiaopin wen di weiji" (The Crisis of *Xiaopin Wen*). In *Xiaopin wen yishu tan*, edited by Ning Li, 68–71. Beijing: Zhongguo guangbo dianshi chubanshe, 1990.

———. 1935. "Zatan xiaopin wen" (Casual Remarks on *Xiaopin Wen*). In *Xiaopin wen yishu tan*, edited by Ning Li, 287–289. Beijing: Zhongguo guangbo dianshi chubanshe, 1990.

Mao Dun. 1934a. "Guanyu xiaopin wen" (About *Xiaopin Wen*). In *Xiaopin wen yishu tan*, edited by Ning Li, 111–112. Beijing: Zhongguo guangbo dianshi chubanshe, 1990.

———. 1934b. "Xiaopin wen banyuekan *Renjianshi*" (*Renjianshi*: A Biweekly of *Xiaopin Wen*). In *Xiaopin wen yishu tan*, edited by Ning Li, 113–117. Beijing: Zhongguo guangbo dianshi chubanshe, 1990.

Miner, Earl. *Comparative Poetics: An Intercultural Essay on Theories of Literature.* Princeton: Princeton University Press, 1990.

Pollard, David. *The Chinese Essay.* London: Hurst and Company, 2000.

Qian, Gechuan. 1935. "Women suo yao du di xiaopin wen" (The Kind of *Xiaopin Wen* We Want to Read). In *Xiaopin wen yishu tan,* edited by Ning Li, 199–201. Beijing: Zhongguo guangbo dianshi chubanshe, 1990.

———— (psuedo. Wei Gan). 1948. "Tan xiaopin wen" (On *Xiaopin Wen*). In *Xiaopin wen yishu tan,* edited by Ning Li, 308–311. Beijing: Zhongguo guangbo dianshi chubanshe, 1990.

Qian, Zhongshu. "Zhongguo xin wenxue di yuanliu" (Review: Zhou Zuoren's *Zhongguo xin wenxue di yuanliu*). In *Zhou Zuoren lun,* edited by Mingzhi Tao, 154–162. Shanghai: Beixin, 1934.

Scoggin, Mary. "Ethnography of a Chinese Essay: *Zawen* in Contemporary China." Ph.D. diss., University of Chicago, 1997.

She, Shusen. *Sanwen chuangzuo yishu* (*The Art of Prose*). Beijing: Beijing daxue chubanshe, 1986.

Shi Wei. *Xiaopin wen jianghua* (*Remarks on Xiaopin Wen*). Shanghai: Guangming shuju, 1941.

Sun, Xizhen. 1935. "Lun xiandai Zhongguo sanwen" (On Modern Chinese Prose). In *Xiandai zuojia tan sanwen,* edited by Shusen She, 217–224. Tianjin: Baihua, 1986.

Wang, Bin. "Qian yan" (Foreword). In *Xiandai sanwen jianshang cidan,* edited by Bin Wang, 1–21. Beijing: Nongchun duwu chubanshe, 1988.

Wang, Tongzhao. 1923. "Chun sanwen" (Pure Prose). In *Xiandai zuojia tan sanwen,* edited by Shusen She, 5–6. Tianjin: Baihua, 1986.

Woesler, Martin. *Modern Chinese Literary Essay: Defining the Chinese Self in the Twentieth Century, Conference Volume.* Bochum: Bochum University Press, 2000a.

————. *Twentieth Century Chinese Essays in Translation.* Bochum: Bochum University Press, 2000b.

Xia Yan. 1954. "Tan xiaopin wen" (On *Xiaopin Wen*). In *Xiaopin wen yishu tan,* edited by Ning Li, 312–316. Beijing: Zhongguo guangbo dianshi chubanshe, 1990.

Yu, Dafu. 1935. "Zhongguo xin wenxue daxi sanwen er ji daoyan" (Preface to Volume II on Prose of *The Collectanea of Modern Chinese Literature*). In *Xiandai zuojia tan sanwen,* edited by Shusen She, 256–280. Tianjin: Baihua, 1986.

Zeiger, William. "The Exploratory Essay: Enfranchising the Spirit of Inquiry in College Composition." *College English* 47, 5 (1985): 454–466.

Zheng, Mingli. *Xiandai sanwen leixing lun (On Types of Modern Prose)*. Taipei: Da'an chubanshe, 1987.

Zhong, Jingwen. 1927. "Shi tan xiaopin wen" (Preliminary Remarks on *Xiaopin Wen*). In *Xiaopin wen yishu tan*, edited by Ning Li, 30–34. Beijing: Zhongguo guangbo dianshi chubanshe, 1990.

Zhou, Muzhai. 1935. "Xiaopin wen zashuo" (Casual Remarks on *Xiaopin Wen*). In *Xiaopin wen yishu tan*, edited by Ning Li, 126–131. Beijing: Zhongguo guangbo dianshi chubanshe, 1990.

Zhou, Zuoren. 1921. "Meiwen" (Aesthetic Writing). In *Xiandai zuojia tan sanwen*, edited by Shusen She, 3–4. Tianjin: Baihua, 1986.

———. 1923. "Ziji di yuandi" (A Garden of One's Own). In *Ziji di yuandi*, 6–8. Beijing: Renmin wenxue chubanshe, 1988.

———. 1928. "Zaban'er ba" (Postscript to *Zaban'er*). In *Zhitang xu ba*, edited by Shuhe Zhong, 313–316. Changsha: Yuelu shushe, 1986.

———. 1932. *Zhongguo xin wenxue di yuanliu (The Origins of Modern Chinese Literature)*. Shanghai: Shanghai shudian, 1988.

———. 1935. "Zhongguo xin wenxue daxi sanwen yi ji daoyan" (Preface to Volume I on Prose of *The Collectanea of Modern Chinese Literature*). In *Xiandai zuojia tan sanwen*, edited by Shusen She, 235–255. Tianjin: Baihua, 1986.

Zhu, Guangqian. 1936. "Lun xiaopin wen" (On *Xiaopin Wen*). In *Xiaopin wen yishu tan*, edited by Ning Li, 290–296. Beijing: Zhongguo guangbo dianshi chubanshe, 1990.

Zhu, Ziqing. 1928. "Lun xiandai Zhongguo di xiaopin sanwen" (On Modern Chinese *Xiaopin Wen*). In *Xiandai zuojia tan sanwen*, edited by Shusen She, 43–47. Tianjin: Baihua, 1986.

———. 1947. *Shi yanzhi bian (Delineating the Shi Yanzhi Tradition)*. Shanghai: Huadong shifan daxue chubanshe, 1996.